THE VERBAL ART OF MOBILITY
IN WEST AFRICA

THE VERBAL ART OF MOBILITY IN WEST AFRICA

Nikolas Sweet

INDIANA UNIVERSITY PRESS

This book is a publication of

Indiana University Press
Office of Scholarly Publishing
Herman B Wells Library 350
1320 East 10th Street
Bloomington, Indiana 47405 USA

iupress.org

Manufactured in the United States of America

First Printing 2024

Cataloging information is available from the Library of Congress.

ISBN 978-0-253-07146-0 (hardcover)
ISBN 978-0-253-07147-7 (paperback)
ISBN 978-0-253-07149-1 (epub)
ISBN 978-0-253-07148-4 (ebook)

CONTENTS

ACKNOWLEDGMENTS

THIS BOOK EMERGES FROM LIFELONG RELATIONSHIPS THAT BEGAN in 2006 during my time in the Peace Corps. I feel unable to properly express gratitude for the hospitality, openness, and care that I witnessed in almost a decade of living in Senegal. Peace Corps colleagues nurtured my curiosity and offered community during these formative years. Robyn d'Avignon was responsible for getting me into anthropology in the first place. Matt McLaughlin led us through many adventures and fostered a sense of curiosity. Steve Wood has been a partner in building community over the long term. I first came to know the richness of Kédougou with others: Kay Stones, Jordan Welty, Andy Jondahl, Amy Truong, Roxy O'Connell as well as Alexa Shaw, Micah Thomas, Jed Fix, Mary O'Brien, Travis Ferland, Sarah Lee, and Michele Lehman. During my anthropological research, I appreciated the companionship of Mike LaChance and Anna French. A dedicated Peace Corps staff supported our efforts there, including Mark Gizzi, Bamba Fall, Chris Hedrick, and Karim Diallo.

This research was possible due to the incredible people on top of the mountain. Many thanks go to everyone in the *funnaange* and, in particular, to Samba, Sakamissa, Ben Idi, Mumini, Ruby, Wurije, Adama and everyone else for making the *hirnaange* a home. My deepest gratitude goes to Doba (my *koto*) and his family—I am proud of our enduring friendship. I am indebted to Harouna and Khadiatou for so many evenings of laughter, and companionship. Doba's family in Kédougou, Ibrahima, Fatou, Aicha, and Oumar, provided companionship back in Kédougou. I honed my Pular from the kola nut sellers and merchants of Kédougou's downtown market. Alhoussainey, Thierno Ibrahima, Alpha Oumar, Boubacar, Siradio, Ablaye, and so many others brought me into so many enriching conversations under a sunshade. Kédougou was the home of curious and engaged minds: people like Waly Cissokho, Oumar Sall, Famakhan Dembele, Ibrahima Ba, Bocar, Diallo, Djiby Diallo, and Hassana Diallo. My time in Kédougou all began with my host family from the neck of the river. Bintou, my host sister, has been a pillar of support. Everyone else in Daande Maayo—including Ousmane, Fatima, Dioukou, Mamadou, Ami, Mami, Sali, and Mory—was so gracious in opening their home to me.

I have continually returned to Senegal because remarkable people kept pulling me back. During my time in Saint-Louis, I was so lucky to meet Daouda Mbaye, whose curiosity and wisdom is awe inspiring. I found friendship with the Bindias, Biesses, and Boubanes in the compound behind the Peace Corps. Kali Américain, Tonton Kali, Bebe, Jimmy, Odette, Taki, Marie Christine, and Ipene offered companionship and hospitality. Alexi, Michel, Barthelemy, Gerard, Olivier, and company, organized restorative block party feasts. Mamoudou Djembe brought so much rhythm into my life. Adama Diaby has been an insightful interlocutor and a keen witness to changes in Kédougou region. Analyzing the back and forth of everyday talk was a difficult and a humbling task. Vieux Diallo was also an exceptional research assistant who helped with translations and offered insight on complicated material. Some amazing friends such as Cellou, Yaaye Aissatou, and Baylo left us too soon. To everyone in Kédougou, I hope that this book does justice to the incredible richness of your life worlds.

This intellectual journey began for me in the French Department at Virginia Tech, where I began to explore French outside of continental Europe. Sharon Johnson and Richard Shryock set me upon my path. Fabrice Teulonand and Janell Watson offered encouragement in my study of French. Medoune Gueye was a large influence on me, first introducing me to the rich world of African cinema through films like *Touki Bouki*. Little did I know that I would spend much of my future life there. Peter Stirling and Laura Burke made me feel at home in theirs. Babacar, Kine, and everyone at Daara Yacine made Yoff a place of refuge and wisdom. Periods of recuperation in Dakar were made possible by Elke Schmidt, who opened her home and the Where There Be Dragon community to me. Liz Conner and Megan Fettig helped me find the simple joys teaching. I appreciate the support of Fiona McLaughlin who offered support and encouragement.

I owe so much to my mentor, Judith Irvine, who guided me through extremely formative years of graduate school at the University of Michigan. Her continued support and keen counsel have opened me to the rich world of language. My graduate committee, Michael Lempert, Mike McGovern, Barbra Meek, and Derek Peterson supported me along my academic journey and gave me so much valuable feedback. Butch Ware reminded me that this work is also an ethical commitment and a humbling opportunity. The University of Michigan is the home of a vibrant intellectual community that has deeply informed my work: Webb Keane, Gillian Feeley-Harnik, Erik Mueggler, Andrew Shryock, Bruce Mannheim, Laura MacLatchy,

Henry Wright, Thomas Trautmann, Kelly Askew, Jason De León, Kriszti Fehervary, Gayle Rubin, Damani Partridge, Matt Hull, and Alaina Lemon. Sally Thomason and Marlyse Baptista welcomed me into the field of linguistics. John Mitani, Stuart Kirsch, and Tom Fricke made West Hall a happy place to come to work. I had the pleasure of teaching with Thomas Chivens and Andrew Shryock, and Holly Peters-Golden. Many incredible scholars are doing work in Kédougou; I have learned much from conversations with Ibrahima Thiaw, Cameron Gokee, Moustapha Sall, Backary Doucouré, Mouhamadou Lamine Diallo, Alioune Dème, and everyone in the Kédougou research group.

I am grateful to have been surrounded by a caring and compassionate cohort in Ann Arbor: Aleksandr Sklyar, Cheryl Yin, Courtney Cottrell, Travis Williams, Maire Malone, Aaron Sandel, Allison Caine, Heyeon Lee, Laura Yakas, Cyrus O'Brien, Chelsea Fisher, and Anna Antoniou. Drew Haxby and Brenna Murphy were pillars of friendship and care. Michigan anthropology fostered a compassionate group of inspiring scholars like Jessica Lowen, Yeon-ju Bae, Prash Naidu, Chris Sargent, Amanda Kemble, Punnu Jaitla, Meghanne Barker, Sandhya Narayanan, Vincent Battista, Bree Doering, Adrian Deoanca, Georgia Ennis, Adrienne Lagman, Promise McEntire, Anne Marie Creighton, Matthew Schissler, Onyx Henry, and Sheng Long. Chip Zuckerman and Michael Prentice offered timely feedback and support. The Michigan Ling Lab community was always ready with insightful feedback on my work. Michigan's AHAW shared their rich work with me. I am grateful to Costas Nakassis, Kristina Wirtz, Susan Philips, Kate Graber, Michael Silverstein and the entire Michicagoan community for their engaged scholarship.

Beginning to teach during the pandemic was difficult, but my colleagues at Grinnell College offered support during uncertain times: Josh Marshack, Brigittine French, Jon Andelson, Monty Roper, Cynthia Hansen, Tess Kulstad, Katya Gibel-Mevorach, John Whittaker, Kathy Kemp, and Maria Tapias. It is in these times of isolation that this book project began, which was both a challenge and an opportunity. This book was completed at the University of Wyoming, where I am deeply indebted to my colleagues for their friendship and support: Todd Surovell, Marcel Kornfeld, Melissa Murphy, Jason Toohey, Randy Haas, Lauren Hayes, Jessica Nelson, Jim Johnson, Allie Kelly, Sean Field, Bree Doering, Bob Kelly, Pam Innes, Jim Ahern, and Steve Bialostok. I feel grateful to be in the company of such generous and empowering colleagues. UW graduate assistants helped me in my teaching so I could have time to write: Mac Larimer, Fox Nelson, and Josh Rutledge; Aubrey Edwards, in particular, offered timely and intentional during a critical semester. Todd Surovell and Melissa Murphy helped cultivate an inspiring place to work as department heads. I relished the opportunity to participate in the Wyoming Institute for the Humanities Research fellowship, where I was reminded that writing is a craft. Allison Caine, Dan Auerbach, Trisha Martinez, Kent Drummond, Alyson Hagy, Katharine Tekyl, and Scott Henkel provided so much generous insight on my work.

Research was made possible with generous support from the National Science Foundation's Doctoral Dissertation Research Improvement Grant, the Wenner-Gren Foundation's Dissertation Fieldwork Grant, the National Science Foundation's Graduate Research Fellowship Program, and the University of Michigan Rackham International Research Award. This work has benefitted from the financial support from the following centers and institutes at the University of Michigan: The African Studies Center, the Department of Anthropology, Rackham Graduate School, the Department of Afroamerican and African Studies, the Mellon Institute, and the Michigan International Institute. Wyoming's Center for Global Studies, UW Arts and Sciences, as well as the Wenner-Gren Foundation funded collaborative and follow up research in Senegal. The Wyoming Institute for the Humanities generously funded the indexing of this book. Senegal's Ministère de l'Education et de la Recherche authorized my research in Kédougou. I am grateful to the West African Research Center (WARC) and to Mariane Wade, in particular, for hosting me as a scholar and providing support during my intermittent trips to Dakar.

This book would not be possible without the insightful and generous comments from two reviewers, who helped me hone my argument and my engagement with important scholarship. I thank the faculty board and the editorial staff at Indiana University Press for their direction and professionalism: Bethany Mowry, my editor for helping bring this work into being; Nancy Lightfoot and Laura Abrams for their careful attention to the manuscript; and Samantha Heffner for helping share the book into the world. I am appreciative of Thomas Vecchio's help in producing an amazing index.

This book emerges from a lifetime apprenticeship in critical thinking fostered by my parents, Monika and Philip Sweet, who supported me through years of discovery. I am grateful to my brother, Matthias Sweet for shared advice and encouragement. I am thankful for my new family,

Pam, Brian, Liam, and Melanie, who made Maine a place of rest and re-covery. This book came into being over many years, and much of it was written while I became a father to Rowan and Sophie. I love you two more than anything. My deepest thanks go to my wife and fellow scholar, Alli. Although we almost never talk about anthropological theory together, everything here bears traces of our love.

NOTE ON TRANSLITERATION AND TRANSCRIPTION

THIS BOOK EMPLOYS SOME SPECIAL LETTERS USED IN the writing of West African languages, primarily Pular.

Ŋŋ voiced velar nasal

Ɓɓ voiced bilabial implosive

Ɗɗ voiced alveolar implosive

Ƴƴ liquid velar implosive

Ññ palatal nasal

Xx voiceless velar fricative (most often in loanwords from Wolof and occasionally written as a *kh*).

A minimum of transcription conventions have been included for sake of readability.

(( )) double parentheses indicate transcriber notes

( ) empty parentheses indicate that something is said, but it cannot be discerned

(this) speech in parentheses indicates uncertainty on the transcriber's part, due to interference or unintelligibility

—dashes, as in "ma—," indicates speech that is broken off

: colons indicate lengthening

... indicates some text is missing

key underlining for emphasis through pitch and volume

THE VERBAL ART OF MOBILITY
IN WEST AFRICA

INTRODUCTION
The Verbal Art of Mobility

The Blind Man and the Boy

Hunched over at the midback, a slim elderly man takes small but assertive steps throughout the crowded market of downtown Kédougou. Although it is early in the morning, he is wearing sunglasses. Small caps of white hair emerge at the end of the man's delicately matted beard. The man is blind. Despite this, he traces a slow but sure-footed route between market sellers, avoiding a crowded field of protruding umbrellas, stools, and motorcycles. People call out to him, and he responds with the confidence of someone who is firmly rooted in time and space. But the elder is not standing alone. He is holding on to one end of a stick whose other end is in the hands of a young boy walking in front of him. Connected to the old man, the boy makes fluid motions and pauses at different times as he considers the path forward. At a short distance away, I occasionally overhear the man murmuring the names of places and people to the boy. These names trace out an inhabited landscape that they will encounter together.

Although the old man and the boy are moving at the same speed, each body has a slightly different rhythm. It is the boy who can see, but it is the old man who appears to be open to the world around him. His trip to the market is one of intense greetings and sociality. He calls out kola nut sellers by last name and politely but persuasively asks them for something to chew on. While the blind man basks in the exchange of these greetings, the young boy maintains his steady silence in a sea of effervescent talk overflowing with haggling, hellos, and good-natured jibes. Moving in concert, they appear to be inhabiting very different places. At the same time, however, they are inextricably linked: each of their experiences in the market is facilitated by the other.

At a basic level, this example draws attention to ingrained assumptions about the nature of what mobility is.[1] In this book, I examine mobility as a relational activity that is frequently underwritten by an individual's perspective. I will show that careful attention to linguistic practices and interactions reveals important insights about mobility, foremost of which, perhaps, is that viewing mobility as a physical experience that language renders meaningful through description hides the ways mobility also emerges through language use and interaction. We are all more like the blind man than we think. Our mobilities are mediated through our connections with others and through the linguistic exchanges we have with them. It is these calls, alongside the guiding stick, that afford this blind man the capacities to move and circulate. Not merely naming places and people, these calls forged a path ahead that these two could follow together. Interactions between the blind man, boy, and those around them shaped the market into a lived and familiar space.

Notice that the blind man's ability to move is not merely a function of his own body. His movements about the market emerge through a relationship between the boy and himself. These are articulated not only through the physical connection offered by the stick but also through hushed, repeated calls between the elder and his young helper. I suggest, however, that we should use the image of blind man and child as a metaphor for how we consider mobility to happen more broadly. It is an inherently social, relational process. The blind man's mobility is facilitated through this linguistic and embodied connection. There is no unmediated mobility—places become available to us through our interaction with other people.

Across West Africa, one often sees familiar scenes of blind men and women led about by young girls and boys—each holding on to one end of a stick rubbed smooth from steady contact. This relationship is a rich glimpse into the lives of West Africans and offers insights into respective access to time and technology, communities of care, and what people value. In much of the United States, many physical infrastructures like ramps enable differently abled individuals to navigate built environments. Throughout West Africa, even more of these accommodations must be made through communities of care and human labor. Throughout this book, I hope to break down existing distinctions between language and interaction on one hand and material infrastructure on the other.

The example of the blind man and his guide also reveals assumptions about the autonomous self—the boundaries of the body and assumptions about what its capacities should be. At first glance, it may likewise appear to be a special case in which an individual bereft of the capacity for movement because of blindness is able to move thanks to exceptional help from another. However, this example distills some broader truths of movement and mobility that figure centrally in this book: mobility is relational and therefore enabled through social relationships; it is intertwined with the communicative capacities that facilitate it. Anthropology has long argued that the individual—often assumed to be independent and autonomous—can be better understood as relationally emergent. Our perceived independence is a product of situated worldviews that further political, moral, or ideological projects. Marilyn Strathern (1988), for instance, spoke of *dividuals* to explore this interdependence in the case of Melanesia. The blind man and his young companion could be thought of in this way. In a more limited sense, the stick can be understood as a channel of communication between two individuals or, more fundamentally, as a relationship that raises doubts about the independence of autonomous personhood. While relational dividualism is useful for conceptualizing this issue given the historical weight of ideologies of individuality, this is not necessarily a question of separate ontologies. Edward LiPuma's (2000, 132) insight that "persons emerge precisely from that tension between dividual and individual aspects/relations" equally captures the complexity of these questions in West Africa.

The example of the blind man can be traced at least to Gregory Bateson, who meditated on a similar case of a blind man tapping a stick ahead of himself to walk. Bateson (1972) used this example to argue that we should expand the notion of what constitutes a self beyond the confines of a physical body, narrowly construed. For Bateson, the blind man's stick constituted a pathway of communication that was a central part of his locomotory capacities. Matthew Wolf-Meyer (2020) builds on Bateson's example and his own case studies to argue that any communication is facilitated through material objects and technologies. I find these debates useful because they help us realize that movement and mobility are practices that are not independent of the things and people around us but mediated through them.

In the first part of this introduction, I will offer an initial sketch of the relational character of mobility in West Africa. I will begin with an intuitive example of mobility that shows how it is experienced and construed in a local context and from local perspectives. The rest of this book will build on these insights to show the importance of language in studies of mobility. I will argue that linguistic practice is a constitutive aspect of mobility and not merely a medium through which it is represented. Some of my examples may not appear to be classic ones of mobility, for instance, that of migrant

Senegalese Mouride traders hawking sunglasses on the Spanish Steps in Rome. However, mobility as an analytic frame helps us understand broader social formations that are affected by the circulation, exchange, and movement of individuals and communities. In this analysis, it is equally important to account for the roles and positionalities of those people who remain stationary, as they are key players in these communities (Gaibazzi 2015). A close analysis of the language of interactions helps reveal mobility's relational dimensions.

The *Garandaaru* Caught Him

Throughout this book I offer a new analytic perspective for studying mobility that reframes linguistic practice. To begin with, I offer an example that begins to sketch out mobilities emerge in a local context. Twenty kilometers to the southwest of the downtown market where the blind man did his daily shopping sits a cluster of villages on the Senegal-Guinea border in southeastern Senegal. This place of patchy forest and brushy savanna is where I conducted linguistic anthropological fieldwork between the years 2014 and 2016. A few months into my time there, a young boy from the village went missing. The explanations and reactions to this episode taught me a lot about how people conceive of mobility in West Africa.

It was the dry season—a month and a half before the seasonal rains would awaken the parched landscape and bring forth unearthly shoots of neon green grasses. The field crops were long harvested. This was a time of taking stock—of food stores, neighbors, and flocks. Residents of the small village of Taabe on the border of Senegal and Guinea did what they could underneath such an unyielding sun. Women tended a dry season garden next to a small stream, trying to coax vegetables from the silty soil. Work was only possible in between drawn-out tea breaks that offered respite from the hot day. During this time of year, sweat-soaked skin searched out for any possible breath of wind; squinting eyes scanned for patches of precious shadow.

We had just returned from another awareness-raising meeting hosted by an international NGO that had attempted to warn the plateau residents of the dangers of eating bushmeat. As we dispersed and the village residents disputed the NGOs warnings (though they had not countered them publicly during the meeting), I suddenly heard news that Didi, an eight-year-old boy, had gone missing. He had disappeared, as if swallowed from the earth, near a mango orchard by a little stream where village women tended a vegetable garden. My friend and village host, Rune (nephew of the village chief), went to Didi's large family compound to hear if it was true. Normally very emotive and prone to laughter, Rune returned in a state of somber alertness. "It's serious," he uttered, "ko sobee."

Nearly the whole village went out to look for Didi. Messengers were sent out to surrounding villages to alert them of Didi's disappearance. I went out with Rune, meeting up with residents from all corners of the village to organize our search efforts. The next afternoon, hours were spent in small fission-fusion search parties. We fanned out into the surrounding groves, riverbeds, and fields, occasionally encountering another group of concerned, sweaty faces. Didi was not found that day, but his father and other close kin continued to look for him through the night. I went back to my hut to round up precious flashlights, which served as essential equipment in an area without electricity. My headlamps—filled with brand-name Duracell batteries—were particularly sought after.

Skipping breakfast, Rune and I woke up early the next morning to look again for Didi. Although it was cooler, we were tired from a long day of traipsing around the bush. We met up with more and more villagers as we left Taabe, prepared to renew our search for the poor boy. As an anthropologist studying everyday language use in this southeastern corner of Senegal, I found my ears perked up when a word I had never heard before peppered the concerned conversations: "garandaaru nangi mo" (garandaaru got him). I heard this phrase over and over again during the course of our search efforts. A *garandaaru*, I gathered, was something that could occupy or overtake someone and cause them to get lost or move in unhabitual ways. "It could be right by you and not respond to your calls," someone explained to me. It was something that would make you lose yourself and your way, like a spirit that confounds you.

It soon struck me that the places where people were looking for Didi were anywhere but the places that people would ordinarily go. Fearing Didi had been possessed by garandaaru, family and friends were looking not primarily on the paths between human settlements or places where individuals harvested wood or food. Instead, they began to scour the so-called wild places that an individual would be least expected to visit. Locals here did not ordinarily go rambling about the bush in search of adventure and natural beauty. Most stuck to the paths and inhabited spaces that were hewn out of this potentially precarious environment. The wild animals and uninhabited spaces around these villages were generally approached with respectful caution. And yet this search was the first time that I felt like I was exploring with members of the community. We bushwhacked along streambeds, in the underbrush of palm groves, and through the scrubby bushes that interspersed the termite mound–pocked plains. During these hours of searching, I came upon clearings, forests, and streams I had scarcely imagined during my time in southeastern Kédougou.

Viewed in this way, garandaaru can be understood as the decoupling of the boy's trajectories from his habitual human context. New forces in the forest might attract Didi, and the unsettling thing for Didi and his family was that neither he nor they might be able to predict where he would have gone. If Didi had been taken by the garandaaru, locals feared that he would respond not to socialized pathways of movement but rather a world that is devoid of shared paths and waypoints. The ways people engage with space and landscape have been rich topics of anthropological discussion. Tim Ingold (2000), for instance, understands wayfinding as movement in a landscape in relation to lived, habitual activities, which draws attention to the connections between mobility and personhood. Garandaaru seemed to sever these habitual moorings, letting Didi loose in an entirely differently constituted landscape (cf. Caine 2022). What scared people about Didi's absence was that he had lost all grounding in the habitual social world and was roaming about the landscape in a way that they could not understand. To the great relief of his family and us all, Didi was finally found in the outskirts of a village some fifteen kilometers away at the end of this second day of searching.

The first two examples here show how inherently social and relational the process of mobility is. For instance, even as Didi is possessed by garandaaru, his condition can be understood as a relational one. Didi is not merely someone who lost his way but someone who has been led astray by a spirit that has him in its clutches. Like the aforementioned example of the blind man and the child, Didi's story reveals why it is useful to think of movement and mobility as inherently social, and recognizing how mobility emerges through relational, interactional processes is a first step. Throughout this book, I argue that mobility is not merely an experience of movement or migration—in this case Didi's wild roaming throughout the bush. The conversations about his trip, contestations about what happened to him, and claims about his journey were themselves at the heart of mobility; these linguistic practices bring mobility into being.

Furthermore, mobility offers a more expansive way of framing fundamental questions of social life and its interconnections. Scholars of mobility have uprooted assumptions of social life as stationary, using mobility as a lens for capturing human activity and thereby emphasizing process and flux. This approach helps to look across borders, examine connections across space and time, and avoid the reification of identity and community as local constructions. Part of the field of mobility's productivity lies in posing questions that go beyond the frame of mobility as mere physical movement.

In essence, the study of mobility is the study of movement layered over time with social and symbolic meanings. Tim Cresswell (2006), for instance, uses the frame of mobility to account for power and social meaning, while Peter Adey (2017, 102) mused, "Perhaps mobility is always meaningful and therefore never simply movement. Even approaches that characterize mobility in the most abstract of ways see mobilities as imbued with value-laden judgements and labels." These considerations ultimately point to the recognition that there is perhaps no movement without meaning. Any form of mobility or motility, such as walking or running, are socially learned techniques of the body rather than natural capacities (Mauss 1935). Language is often implicitly identified as the process through which we give meaning to the experiences of mobility. The danger, however, is to see language only as an immaterial, conceptual process of coded meaning that sits in contrast to the "real," material experiences of mobility.

This book argues that many theoretical issues can be resolved if we avoid separating mobility dualistically as an experience that is then rendered meaningful through linguistic and social representations. Situating language as a core component to mobility, rather than a mere reflection of it, helps resolve many of the theoretical tensions of this referentialist ideology of language and helps make sense of ethnographic encounters. Didi's wanderings caused by garandaaru, for instance, show that the physical experiences of mobility as movement should not be understood as independent from how they are articulated through language and interpreted through forms of relational possession as personhood. His movements were not independent phenomena but came into being partly through the local conceptions of garandaaru that community members articulated together.

Across West Africa, children like Didi are sent on errands to make small purchases at stores, transmit messages, or check on the status of visitors and events. The way in which they must report on their trips when they return demonstrates the importance of viewing mobilities as articulated action in relation to others rather than as a transparent representation of experiences. Gracia Clark (2010) discusses the local term used to understand this process in Ghana:

> Every time children go on an errand or adults pay a visit, they are asked on arrival to present their ɔkwansu, the story of their trip. This narrative should not be interrupted. It starts with the circumstances that led up to their making the journey and ends with their arrival. *Relatives and neighbors judge a child's maturity and intelligence by the coherence of the ɔkwansu. The story also sets the stage for any subsequent request by describing the circumstances which created the need for it. Ideally, it should alert listeners to the intended request before it is voiced explicitly, so that they can be ready with a response or an alternative solution.* (9–10, emphasis added)

At first glance, this "narrative" may appear to be only a representation of experiences or facts as they happened on this journey. However, notice that the results of the ɔkwansu condition future actions and responses, thereby articulating the children's movements in relation to requests and activities of the adults. In so doing, these stories provide platforms for shaping future interactions and relationships between children and adults in which the child might be characterized as a certain kind of person; for instance, as an unreliable child who would not be asked to complete similar errands in the future or a dependable child who understands the stakes of the errand and may be trusted as a page. The story told thus offers a form of social action where the child is articulating a narrative in relation to the expectations and anticipated counteractions of the adults. Not merely a feature of youth language socialization, these features of narration as social action are true of linguistic practices more broadly. Building on the previous examples, which showed the relationality of mobility, the custom of sharing ɔkwansu offers a first example that demonstrates how linguistic practices can be understood to constitute mobility in a meaningful sense.

Language as Infrastructure

Examining language as a material process makes better use of mobility as an analytic device. Doing so also helps us understand how local communities of migrants live their lives distributed across space. In the previous section, I begin to show how linguistic practices are not merely a representational technology through which migrants share information. Applying this insight one step further, we can say that they are also a material means of forging pathways and channels along which people and objects circulate. In his stimulating essay on African cities, Abdou Maliq Simone (2004) called for an increased consideration of human creativity within a discussion of infrastructure in what he called *people as infrastructure*, a term that captures how people's situated actions are not merely layered on but also radically change material forms in our world. Such frameworks also challenge stark nature-culture boundaries that provide a cultural blueprint based on keeping objects and humans conceptually distinct (Latour 1993; Descola 2013). Drawing on Simone's analytic, *people as infrastructure*, this chapter explores what we can learn about mobility and social change when we examine linguistic practice as a form of infrastructure.

Other literature from urban anthropology, such as the fascinating study of West African migrants in Paris's Gare du Nord shows how a train station constructs pathways for durable social infrastructure (Kleinman 2014, 2019). Building on the question of how physical space mediates social and linguistic exchanges, however, this book interrogates the material implications of linguistic practice in the context of mobility. These qualities of language emerge even more fully in published responses to Julie Kleinman's work: "Stories, and even practices associated with particular urban forms, continue to exist after buildings and neighborhoods are demolished or re-identified after gentrification" (Newman 2021, 3). In other words, places are laminated productions of their overt material properties and other conceptual layers constituted through language as a material, symbolic infrastructure. These latter processes and can sustain a place long after they are "gone." In the same set of responses to Kleinman's work, Rudolph Gaudio (2021) examines the way in which language sustains and is materialized through infrastructure. Grounding language as a material practice, he defines what he calls discursive infrastructure in two ways: "1) the ways in which language is materialized—that is, mediated by material forms—and 2) the ways people and institutions use language to comment and act upon physical and social infrastructures" (3). This book expands these important foundations to examine language as a material channel that mediates and constitutes mobilities.

It is useful to consider language as a kind of infrastructure in several senses. Firstly, contrary to popular conceptions in which it is held to be a purely symbolic technology, language is a material thing and process. Its frequency and force can be measured by instruments, and it is produced by the physical body as instrument. Our bodies thus offer physical channels of this embodied practice, producing vibrations in our lungs and vocal apparatuses that are captured by other interlocutors through measurable processes. Alongside other infrastructures like internet cables, electric wiring, or roadways, language is "matter that enable[s] the movement of other matter" (Larkin 2013b, 329). Language's separation from the material world can be located in intellectual histories going back at least to Ferdinand de Saussure, who proposed a separation from the denotational sign and the material world, a conceptualization that parallels broader Cartesian distinctions between mind and body (Irvine 1989). As discussed by Webb Keane (2005, 185), "Saussurian semiology fails to see the role linguistic practices play in the objectification of things." It is for these reasons that linguistic signs as material things can interact with other forms of materiality to wear down or fail such that linguistic signification is disrupted (Keane 1997). Drawing on work from coastal Senegal, Judith Irvine insisted on the material qualities of language and their consideration alongside issues of political economy by examining, for instance, how praises sung by West African griots constituted a material form of exchange (Irvine 1989).

A material thing in its own right, language also enables the circulation of other material, social forms. Other anthropologists of media have offered a broader framework for examining infrastructure's capacity to enable circulation and exchange—in addition to a technical process, it is one that is intertwined with political, aesthetic, and social concerns. Brian Larkin (2008, 6) looks to infrastructure as material forms that enable broader circulations across channels: "Infrastructure, in my usage, refers to this totality of both technical and cultural systems that create institutionalized structures whereby goods of all sorts circulate, connecting and binding people into collectivities." The forms of verbal art I describe in this book establish channels of communication and circulation across which mobility is made possible. Alongside quintessential forms of infrastructure and media such as radio, internet, or cell networks, language in interaction offers a form of mediation that "bring different people, objects, and spaces into interaction" (Larkin 2013b, 330). Alongside that of Simone, the work of Julia Elyachar (2010) demonstrates the infrastructural aspects of linguistic exchange and practice. She shows how *phatic labor* in the form of social exchanges establishes an "infrastructure of communicative channels" that can further other social, political, and economic projects (452). In so doing, she demonstrates that language can be examined on the same plane as other forms of conventional infrastructure. In this book, language emerges as a particularly useful lens for investigating mobility precisely because it has an intersubjective character that emerges *in between* people rather than as the property of one person. In the second half of this book, I draw more heavily on the perspective of language as infrastructure to explore how linguistic exchanges in mobile settings form a material infrastructure through which migrants bring homes, markets, and borders into existence.

Linguistic practice can etch lines into the ground, so to speak, giving rise to the emergence of socially meaningful sites, places, and mediating material connections along which people and things circulate. I offer two short examples of what language as infrastructure may sound like. For instance, the language traded between migrant merchants in Kédougou's downtown market was a key practice through which they rooted themselves in a new place. Merchants and laborers from Guinea, the Gambia, and Mali frequently tried to take advantage of Kédougou City's place on a busy road to make money away from home. Here, among kola nuts and ready-to-wear clothes, in-law talk was very productively used among individuals to build relationships of futurity between individuals who weren't always in-laws in a technical sense. Traders hoping to build long-standing relationships with customers often yelled out "esiraaɓe!" (senior in-law) to passersby. The bamboo stools or wheelbarrows on which they were sitting became a domestic space partly through the way they used honorific and teasing registers of in-law talk. This talk was not merely bouncing off the surface of an already constituted place; it shaped the market in domestic space, which emerges as a hybrid of physical and conceptual layers. Eating large plates of meals together from their selling spots, these merchants could disperse patronage and favors from a place that had become more like a new home than merely a market of buying and selling.

Viewing language as infrastructure also helps understand our desperate search for Didi in the land surrounding Taabe village. Although all I could see was an unfolding landscape, the area we had been scouring was overlaid by a social infrastructure. What appeared to me to be rivers and clearings were often highly saturated sites of human activity, constituted through iterative stories told and distinctions made by inhabitants who discursively shaped this into a built environment: places where oil palms were harvested; a site where a young couple had been discovered; areas where spirits still dwelled; and caves where traces of the autochthonous residents were to be found. To have been a part of these previous chains of speech events was to be able to see the linguistic infrastructure that shaped the land in front of it. As a newcomer to this, I did my best to try to navigate the same landscape, awkwardly entering into incomplete and broken chains of language-as-place saturated with meaning.

Mobility as a Verbal Art

When I speak of language in this book, I do not speak of it primarily as a formal system of representation, as it is frequently approached in linguistics. Instead, I consider language a socially infused, material practice in everyday life, not merely a symbolic system (Irvine 1989; Miller 2005; Keane 2005). These approaches to language guide linguistic anthropology, a field from which this book emerges. Close attention to language can show how people become successful migrants—as a way to expand or contract their life possibilities—but it can also reveal how we should be thinking of mobility from a broader perspective. My research suggests that it is useful to view mobility as a kind of verbal art. Doing so takes emphasis away from individual capacities and movement and shifts it toward the social and linguistic contexts that render people and places available and knowable to one another. Linguistic practices enable migrants to be successful—to build relationships with others far from home or to articulate their stories to others. Not merely a semiotic system for encoding referential statements, my ethnography among migrants in Senegal has demonstrated language to be an interactional, performative medium that can impel changes in the world. In this first sense, perspectives on language as social action (and not mere reference) allow us to see the negotiation of relationships, identity categories, and status.

Thinking of language as verbal art can help us view an international border as a joint construction of the material environment and talk. The border between Senegal and Guinea, for instance, was formed not out of physical barriers but rather through the exchange of talk by local residents, border police, and travelers. Boundaries between those living in Senegalese and Guinean villages were established through repeated stories told about who had rights to harvest straw and other natural resources in certain areas. The story of a conflict between border dwellers offered a narrative site through which interlocutors agreed on long-standing boundaries between areas. As people came and went, reports on their movements included deictic expressions like *here* and *there* through which individuals made distinctions between places that were held to be distinct. As such, appearances of an objective, Cartesian space were transformed into a lived landscape through talk. These distinctions helped established spatial boundaries such that one could be away in the first place. Physical distance thus does not always map onto space as it is socially experienced. Being a migrant is not merely a question of spatial distance expressed in kilometers but also an issue of inhabiting socially constituted spaces and roles that are negotiated through talk. I develop the verbal art of mobility more fully in the first half of this book, and in the second half, I build on these insights to show the language as a form of infrastructure.

Describing linguistic practices as a verbal art draws attention to the important social consequences that everyday language can have in the lives of migrants. I adopt the term *verbal art* in this book to capture commonsense understandings of the value of everyday linguistic practices. However, this work significantly departs from the ways that scholars have approached verbal art in the past. Most frequently, verbal art has become shorthand for the jokes, proverbs, or folktales that were shared in communities. Currently, most linguistic anthropological approaches eschew this kind of cataloging approach because classifying generic forms tends to reify an expressive culture rather than showing its sociocultural dynamics and its situated functions. Scholars such as Richard Bauman (1975) have attempted to build bridges between folkloric studies and verbal art, on one hand, and linguistic anthropology, on the other, by eschewing a text-centered approach and looking to performance as an analytic. Performance helps explore the mediated doing of verbal arts, how roles, audience, and manner all matter and offer creative opportunities for social action. For instance, work by Sabina Perrino (2020) examines the narrative processes through which migrants are performatively excluded from northern Italy. Her analysis employs concepts like stance, chronotope, and scale to tease out how speakers position themselves with respect to migrants. Using the analytic *intimacies of exclusion*, Perrino examines the affective dimensions of these processes, wherein authenticity, food, and history are suffused with often racialized feelings of belonging.

Examining mobility as a verbal art offers critical insights on power and precarity in migrant lifeworlds. For instance, consider the example of an international refugee (Jacquemet 2009). Even becoming a refugee entails the successful performance of what precarity and destitution look like in the eyes of a state. What does a refugee talk like? What do they look like, and what kinds of things should they know? Many of the international migrants I met were intensely aware of such issues, even if they could not always navigate them perfectly in highly unequal interactions. Using language in particular ways could thus quite literally make someone into a refugee. This was a question of performance—an interactional frame between an individual and their interlocutors driven by certain assumptions about language.

The linguistic varieties individuals wield impact the ways people are interpreted and the opportunities they might have. This is a question not just of codes but of specific competencies—knowledge of contexts and of norms of usage. According to Paul Stoller (2013), a foundational scholar of West African diaspora in the United States, language and its related cultural competence were the most important factors determining the success of West African migrants. The performances of migrants—their possible missteps, interactional disjunctures, or use of stigmatized varieties—were closely monitored. As Jan Blommaert (2010, 6) has remarked, "movement of people across space is therefore never a move across empty spaces. The spaces are always someone's space, and they are filled with norms, expectations, conceptions of what counts as proper and normal (indexical) language use and what does not count as such." For these reasons, it is just as important to study how language is interpreted as it is to track how it is produced. For instance, the borderlands of Senegal and Guinea offer a field of evaluation in which certain linguistic signs became highly salient and policed. In the multilingual context of West Africa, to speak certain varieties—and not others—is to encounter an entirely different kind of place. Speaking different languages and being a part of different networks can thus mediate experiences in distinct ways, such that the same "place" could appear very different to a newly arrived migrant in contrast to a long-standing local. In contrast to visuality, language as aurality presents one of the most shrouded and underappreciated forms of power and evaluation (Lippi-Green 2011).

In sum, linguistic practice should be seen as more than a representation of mobility, in terms of coded meaning, as it is a core part of mobility itself. At first glance, dodging law enforcement in distant lands, perilous maritime voyages, and other precarious leaps across space appear to be the experiences on which becoming a migrant are founded. However, the true craft of a migrant often emerges in the capacity to manage contingent social relationship with hosts, friends, and kin. In a basic sense, the study of mobility entails the resources, infrastructures, and social contexts that render it feasible. Being a successful migrant in West Africa, as throughout the world, requires an ability to manage relationships through idioms of kinship, commonality, or destitution. Ethnic identification, kinship relationships, or other form of community building in mobile contexts should not be questions of automatic affiliation but, instead, are contingent on creative acts of linguistic performance. This entails the capacity to articulate oneself as a certain kind of legible person, such as guest, kin, or worker.

However, this relational work was also a double-edged sword. Building relational connections with others through interaction could enable migrants to succeed, but they could also be exploited by others to make demands on a person's time and resources. For instance, many across West Africa shared a concern with the power of language and gossip to bring unwanted attention to one's possessions. A jealous eye might threaten one's successes and desired possessions such as expensive phones or automobiles. For this reason, aspiring migrants often hid their imminent travels carefully from their communities. There was thus a danger of bragging about or talking about one's plans to move abroad for fear that this talk would bring unwanted attention to one's possible fortune. Young aspiring migrants would frequently "disappear" overnight, having launched a migratory adventure many months in the making. Even knowledge of their whereabouts abroad was not always shared with those back home. News often came in the form of Western Union and MoneyGram transfers, which offered steady streams of support to extended families. In an important sense, being away didn't manifest itself until such gifts back home made this migrancy a reality.

From Representing Mobility to Articulating Mobility

Becoming a migrant thus constitutes an act of social articulation that is performative rather than narrowly communicative in that it constructs relationship with others and facilitates access to other social spaces. For these reasons, I prefer to use the term *articulation* rather than *representation* to better show the work of language in mobility. Articulation draws on the dual meaning of making connections and making propositions or references. By entailing meanings that emphasize both material processes and social labor, articulation provides a theoretical middle point to my discussion of language as verbal art and as infrastructure. This term builds on long-standing work in linguistic anthropology that has critiqued a referentialist ideology of language in which people ignore language's connective, affective, or poetic capacities in favor of viewing language as mere reference. As such, migrants don't come to places as complete persons but learn to articulate and identify themselves in relation to new people and places. Capturing the emergent character of interaction helps move away from a view of unchanging, autonomous people who simply move around to new spaces. In speaking and connecting with others, migrants learn to adopt new voices and retool how they present themselves in different contexts. Another way to think of this concept is to consider identity and place as emergent productions. People make the places they move through, and respective identities emerge in relation to one another. The task before us is to examine not only the political or economic contexts in which mobility happens but also the social and linguistic contexts that render people and places available and knowable to one another.

Approaches to mobility have often been separated into two separate processes: the movement and experience of mobility, on one hand, and the construction of meaning, on the other. Here movement is often conceptualized as an embodied, physical, or material sense, and the construction of meaning and its representation is held to be the purview of language. When language does figure in approaches to mobility, it becomes tacked on to ask how acts of mobility are represented or reflected. Meaning as investigated through language is treated as a separate calculation that occurs before or after mobility has happened. Such approaches often employ terms like *representation, imaginaries,* and *fantasy.* Methodologically, the model here is the interview or story told that represents the faraway travels of migrancy as it happened. Although mobility studies have often insisted on the importance of exploring the meaning of mobility,[2] these approaches risk separating out mobility in terms of experiences and their representations. As such, language is often held to be a mere representation of a preexisting experience. Throughout this book, I insist on language as a form of social action in its own right and not merely a representation of the world. Language does not merely reflect "experiences" in the world but can also bring things into being.

Viewing talk on mobilities in terms of articulations rather than representations helps resolve tensions in the scholarship around the purported "accuracy" of migration realities. Beneath the gilded allure of emigration, there is an increasing recognition that Europe and the United States are also places of hardship and suffering. However, these difficulties are often hard to express to those who remain in Senegal partly because they must be shown and not merely told. As such, a migrant telling their family back home how hard it is over there is often accused of protecting their successes. In this way, many scholars have noted a disjuncture between the stories told of migration and the realities that migrants face when they get there. Based on work between Mali and the Congo, Bruce Whitehouse (2013, 25) notes how "migrants frequently misrepresent their circumstances in the place of destination, exaggerating successes and playing down hardships." Viewing such talk of mobility as an articulated form of social action shows how it is a force for broader interactional or political designs rather than a narration to be examined in terms of mere truth value. At a broader geopolitical level, the way in which African migrants to southern Europe have been narrated in terms of civilizational invasions provides another example. Not mere representation, this discourse constitutes a form of exclusion and alienation rather than a mere reporting on the state of things (Triulzi and McKenzie 2013). In the work of Caroline Melly (2011), migrants discussing the disappearance of an infamous clandestine vessel bound for the Canary Islands is not merely a story told as an imaginary; it structures future possibilities for mobility and action. These effects are also important to track at the level of face-to-face encounters. Even the term that West African migrants or media employ to discuss their migrations encode stances and situated ways of experiencing mobility: terms such as *aventure* or *aventurier* that encode notions of risk, uncertainty, and possibility (Bredeloup 2008, 2014).

These arguments about articulation and the materiality of language may at times appear to be abstract. The stakes are most apparent in an example I describe in chapter 3. Simply put, I show that a young Guinean trader can leave his homeland, be abroad for four years before returning, and yet not be a migrant. At first, this might seem like an impossibility. However, this apparent conundrum can be explained by thinking of language as not merely a representation of existing mobilities but something that brings migrancy and mobility into being. In this example, a Guinean laborer makes his way to Mauritania, where he is exploited as a domestic servant—a slave almost—for four years in the compound of a wealthy family. After he returns, his story is told and interpreted by his peers in a downtown Kédougou market. They evaluate the signs of his mobility, including whether he had learned any local languages, returned with any money and new belongings, or had knowledge of the neighborhoods of Nouakchott.

As proof of his lack of mobility, his peers conclude that he hadn't acquired any new things or money and had displayed little local knowledge of the area. Mocking him with a customary teasing nickname, the friends of this young Guinean trader in effect deny him the status of migrant; thus, mobility is negotiated through language in interaction. The approaches adopted in this book resonate with studies of mobility around the world where a frequent preoccupation with economics and material resources as accumulation belies central concerns of becoming "somebody" (MacGaffey and Bazenguissa-Ganga 2000). This process cannot be captured as a single, individual telling of a "story." Becoming somebody entails a translation of cumulative experiences in relation to others through everyday interactions.

Chapter Summaries

This introduction has set the stage for thinking about language and mobility in new ways. Approaching language as material and as negotiated decenters assumptions about the primacy of human autonomy and intentionality in which language is held to be a transparent window on people's thoughts and personhood. Instead, we must look to language as a material, embodied practice through which mobilities are articulated. Talk on the move does not flow unimpeded as self-evident representations. It becomes snagged on the contingency of multiparty interactions; it is entangled with objects and places, and through it, the shards of many a migrant's personhood become distributed across time and space. Navigating this interactional, material landscape through creative performances is the verbal art of mobility in West Africa.

Chapter 1 (Navigating Change in a Rural Borderland) examines cross-border treks from Senegal to Guinea as starting points for considering language and mobility as well as the regional histories within which these arguments are made. While conventional approaches to mobility emphasize material resources and physical movement, mobility is rendered possible through the relationships negotiated along the way. This chapter situates this book's linguistic anthropological approach within the processes of social change that have fundamentally shaped southeastern Senegal. Within the past decade, a gold mining boom, the construction of an international highway, the 2014–16 Ebola epidemic, and the establishment of Kédougou as a region have all contributed to significant social and economic challenges for Kédougou's communities. These changes sit alongside a deep history of seasonal, regional mobility that have allowed communities to thrive amid economic and environmental precarities. First grounding these issues in a cross-border trek to establish initial conceptions of mobility, this book goes on to explore more complex forms of mobility constituted through language.

In chapter 2 (The Pursuit of Relations in a Time of Social Change), I take a step back to discuss the broader repertoire of social idioms and routines West Africans creatively adopt to thrive in mobile contexts. While kinship, affinity, and other forms of mutuality are often presented as static social structures that push people into migration, this chapter demonstrates that these idioms in interaction can also be used to creatively navigate and build relationships. Local migrants, keen observers of their own social worlds, understood this relational work to be fundamentally mobile and described it as the *pursuit of relations (jokkere endam)*. To study mobility is necessarily to account for different forms of personhood and identity that emerge from varying contexts. The ability of migrants to present themselves across time and space is mediated by the specific kinds of resources, routines, and understandings that are shared in distinct environments. Migrants do not transport themselves as autonomous, complete people from place to place but emerge in relation to existing sociolinguistic understandings. At the end of this chapter, I show how technologies of statecraft like ID cards, birth registries, and surveillance initiatives on the border also are a part of these flexible social practices.

Chapter 3 (Articulating Mobility: Migration in Interaction) offers a toolkit for exploring how mobility is negotiated and articulated in multiparty social encounters. Whereas individual narratives or interviews might appear to transparently represent the experiences of migrants, tracking negotiated interactions better accounts for mobility in the lifeworlds of migrants. This approach is grounded in the recognition that communicative acts bring things into being at the same time that they represent experiences. To do this, the chapter develops the term *articulating* as an alternative to *representing* to emphasize the dual meaning of expressing a proposition and making relational linkages. Articulating mobilities entails a social practice that can shape relationships, mediate the formation of collectivities, and enable the movement of people, bodies, and ideas. This shift of perspective is a useful complement to other approaches to meaning making in mobility studies that draw on nonmaterial concepts such as representation, imaginaries, and fantasy. Linguistic representations of mobilities might first appear to be communicative acts of reporting on existing "events" or "experiences." However, ethnographic encounters show how articulating mobile experiences should also be seen as a form of social action—a practice of mobility itself. While most studies have looked at language as a source of information about mobility and examine these as texts based on interviews, I look at the textures of interaction through which migrants become legible in different places. Rather than only reflecting worlds and experiences, language creates them.

Chapter 4 (Kola, Salt, and Stone: Forging Pathways of Belonging through the Materiality of Language) shows how the exchange of talk and objects grounds more durable social infrastructures that help migrants connect with dispersed communities. As such, it tracks the material webs of exchange through which migrants manage their presence in distant hometown communities. In a first example, it zooms in on a naming ceremony in a small rural village to explore how communities account for the participation of migrants who are often absent from village life. This tells the story of an increasingly mobile woman who resorts to creative performances of teasing and reenactment to reassert herself as a central community member. With strong methodological implications, it shows that participation needs to be studied from perspectives that combine the exchange of language and material objects on the edges of ritual action. In a second example, this chapter examines my journey in founding a field station in the outskirts of Kédougou with a local collaborator. Not merely a question of stones and mortar, this enterprise is also dependent on the distributed attunement of neighbors to succeed: a process achieved through material ritual blessings.

Chapters 5 and 6 draw on central concepts of the book—articulation and language as infrastructure—to reinterpret central sites of mobility: the international border and the market space. Chapter 5 (Constituting a Border through Linguistic Practice) shows how the border between Kédougou and Guinea came into being through situated interactions during the Ebola pandemic. I argue that firstly, this amorphous border was constituted through distinctions that emerged in routines of storytelling and surveillance. During the Ebola epidemic of 2014–16, this zone became the site of intense scrutiny by the Senegalese state and international communities who were concerned with the spread of Ebola. The border simultaneously offered a zone of discernment in which marked distinctions based on provenance, linguistic usage, and demeanor could affect one's ability to travel, trade, and thrive. Drawing on scholarship in medical anthropology, this chapter argues that Ebola should be analyzed alongside sociolinguistic practices as a force for shaping the interactions of mobile individuals in these borderlands.

Chapter 6 (Kédougou Market: A Place of Wares and Words) examines how migrants made a place out of Kédougou's downtown market. Through the exchange of wares and words, migrants performed routines of verbal creativity that include teasing, storytelling, and greeting to negotiate relationships with one another and ground themselves in a fickle place. The performance of in-law talk, for instance, enabled migrants to constitute a domestic sphere from which they could dispense hospitality and enjoy in the comforts of home. Markets were profitable but potentially risky places that could eat your money just as quickly as you could make it. Succeeding here required migrants to monitor their language and wealth so as to benefit from connections with others while also not revealing too much of themselves. The conclusion discusses the implications these approaches on mobility carry for questions of power and precarity. The appearance of autonomy in the context of mobility—in which mobility appears to be a mere technical, logistical question—is often a gauge of power relations. Having to account for social others in contexts of mobility is thus indicative of an individual's power and position with respect to those others.

Notes

1. Some scholars might call this level of movement at an individual level *motility*. Although this term can also be useful, I prefer to speak of *mobility* because even at an individual, organismal level, our capacity to move and migrate are relational and therefore not merely a question of natural bodily movements. Furthermore, the way we *scale* human activity (in terms of duration, collectivities, and other complexities) should be seen as a question to investigate processually rather than an a priori assumption. In this initial example, I draw out some insights at an individual level that I will apply to more encompassing questions later.

2. The term *mobility* can be approached in a couple ways: in one sense, mobility provides an analytical perspective through which scholars study human practices in a new and useful way. In another sense, local communities of practice have understandings of these phenomena—who is a migrant, what this means and the local significance of migrations, movement, and circulation.

1

NAVIGATING CHANGE IN A RURAL BORDERLAND

Limping across the Border

My right leg had been aching for kilometers. It wasn't the kind of pain you get from muscle fatigue. It was the pain of a joint giving out. Not the casual fatigue that slowly crept in after a hard day's hike, this was an existential exhaustion that fixes your gaze no further than a few inches in front of your feet. Local speakers of Pular (a lingua franca in southeast Senegal) have a word for this form of extreme exhaustion—they call it *mboggegol.* This word was not infrequently heard in the inaccessible plateaus and mountains of the Fouta Djallon range in southeastern Senegal and northern Guinea. Borderlanders used it describe their long journeys up and down steep inclines to access markets and go to school. We had been navigating these paths from sunup to sundown, and my walking companions and I had grown desperate. But seeing small, thatched goat paddocks next to a cleared path, I knew we could not be far away from the village. We mustn't be because I couldn't go any further.

This was the second or third time I had set foot in the village of Ta-abe, but I had never been more thankful to recognize a place. As I at last glimpsed a few human outlines in the dark path ahead, my right leg collapsed on the rocky earth. A familiar face emerged out of the shadows calling my name, and I have never been happier to see anyone in my life. It was Mamadou Diallo, my friend. Hobbling over to a bamboo platform, I frenetically began to tell the news of our arduous trip across the border. Nervous laughter flowed out from my throbbing body. In the hopes of putting this all behind us through a ritual of deprecatory storytelling, I began to tell him of our ordeal.

I had just walked nonstop from Maliville, Guinea, to Senegal with two former Peace Corps colleagues, Robyn and Steve. Robyn had a later plane to catch in Dakar, and we had hoped to walk from Guinea to Kédougou City by that evening. Given the sporadic public transportation on the border and the enthusiasm of our youth, it seemed like a good idea at the time. Although some trucks with massive ground clearance were able to navigate the roads across the Fouta Djallon mountains, the road from Maliville to Senegal was frequently little more than a muddy track. We set out well before sunrise from the hills of Maliville, hoping to make it across the border to Senegal by nightfall. We had walked what we later estimated to be over sixty kilometers in one day—much greater than the true distance due to our frequent backtracking. However, this wasn't some heroic feat. We had begun the trek with a group of local merchants who were transporting woven indigo fabrics from Guinea to Senegal on their heads and slung across their sides. Along with them walked a man and his young daughter, a girl no older than eleven or twelve. Although we separated from this group early in the trip, this man and his daughter likely crossed the Senegalese border at Takkopellel by sundown, just as so many before them had done. Although there were Guinean and Senegalese border stations between Maliville and Kédougou, a web of quicker and more efficient routes bypassed these official posts. Without the aid of maps or GPS, these travelers drew on an accumulated knowledge of the terrain to make their way to Senegal.

Confident in our local language skills after two years in Senegal, we thought we could manage on our own. Although we set off with a few other Guinean travelers, we weren't concerned when we split up. When we were unsure of which path to take, we asked for directions from those we met. In the end, we probably followed every detour, dead end, and cattle path between Maliville and the Senegal-Guinea border. Since we did not know the most efficient route, we relied on guidance along the way from farmers and villagers, whose accommodating directions resoundingly assured us that the next town was "not far," no matter the distance that remained. Although "not far" often meant many weary kilometers to go, these assertions offered a palliative attempt to accommodate strangers rather than information that should be assessed in terms of its truth value. To this day, I imagine these surprised Guinean farmers telling stories about the time three Americans suddenly turned up in their fields, flustered and confused. One might have called our adventure a survey of some of the loneliest cows in the borderlands. The few liters of water we brought with us were soon

Figure 1.1. Looking down on the Fouta Djallon foothills.

consumed, and in the kilometers between habitations, we quickly became thirsty. When we eventually made it to the border, we were dehydrated and on the verge of utter breakdown. Meanwhile, the families we set out with had seemed to navigate the journey with ease, passing from village to village, where they drank water and rested until the next stop.

I remember thinking halfway through our trip that I couldn't go any further. And then I realized what a body does to continue when it has to. To this day we joke that Steve's mind slipped halfway through—his talk turned into loopy riddles, and he began quaffing water out of muddy puddles. But maybe I'm not remembering things clearly either. Sometimes I forget if we were just teasing him or if this all really happened. Thinking back now, you might even say that we were possessed by garandaaru, as Didi was said to have been. We soon realized that we needed to keep talking to keep the exhaustion at bay. Chatting together helped us keep our minds sharp and reminded us to remain present in our bodies. Talk was integral to keep us moving.

In this sense, language is not merely something that is layered onto movement and mobility but a constitutive part of them. Jason De León exposes the hardship and mortal danger faced by border crossers on the US southern border who are set up to fail in a context where the desert does the dirty work of broader policies of exclusion and xenophobia (De León 2015). Although my friends and I were crossing the border as part of a trip of exploration, border crossers in the United States must navigate precarious borderlands just to maintain connections with fragmented families. De León's work shows that linguistic practices of border crossers—the jokes they tell themselves along the way—help them reshape their mobile experiences. They make the best of their journeys by telling each other that they are having a picnic or using humor to rearticulate their experiences (De León 2015, 94). Not only can such linguistic exchanges be thought of as conceptual forms of representation, but in an important sense, they can also materially impact the travelers' experiences. Words can quite literally help people move ahead; they can reshape the land. More broadly, we talk and sing to each other during periods of work and physical hardship to move ourselves along. It is in this way that language can also be understood as an embodied practice that has real, physical impacts on body and landscape.

On Mobility, Language, and Nature-Culture Boundaries

West Africans traveling in the bush (Pular *ladde* or *buruure*) from Senegal to Guinea do not often bring water, food, or other backwoods amenities with them. They don't need to. Instead, they move from village to village, using islands of human settlement as relay stations as they trek across what outsiders might perceive to be great natural expanses. The most important thing is not necessarily to know the way as an independent traveler but to follow the footsteps and the advice of those who do. In every village that we came across, polite greetings were returned with offers of water and rest. The moment of arrival at a village is therefore significant. Extended greetings often involve the exchange of one's last names, accounts of one's destinations or origins, and declarations of one's intent. "Ko honto wonuɗaa yahde?" ("Where are you headed?") we often heard travelers asking one another. Their answers often intertwined people and communities, placing fellow travelers into social frameworks. These greetings—a recognition that you were occupying the same world—were followed by hospitality in the form of food, water, and sharing of news. At moments such as these, West African travelers also fill up on water. Rather than taking small sips, most guzzle a liter of water from giant plastic cups in one fell swoop. I can still taste its earthy minerality—water steeped in large clay jars that remain cool even in the hottest temperatures. Hydrologic systems are not just a function of streams, lakes, and other natural formations. On the journey from Maliville to Taabe, water slowed not merely along depressions in the earth but also along the channels of reciprocal human interaction and exchange.

Although this first story ostensibly happened en brousse—in the so-called wild spaces in between—these transborder travelers employed the same strategies that allowed other migrants to succeed in the more densely inhabited regional hubs, mining villages, and European cities that many mobile West Africans now call home. Rather than a practice of self-sufficiency in a natural environment, movement entails the critical skill of navigating social relationships to leverage one's mobility across vast spaces. Anthropological perspectives show no untouched nature remaining free from human influence. Nature-culture distinctions instead offer situated perspectives on the world as part of constructed human categories (Descola 2013). There are other ways to divide up the world. To call something a natural disaster is to practice the erasure of systemic social issues that distribute calamity (Cox and Cox 2016). Most of those traveling in West Africa don't pretend to be self-sufficient travelers who charge through an untouched forest. They instead rely on existing oases of relationality, bootstrapping from place to place as they navigate the social landscape. The work of being mobile is not primarily the capacity to move about but the ability to traverse relationships within a world of others. This is the work of mobility as a verbal art—of creatively inserting yourself into a social scene, making oneself intelligible as a person, and growing out from these pockets of human sociality.

Viewing mobility as social negotiation achieved through the verbal art of self-presentation helps us get away from existing approaches that focus on the movement of things, people, and objects independently of their social situatedness. Attempting to sift out the inherent social from mobility has important consequences for our interdependent societies. While explorers and colonial agents often imagined themselves to be traveling through uncharted, wild places in the New World and across Africa, they were in fact moving through intimately inhabited, social worlds. Rather than building ties with communities along the way, many imagined themselves to be self-sufficient, with only the occasional need for "resupplying" and "restocking." Their (willful) ignorance of these networks is perhaps reflective of their broader imperial ambitions. Tracking mobility through the verbal art of social negotiation helps us cut to the heart of what mobility is all about.

Introducing the Village of Taabe

Mamadou Diallo, my savior in the village of Taabe at the end of this grueling trip, ultimately became my closest friend during my time in West Africa.[1] Although I visited his hometown of Taabe only a few times in my time in the Peace Corps, I came back to this small Senegalese village on the Guinea border for longer stretches during my fieldwork, using it as a base to explore mobility and language practices in the rapidly changing region of Kédougou. By the time I had met him, Mamadou was beginning to develop a reputation as a knowledgeable guide for Spanish and Catalan tourists who occasionally made their way as far inland as Kédougou. His linguistic and professional capacities—the ability to speak to tourists and figure out what they wanted out of a week in West Africa—had enabled his own mobility. He was someone who frequently traveled between coastal Senegal and Kédougou, and through this became known as an important individual who could mobilize people and things.

Our friendship started when I began to give Mamadou English lessons and help him conceptualize his expanding guest lodging in Taabe, a small compound of huts on top of a plateau where he welcomed tourists looking for a rustic experience. When Mamadou later managed to buy a parcel of land just outside the nearby city of Kédougou, we used his new place to hang out during his trips to town. We would sit underneath a small baobab tree on a plastic mat, brewing green tea and chattering away in Pular, English, and French while gazing on a star-filled sky free from light pollution. Years later, this land at the edge of town where we used to find the spent shotgun shells of quail hunters would become a bustling and expanding new neighborhood for the growing families of people like Mamadou.

Mamadou's hometown of Taabe sits on one of the northernmost mountainous plateaus in the Fouta Djallon mountains along the border between Senegal and Guinea. Mamadou and most others in this area (and into Guinea) considered themselves ethnically Fulɓe Fouta. Inhabiting the first rises in the Fouta Djallon mountain range that spilled over into Guinea, the Fulɓe Fouta here spoke a dialect of Pular that was very similar to the varieties spoken across the border in Middle Guinea, an area that was often held to be the authentic origin of these Pular varieties. Residents here frequently had business with family across the border in Guinea. The *hoore fello* (on top of the mountain) included Taabe and several linked villages sitting on a plateau in these northern reaches of the Fouta Djallon mountains. Covering

Figure 1.2. Kedougou's new neighborhoods.

an area of approximately fifteen kilometers, these villages were interspersed by fields of mushroom-like termite mounds, low scrubland, and patches of forest. A web of paths was etched into the savanna, many branching off toward small hamlets or fields that were reclaimed from the surrounding vegetation. Taabe's residents were primarily agriculturalists who grew fonio, peanuts, and corn on the rocky, ferrite-rich soil of the plateau. A prized grain that is often eaten throughout West Africa on special occasions, fonio provided the most important source of revenue for these farmers. Its cultivation necessitates a great deal of coordinated labor and these agriculturalists traditionally relied on support from extensive in-law networks and work parties at critical times of the harvest. As such, mobilizing people and labor was a central concern of Taabe residents in an area where moving around was hard and people had a tendency to leave.

Yet it would be a mistake to view these farmers merely as provincial residents. These same individuals balanced farming with seasonal work in Kédougou City and Dakar, and in mining areas throughout the region. Taabe represented one node in a broader network of places held together by the repeated social and material investments of mobile individuals inhabiting distributed communities. Across these sites, those connected through

Figure 1.3. The village of Taabe.

Taabe could be found mining gold, selling grains or manufactured goods, or laboring in the expanding suburbs of Dakar. Many of the residents of these villages can trace their origins throughout the region and most settled here to escape the same kinds of repressive economic and political conditions that impelled Fulɓe Fouta across Guinea to seek opportunities elsewhere (Fioratta 2020). With Taabe sitting only a few kilometers from the border between Guinea and Senegal, residents also traveled back and forth to the regional capital of Kédougou City. Beginning around my arrival in 2006, the region of Kédougou witnessed accelerating social, economic, and political change at the intersection of infrastructure development, political decentralization, and a mining boom—all compounded by the Ebola epidemic of 2014–16, which threatened Senegal during the period of my field work.

During my time in Taabe, I lived with the family of the village chief, Jom Wuro, who was the younger brother of my friend Mamadou's father. It was Mamadou's deceased father, Diao, who had been the village chief before his younger brother. Diao was a remarkable leader who rallied the entire plateau around him. In a place where the machines often came to die, eaten away by dust and overuse, he put an array of technological advances to productive use. His was a creative mind; for example, he was the first to experiment with plowing and food processing technologies in the village. At the same time, he held the mantle of village authority and commanded deep respect across the plateau. When I had the honor of meeting him during one of my first visits, his compound was a dense social node. People from all over the plateau were in attendance, discussing his recent farming innovations and sharing in his artful storytelling.

I found the shards of this great village chief's personhood in the subsequent generations still present in Taabe. Many young boys in village were named after him and this connection was not merely a symbolic one. To share a connection with a powerful namesake was to inherit a part of this person's character—an inheritance not only of blood but also of name as linguistic substance. A son of Diao's younger brother was one of those who carried along his Diao's name and was often referred to with deference for these reasons. I saw various qualities of the deceased village chief distributed across his three sons, Mamadou, Ibrahima, and Rune, who were generous with their friendship during my time in West Africa. Sometimes I think that each of them was gifted with an aspect of their father's vitality. Mamadou inherited his father's long-term vision and seriousness of purpose. Rune embodied his playfulness and his love of life and storytelling, while future-oriented Ibrahima expanded on his father's ambition through his own economic ventures and ambitious plans to travel abroad.[2] The generosity of this extended family immeasurably enriched my life in West Africa.

To walk through the village of Taabe was an act of social navigation. Rather than throughways, the paths winding throughout the village often led from one door of a family compound to another. These traces led to people rather than to places. You had to account for these relational geographies if you wanted to go anywhere. Directions were given in terms of people and habitations as much as street names and landmarks. These paths were not drawn as marks on a map but rather worn into the ground through the overlapping footprints of those seeking out or avoiding one another. As such, one could not simply walk north and east to reach the other half of the village. One had to travel first through the compound of Goro Talla (a respected, yet often lonesome elder who relished long greetings), then through the field of many cashews owned by the Barry family, and finally along a path that led between the homes of Old Man Diallo and his brother's wife (a place where one was often ambushed for news of the wider world). The choice of which path to take was a decision about which family networks one would encounter on one's way: people in places and places into people.

In talking about Taabe's history with its longtime residents, I learned that many saw the past decades as a period of decline. The population had decreased as residents increasingly turned to work outside the village, and recruiting a network of villagers capable of cultivating extensive fields was becoming an increasingly challenging activity. Whereas scores of youths had previously participated in regularly occurring initiation ceremonies, now these rituals only happened every few years, with fewer mentors able to take up the mantle of leading them. Or at least so it seemed in the memories of Taabe elders. As many as five Koranic schools used to be active in Taabe, with now only half as many available. The vitality of the Koranic schools could be gauged by the state of the fire pits around which *talibé* studied at night. Many still burned bright, while young students recited Koranic verses among the shadows that flickered on massive baobab tree trunks, but some were now dormant and kicked over with sand and dust.

Accounting for Taabe's population, however, requires understanding matters of time and cyclicality. Taabe had become a new kind of hometown for many who now spent months if not years in other towns trying to make new livelihoods. As in other West Africa contexts, mobility was distributed across a person's lifetime. Children often grew up in a rural village, experienced mobility in their youth and young adulthood, and then chose to return to their village or build a livelihood elsewhere as they grew older (Jonsson 2012). Tracing social formations across the rural-urban axis has been a preoccupation of many scholars of West Africa for some time (Geschiere and Gugler 1998; Gugler 2002; D. J. Smith 2004). Other anthropologists have discussed how families have negotiated kinship and affinity transnationally (Buggenhagen 2012; 2011b; Yount-André 2018; Fioratta 2015) for whom the hometown became the social arena even while they were abroad (Kane 2011). These incomers—not without some pressure from folks back home—could triple the population of Taabe overnight during holidays, at which times Taabe reclaimed some of its past vitality of legend. As I spent more time there, I learned to look past these narratives of decline. I began to see a nexus of distributed communities, drawn together at different moments by the push and pull of life and held together by the verbal art of maintaining relationships in a state of mobility.

Although most Taabe residents farmed during the rainy season, many also spent significant time outside of the village in order to explore economic or educational opportunities. At times this meant that they would try their luck at jobs away from the village for several seasons, only to return and work the land again for several years. Most men had learned trades and continued to practice them in spaces between Taabe and Kédougou. The village chief, for instance, had worked for many years as a baker in southwestern Mali. Many enterprising women supplemented their farming income by selling grains and other products across the region. Although game was becoming increasingly scarce, some hunted deer and other small mammals in the bush for food. Mouth-puckering bush fruits such as tamarind and *laare* (*Saba senegalensis*) also provided side incomes for families, which often meant that intermediaries from the surrounding villages traveled broadly to Kédougou and mining towns to sell products.

Given this social porosity and mobility, how should one conceive of community? Rather than positing the existence of community as bounded or singular, anthropologists have increasingly studied the processes through which communities are conceived of and constituted (Barth 1969; Irvine 2006). Here, the interactional art of managing relationships becomes an important entry point into exploring how increasingly mobile individuals constitute communities across dispersed spaces. Earlier anthropological work often relied on village studies that took them to be representative of larger culture groups. Even further, rural cultures were often held to be the traditional, pristine forms of cultural practice, "unadulterated" by influences from other communities. These ideologies were not entirely foreign to Kédovins (residents of Kédougou), who often contrasted the diverse cultural and linguistic forms of Kédougou City with purer forms in the countryside. Anthropologists have long abandoned these premises, however, and increasingly engage in multisited work that takes transnationalism and mobility to be central to the study of social formations (Amselle 1990). While this book draws from these new approaches, it also shows that there is much to learn from village settings, which must not be ignored merely because older work overemphasized rural contexts. Taabe was hardly a sclerotic site of unchanging traditional practice. This rural place was the site of creative linguistic practice and mobilities. Not only a defining feature of metropolitan and European diasporas, mobility and movement are at the heart of rural life in West Africa as well (Wright 2010).

I soon realized that I had to change my conceptualization of a village like Taabe as a fixed and stable community. Taabe serves as an important cultural touchstone for individuals who anchor their sense of belonging and roots there. During important holidays, marriages, and funerals, these rural homelands attract many individuals who may never have lived there for long and who may not even have been born there. Taabe was a nexus of mobile pathways that required social labor to maintain as a social anchor. It was impossible to count the residents of Taabe with any precision, as each family had several if not a dozen or more family members who were away at any given time, pursuing education or economic opportunities across Senegal, West Africa, and Western Europe. To understand Taabe the village, I needed to understand these broader connections. Often life cycle rituals and holidays offered intense moments of sociality that could multiply the population of the village by two to three times over the course of a couple of days. Negotiating relationships with one's hometown was thus a part of the art of being a successful migrant.

Although the village appears to be a fixed and secure entity, it in fact requires ongoing social labor to hold it together. This art of bringing people together through linguistic and ritual exchange was often called jokkere endam or the *pursuit of relations*. (I discuss this understanding at greater length in the following chapter.) During my fieldwork, Taabe's village chief, Jom Wuro, was a master of the art of jokkere endam. When he was not farming, Jom Wuro would travel across the plateau area, greeting kin in surrounding villages or checking in with hamlets allied with the village. Much of this took place after the harvest, when he would comb the surrounding area to drum up support for work parties and to maintain a census of the area's residents. This work of generating social capital for the village was practiced through the verbal art of social negotiation. Expertly switching between keys of teasing, deference, and political debate, the chief labored incessantly against centrifugal forces that threatened to pull Taabe apart. Engaging community members such as in-laws and colleagues through performances of verbal art—greeting, teasing, and storytelling—was a central practice of cultivating social networks. It is through these everyday linguistic practices that increasingly mobile residents of Taabe were continuously cajoled, prodded, and encouraged to maintain relationships with their hometown. At a time of political expansion in the wake of Kédougou's change from a department to a region, the chief used the bureaucratic methods of statecraft like censuses and birth certificates to inscribe and solidify these connections.

Even in its narrowest configuration as a cluster of dwellings, Taabe as a community defied a constitution based on linear physical boundaries. For instance, in the nearby village of Mariwuro, only six kilometers away from Taabe, lived several family compounds who were in fact part of the village of Taabe. These individuals attended assemblies and counted their names in the registers of Taabe and not Mariwuro. They regularly traveled to Taabe for ritual events and sat out on political discussion in the village of Mariwuro. Similar arrangements can be found in other surrounding villages of the plateau. This might at first seem to be an anomaly. However, this diffusion is a reality that defines West African communities more broadly. This dispersal of families with negotiated links to hometowns is characteristic of what Kopytoff (1987) called the African Frontier. At moments of political division, groups would often splinter off from previous settlements, founding new villages but maintaining overlapping relationships with previous communities. Rather than taking the existence of a singular community for granted, villagers must negotiate how to maintain connections in the context of centrifugal social forces often propelled by increased mobilities.

A Context of Social Change

Mobility has long been a fundamental feature of the deep history of West Africa. Communities spread out along riverine networks and separated by hundreds of kilometers of Sahel were in fact long part of mobile networks that were activated through host-stranger hospitality. These links were rendered possible by the diffusion of relational idioms that were shared across vast areas: "Western Africans opportunistically redefine their identities in response to changing circumstances. Removed, even fictive, kinship ties, special bonds between groups such as 'joking relationships' indeed any social or cultural advantages one can claim or contrive have for centuries facilitated human relationships and expedited trade, travel, migration, and settlement in Western Africa" (Brooks 1993, 28). Viewed from such a long durée perspective, these words are as representative of today's forms of mobility as they are of historic populations. However, the reality faced by borderland Kédovins over the past decades is one of massive social change brought about by a cluster of interrelated political, environmental, and epidemiological factors.

The reassignment of Kédougou from a department to a region generated the first massive shift in the area. This administrative change had significant cascading effects that brought government officials into a place that had previously been at arm's length from administrative and police oversight. Most significantly, this recategorization increased the ability of the state to count populations and manage how landownership happened. This resulted in a more formalized land market. Chiefs such as Jom Wuro began to feel pressure to formalize census and land registers. Whereas land could previously be claimed and effectively owned after material improvements had been made to it in the tradition of homesteading, the expansion of the administrative oversight slowly impacted the way land was controlled and allotted. It became increasingly zoned, monetized, and managed by bureaucratic institutions like the land management office. Even the land around villages, whose boundaries had previously been unformalized, was increasingly being surveyed and brought into a formal land market. This shift of policy essentially gave more power to those who could accumulate capital and enabled coastal Senegalese or foreigners to buy up land in Kédougou and other larger towns. In many cases there were different prices for locals and nonlocals, which reflected ongoing tensions around autochthony in the region.

The update in status of Kédougou also brought with it the expansion of the police, from a skeleton crew of border guards who only monitored major international crossroads to a comprehensive police force. This increase had significant impacts on mobility. Furthermore, with these two bureaucratic changes came an increased emphasis on ID cards (*cartes d'identité*) for all residents. Particularly during the COVID pandemic, documents were increasingly used to control the movement of travelers in town and throughout the surrounding areas. This administrative change thus meant that the state was increasingly counting populations and issuing ID cards as a condition for being a state subject. It managed the access to educational opportunities, transportation, and medical services. The issue of ID cards and population census reveals a tension within the flexible forms of social identification that were long commonplace in this borderland region. Whereas routines of verbal arts, such as joking relationships, and the fluidity of naming long meant that West Africans could flexibly adapt the presentation of themselves to others, these new state mechanisms, if only at first glance, appeared to solidify these identities.

Secondly, an unprecedented mining boom fueled by an industrial mine drew in large numbers of artisanal miners to Kédougou.[3] They came from across coastal Senegal and from neighboring countries, such as Mali,

Figure 1.4. "In the hell of the mines." From the newspaper, *Enquête*, January 16, 2015.

Guinea, Burkina Faso, and Nigeria. During the most intense phase, mining towns of tens of thousands of miners appeared in what had been a village of only several hundred. National newspapers I collected at the time often presented Kédougou as a kind of hell on wheels mining town, a place defined by banditry and environmental degradation.

Although mining has been a long-standing practice in West Africa (d'Avignon 2022), the acceleration of industrial mining in Kédougou radically changed the economy, offering opportunities as well as pitfalls for its residents. By the time of my fieldwork in 2014–16, the pace of the mining boom had temporarily slowed down. At this juncture, Macky Sall, who became Senegal's president in 2012, was instituting a policy of regularization, or formalization, of the mining sector. These policies in many ways attempted to redistribute the wealth generated from mining away from foreign workers and toward Senegalese. This mining economy spurred increased levels of cyclical mobility as residents of Kédougou City made daily trips to surrounding mining towns where they sold food and manufactured goods or got involved in various forms of extraction.

The construction of a major highway that linked Dakar, Kédougou, and Bamako offered a third driver of social and economic change. As a result, Kédougou's downtown market transformed from a relatively calm setting to a hectic constellation of mobile sellers, loaded lorries, and speeding motorcycles. While there have always been a community of transnational migrants working in the market, this economic boom attracted an even larger migrant population from neighboring West African countries. Some Kédovins viewed this economic boom with ambivalence. Although it bought new opportunities for some Kédovins, many others felt left behind. While painstaking and often dangerous, artisanal mining could bring in previously unheard-of funds and was relatively accessible to individuals of any education level. However, those Kédovins who benefited less from the boom-time economy found themselves with a higher cost of living. Issues of autochthony also crept into the city of Kédougou as many debated whether Kédovins were, in fact, benefiting from the new economy or if only foreigners and other coastal Senegalese were. A 2008 youth riot (*soulèvement*) that led to the death of a young man and the burning down of a municipal building were motivated by the central issue of whether the benefits of growth were accruing to outsiders rather than locals.

The experiences of individuals caught in these processes offer important glimpses into Kédougou's waves of change. In what follows, I offer two short snapshots of how people have been navigating these transformations. There were significant differences in what I observed during my time in the Peace Corps from 2006 to 2009 and my return trip for fieldwork from 2014 to 2016 (and indeed in 2024). The first individual who encapsulates many of Kédougou's changes is a young woman I call Jaja. Jaja was a middle sister in the family who hosted me during my first time in Kédougou City. Having immigrated from Mali many decades ago, the family lived in one of Kédougou's older neighborhoods. Jaja was a close friend and companion during this time. When I first met her, she was still in school, but soon she dropped out to help cook and care for her extended family, which included several younger dependents, with few adults around. Jaja's mother was the matriarch of the household, since her father had passed many years ago. Back then, Jaja's two older brothers were around, but as time went on, they increasingly spent time in other parts of Kédougou or Senegal to pursue economic opportunities. Jaja was an exceptional hair braider and spent many long evenings transforming her female peers's coiffures for holidays and parties.

As time went by, their family's changes could be partly interpreted through the architecture of their compound. Mud and thatched huts began to give way to concrete and tin roofing—renovations begun but never completed. A woven bamboo fence—one that fell on my head when I was sick and using the outdoor restroom in the middle of a storm—was replaced with a solid concrete wall decorated with shells. After I left, one brother made it to the United States when he married a Peace Corps volunteer and began working in the northern Pacific deep sea fishing industry. From there, he was able to finance occasional house improvements. Meanwhile, the eldest brother began to focus more on the mining areas, where he mobilized labor and financing to try his luck in the gold boom.[4] In a familial situation where economic opportunities abroad and in mining camps drew away most of the men, Jaja and her sisters found themselves increasingly in charge of the compound. The burden fell especially hard on Jaja and her sisters after mother passed, precluding other opportunities for them. Jaja had long dreamed of studying hair braiding more formally and potentially pursuing it as an entrepreneurial endeavor in Dakar or, even more lucratively, in the United States. Now, however, she was caring for her young son and found herself rooted in place by family responsibilities.

Jaja and her sisters managed the best they could to make money for daily expenses within these new opportunities and challenges. They bought refrigerators and made large ice cubes that they sent on trucks to the mining areas. They sold watermelons (a fruit that is native to Africa) at the market, leveraging their brothers' fish selling spots. Before big festivities like Tabaski, Jaja bought fine cloth or shoes and used her expansive social network to tempt people into new outfits, often until three o'clock in the morning. I sometimes followed her on frenetic, ambulatory trips through the market, where she sold fabric on credit. In one breath, she would leverage her social ties with people to sell them cloth and in another try to coax money owed to her from former clients. She traveled to some of the nearby mining concessions, where she set up a small food stand and sold lunches and snacks to miners. It was her skills as a hair braider that exemplified the tensions within a place where more and more facets of social life were being monetized like land, labor, and building materials. Jaja's hours-long braiding sessions were often done in kind or for small amounts of money. Yet, increasingly, this work was becoming part of the market economy and could be extremely lucrative, especially abroad (Babou 2008). With prices for basic goods increasing along with demand, Jaja and her sisters did their best to make money during the mining boom, riding its ups and downs. When I visited during my anthropological fieldwork, Jaja often sat at the edge of the road across from their house, yelling quick staccato directions to household members while strands of hair were intertwined with her slender fingers. From underneath their neem tree, Jaja and her sister recognized and interpreted people from a distance through their hairstyles and hair textures.

The struggles of a young tailor's apprentice offer a second snapshot of Kedougou's changing social and economic landscape. When I met him in 2006, Samba was learning to sew local outfits in a downtown workshop. At that time, Kédougou's market was still a sleepy place where many men gathered to play *pétanque* or *boule* every day over the course of many hours; however, by 2014, these courts had been taken over by a cluttered grid of food stalls, temporary merchants, and motorcycle parking. When I saw him again that year, Samba had given up being a tailor. As many like him had, Samba had tried his hand at gold mining. With his first modest success, he had invested in a metal detector that someone from Dakar had sold to him. Yet Samba couldn't read the instructions on the machine, so he experimented with the buttons as best he could to comb over the mining sites in the outskirts of Kédougou City. He preferred this *pic-à-pel* method of mining to the more dangerous shaft mining that required machinery and risk. In pic-à-pel, individuals pick through previously excavated areas to find the remaining gold left over from earlier excavations. Working as a metal detector operator, Samba received one-third of every discovery he made, with the other two-thirds reserved for the diggers. His family had a compound on the quickly expanding edges of Kédougou. While they had managed to build a nice cement house with a wall around it, they still were in an area with no running water and no electricity. The city had grown too quickly for the utilities to catch up. Taking the electric grid into his own hands as so many others had, he began investing in solar panels. With some of the money that they had made, Samba's father had been able to go on hajj to Mecca, which was a great honor. Despite some modest successes, Samba expressed increasing disillusionment with the opportunities that the gold mining boom had to offer. What good was having more money when everything simply became more expensive?

These short vignettes demonstrate some of the shared experiences Kédovins were navigating in a time of heightened social and economic change. While new developments were enabling mobilities and economic opportunities, the Ebola epidemic from 2014 to 2016 rendered this mobility increasingly problematic. Most significantly, the Senegal-Guinea border was closed for a majority of the Ebola epidemic to isolate Senegal from contagion. This rendered cross-border travel illegal, despite the continuing and necessary movement in trade and persons. Taabe for instance, maintained close relationships with communities in Guinea that were only a few kilometers away.

Given these increased opportunities and disjunctures, how would a village like Taabe continue to be a place? How would Jaja maintain her household whose members were now spread out over thousands of miles? How would people maintain connections across communities to take advantage of these new opportunities? I suggest that viewing language as a constitutive element of mobility helps us answer these questions and similar ones about how individuals navigated these changing contexts in southeastern Senegal. In the next chapter, I examine long-standing sociolinguistic practices—idioms that draw on joking relationships, affinity, and namesake connections—that have offered migrants a set of tools for mobility that aid them in navigating significant political, economic, and environmental changes.

Notes

1. Taabe, like all other personal names and place names in this book (with the exception of large cities like Kédougou) are aliases to protect the identities of individuals.

2. Personhood in much of West Africa is interpreted through a range of relationships and mediums. Anthropologists have historically focused on important kinship relationships and responsibilities (Radcliffe-Brown and Forde 1950), wherein individuals often traced their place in relation to others; this often was more important than individual achievements. In the case of Fulɓe, corporate belonging was often traced through (often patrilineal) lineages or relatedly, caste groups (e.g., blacksmith, noble, or potter) (Derman 1969). In praising a person, for instance, griot (casted oral historians and musicians) often connected individuals to the achievements of those in their lineage rather than noting their own accomplishments (Irvine 1973). Names also provided an important dimension through which personhood was articulated: last names (patronyms) linked people to lineages through the men in their family (i.e., patrilineal ties), but first names could pass on character traits through the generations. Likewise, people often held that personal traits (*jikko*) were largely inherited through women. Whereas concepts like sense of humor can be used in the West to describe a person's personality traits, these were often distributed to social groups in Sahelian West Africa (Sweet 2019). For instance, certain Fulɓe lineages were held to be easily offended, which demonstrates the inherited nature of these supposed personality traits.

3. While I use the terms *industrial* and *artisanal* here to illustrate distinct parties within the regional mining economy that were also locally legible, Robyn d'Avignon (2018; 2022) has argued that "artisanal mining" is a racialized category. The two types of mining are intertwined in that "industrial" mining is possible only through exploiting long-standing "artisanal" mining knowledge across West Africa.

4. The eldest brother once found me at the compound, where he feverishly asked me for something from the United States to be a part of a sacrifice prescribed by a local Koranic cleric. Combined with ritual objects, practitioners could perform ritual language to initiate exchanges with the subterranean entities that controlled the gold. These practices of exchange and sacrifice form part of long-standing mining practices in West Africa's auriferous regions (d'Avignon 2022).

2

THE PURSUIT OF RELATIONS IN
A TIME OF SOCIAL CHANGE

THIS CHAPTER CAN BE READ AS AN EXAMINATION of the social, interactional resources that allowed people to thrive in a mobile context. Social idioms such as affinity, joking relationships, and kinship (even so-called fictive kinship) have traditionally been thought of as constraining principles that pushed migrants away from their communities to migration destinations. Kinship has commonly been seen as a mechanism of automatic affiliation that mediates the kinds of economic activities one could pursue or the kind of person one could become. The ethnography of interaction reveals how these resources offer migrants mechanisms for negotiating their place across dispersed communities. An attention to interactional dynamics reveals the greater ingenuity with which migrants performed these connections. Emphasizing these emergent social connections places a much-needed emphasis on interaction over interviewing in approaches to mobilities. This interactional perspective also better analyzes forms of power such as identity cards and documents that not only authorized formalized, state-based techniques of control and territorialization but also enabled everyday forms of interpretation and interaction between various mobile actors. As a verbal art of mobility, these interactional idioms facilitated voyages abroad and also helped migrants succeed in difficult contexts of migration.

Interactional perspectives on mobility help us understand how persons come to be socially recognized and how they manage identities at a broader level. Migrants do not transport themselves as autonomous and bounded individuals from place to place but emerge as people in relation to existing sociolinguistic understandings and associations. The ability of migrants to enact and embed themselves across time and space is mediated by the specific kinds of resources, routines, and understandings that can be shared in different contexts. This is a question not merely of codes in the form of established languages (like Swahili, French, or Yoruba) but also of being ratified and knowing how and when to use linguistic knowledge. This includes an understanding of the narratives and characters that are legible to speech communities in different settings. This relational emergence of selfhood flies in the face a common myth of personhood in the West that views individuals as autonomous with identities that emerge from a stable core (Strathern 1988; Bucholtz and Hall 2005).

Names and identity characteristics are thus not fixed but are better understood as borrowed, material signs that facilitate access to different times and places. For example, Gabriele vom Bruck (2006) describes how the adoption of male names by elite Yemeni women afforded them the possibility of moving about the world and interacting with men outside their intimate family circle. Adopting a different name as a mask, therefore, opened up possibilities for mobility and identity as entangled phenomena. Likewise, name-based connections in West Africa afford individuals a social mask that could be worn in order to open up other domains of social interaction. Rather than merely a process of referring to individuals who are assumed to have stable identities, names were starting points for connecting oneself to a world of others.

Narratives of Mobility and Immobility

The historiography of West African mobilities can be understood as a tension between a long-standing distrust and avoidance of undomesticated spaces outside the bounds of a community, on one hand, and a tradition of expansive networks for long-distance trade and mobility, on the other. Discussing this first dimension, Isaie Dougnon (2013, 35) notes that "African societies were characterized by a sharply bounded community [where] any movement of individuals outside this community and environment was understood in terms of a threat or danger to their lives." However, *longue durée* historical and archaeological scholarship on West Africa has also shown it to be an active place of long-distance, cyclical mobility for many centuries (Brooks 1993; Barry 1998; Bruijn, Dijk, and Foeken 2001; Gokee 2011; d'Avignon 2022). Early perspectives on mobility in West Africa noted that "the Europeans had no need to send out overland trade diasporas, much less develop trading post empires. The African merchants had already established trade networks in long distance trade, some of them extending back in time to the thirteenth century if not before" (Curtin 1975, 62). How can these two perspectives simultaneously be true of the same region?

Situating mobility as a social process helps dissolve this apparent conundrum: individuals expanded their trading and migratory reach through building relationships with other individuals and corporate groups. In short, people moved through places by assimilating them into their social networks. My ethnography of border crossing in chapter 1—an act of going from one social island to another—provides a demonstration of this pattern at a granular level. More broadly, shared social knowledge of negotiating kinship, caste, or affinal relations with others has allowed West Africans to expand the range of the familiar and, thereby, to move through it. Arrangements were forged with autochthonous spirits throughout West Africa. In precolonial times an individual's ability to function in a particular activity was a contingent on their integration into a household, kin group, or other type of community (Berry 1989). Social relationships not only enabled mobility, resources, and employment but also made places.

Some common features of this social assemblage were spread by expanding and contracting empires such as the Empire of Mali (1240–1645), whose political dominance spread Mande languages and cultural practices across much of the Sahel and southern Sahara for many centuries. This left many populations with common blueprints for tracing commonalities through social identities. Though not exclusively Mande, these included the significance of last names (often clan names) through which individuals could trace belonging with one another across great distances. Oftentimes these names held equivalencies across different groups such that an individual's social role could be translated into a related social framework (McGovern 2013). Relatedly, a caste system based on conceptions of innate differences between social groups who displayed complementary social roles provided a way for individuals to be rendered intelligible in neighboring communities (Tamari 1991). Together, these demonstrate a widespread social sense of how to interpret ethnic, patronymic, and other name-based keys to identity. They show the traces of long-term mobility in which people translated themselves in new places. In this way, "these clan name exchanges are deeply rooted in the social history and practices of the western savanna. It is a ticket to mobility, a smoothing of the way down the road" (Bird 1999, 276). The practice of joking relationships in Sahelian West Africa (Ndiaye 1993), which I go on to discuss, offers one such common intersubjective technology through which individuals interpreted social connections in interactions (E. Smith 2004; Sweet 2021a).

In West Africa as elsewhere, anthropological scholarship has examined recent mobilities within the context of neoliberal policies and thereby has tracked how individuals are able to situate themselves within broader economic and political systems (Ong 2007). Indeed the earliest work on mobility and migration merely saw these phenomena as push-and-pull factors that moved people around the globe (Whitehouse 2013). Framing mobility in this way is useful and enables global perspectives that highlight systemic inequalities and precarities. But these are not the only lenses through which these stories are told. Equally significant are durable bundles of social practices, which include centuries-old routines of sociality, such as joking relationships, that have enabled individuals to traverse and make their lives across long distances. These practices mobilize locally significant distinctions and narratives to make sense of persisting linguistic and cultural practices. These idioms of relationality continue to offer migrants resources for navigating changing social, economic, and environmental contexts.

Scholars on mobility have emphasized distant migratory destinations as places where individuals seek opportunity away from kin in order to escape potentially constraining social relationships and expectations (Simone 2004; Whitehouse 2013; Bredeloup 2014). Not merely constraining, however, these same idioms of kinship and affinity in interaction also offered migrants tools for building or insulating themselves from important social relationships. In this chapter, I take a step back to offer a broader view of the existing social idioms and routines that West Africans creatively adopt to thrive in mobile contexts. I describe the diverse interactional practices through which mobile individuals in West Africa cultivated relationships across great distance. In so doing, I track the verbal art of building and maintaining relationships with others as practiced by mobile residents of the broader Kédougou region.

The Stakes of Saying One's Name

On my first trip down to Kédougou to conduct fieldwork in 2014, our overland bus broke down on an uninhabited stretch of highway. Crouched in the sandy ditches by the side of the road, we passed the time telling stories of other harrowing overland trips to and from Kédougou. In doing so, we weren't merely passing along tales of travels. These narratives helped fellow travelers steel themselves for the long road ahead. Making it through this ordeal together brought us closer through a shared experience of precarity. Many of us stayed in touch during the years of my ethnographic fieldwork, and some of us still text each other on WhatsApp to this day.

Through this experience, I met a migrant named Duke, an electronics technician from Dakar who specialized in repairing metal detectors. Although Duke's family and children lived in Dakar, he spent much of the year in Kédougou to pursue opportunities offered by the gold boom. Encounters between Duke and his clients demonstrate some of the powerful social idioms through which individuals from distant lands could come to understand one another. Individuals drawn to his remarkable ability to bring broken things back to life would entrust him with electronics that had fallen in disarray from dust, sun, and extended use. He lived in one of Kédougou's largest apartment buildings overlooking the road that led to the industrial mines. In each of the units lived many hopeful migrant entrepreneurs, trying to find their place in the workings of the mining economy. One was a Malian chef known for his meat skewers. We mused that his food must be very good indeed because he was never home. Another neighbor woman washed the dusty clothes of busy miners, ever squatting on a bright plastic stool. Her hands wrung rust-colored water out of colorful fabrics twisted in on themselves. When her knuckles came together in powerful cleansing strokes, a familiar *pitsch, pitsch, pitsch* sound gave auditory evidence of her impeccable technique.

From his dusty cement balcony, Duke and I would watch individuals loading up trucks with building supplies to take to the gold fields. One day, as I was catching up with Duke in the weeks after our fateful bus ride, two Pular-speaking men walked into his shop lobby. They wore colorful but worn robes whose ragged hems gave evidence of long journeys over dusty roads. As they approached Duke, one of them pulled out an evidently broken phone from his pocket to be repaired. After exchanging a short greeting in Pular, Duke soon realized that neither man spoke his native language of Wolof. Duke himself spoke only halting Pular of basic greetings and market phrases—this despite his significant time in Kédougou. Nevertheless, Duke soon understood that they wanted him to repair their cell phone. However, the two parties could not agree on a price, which they negotiated by switching between the conventional French and base-five Pular counting systems.[1] After a minute of difficult negotiations in which Duke refused to budge—either because of a communicative impasse or because of his own intractability—one of the Pular speakers shifted his footing (Goffman 1981) and asked of Duke: "ko honno inneteɗaa?" (What is your name?). Duke pursed his lips and responded in a brusque but animated repartee: "Way yooy il faut même pas commencer avec ça!" (Oh, man, don't even get started with *that*!).

How are we to understand this moment when Duke refuses to utter his name to these potential clients? What was the "that" to which Duke was alluding? Duke's momentary refusal encapsulates many of the questions that drove my curiosity about how West African migrants weave names, ethnicities, or affinities into webs of social connectivity. Was Duke fearing that in uttering his name, others might be able to reveal some connection and then wield it as leverage to advance their aims? I suggest that this seemingly simple moment of self-identification hints at what are highly productive routines of everyday social identification through which mobile West Africans negotiate relationships with one another through names, ethnicity, and kinship. While in this case Duke manages to suppress his name, these were the kinds of encounters in which individuals brought up relation names and identities, thrusting interlocutors into webs of relationality. While these kinds of interactional connections were pertinent mundane social contexts, they became particularly important in the context of mobility wherein individuals from far away might draw on diverse social correspondences to build relationships with one another.

By avoiding the disclosure of his name, Duke was also insulating himself from a joking relationship (also called *sanakuyaagal* in Pular or *cousinage* in French), a routine of teasing and play based on specific correspondences between last names, generations, caste, or ethnic identities that allowed individuals to tease and probe one another interactionally. His refusal is telling and hints at the potent social connections that his solicitors might have established given the affordance of his name. Indeed, after the two clients left, Duke admitted to me that—among other things—he had wondered whether they had identified him as a Serer (which indeed he was) and thus were hoping to play off a Serer-Pular ethnic correspondence to plead their case for a preferable price. While those identifying as ethnically Pular were widespread throughout southeastern Senegal, Serer constituted only a very small minority of traders who were valuable contacts because they served as key nodes in trade with coastal Senegal.

As noted by scholars of social interaction, such as Erving Goffman, communication entails risk. The things you say and the signs you inadvertently give off during interactions all reveal things about yourself that can be exploited by interlocutors to characterize you (Keane 2015; Goffman 1981b). Given the existence of myriad genres of social connectivity in West Africa, speaking one's name thus offers a rich opportunity to establish relationships of privilege, bait others into interaction, and otherwise mobilize identity-based connections. Negotiating relationships with others was a verbal art of mobility that enabled individuals to negotiate connections with a diverse range of others across West Africa.

The Verbal Arts of Mobility

Interactional perspectives demonstrate these negotiated relationships to be achievements rather than merely activated connections. Other approaches to migrant community formation have often posited the connection of individuals based on ethnicity, kinship, or locality. The often-creative performance of relational idioms, such as joking relationships, enables individuals to formulate different kinds of connections with people in mobile contexts. Rather than fixed aspects of social structure, the routines of relationality based on name, kinship, or identity I describe in this chapter enable people to form relationships in innovative ways. Successful migrants were often those who could utilize these connections to gain access to markets, products, spaces for selling, information, and social networks that would prove useful to untethered entrepreneurs.

While not exhaustive, table 2.1 offers a sketch of some of the most common routines of social connectivity that enabled mobile communities to negotiate multiple presentations of themselves and others in diverse contexts. Not merely relational in an abstract sense, these social negotiations of status and identity rooted people to places in material ways and partly served to constitute the places that migrants found themselves in. Through in-law talk, for instance, migrants were turning foreign markets into domestic spaces from which they could perform domestic hospitality, establish patronage, and share food. Linguistic practices thereby ground actors in the infrastructure and spatiality of the everyday, partly constituting the places they move between. Routines of relationality like these are both demonstrations of relationships and interactional stances and infrastructures that etch contours into our built environment.

Though long-standing, the relational routines I discuss in this chapter are not timeless, ahistorical practices. Instead, they have long offered tools

Table 2.1. The Pursuit of Relations through Routines of Relationality

Routine	Idiom	Key Terms
tanagol	generational (grandchild)	taniraawo, taniraaɓe
dendiraayaagal	crossness (cross-cousin)	dendiraawo, dendiraaɓe
sanakuyaagal	joking relationship	sanaku
esirayaagal	affinity (senior in-law)	esiraaɓe (senior in-law) keyniraawo (junior in-law)
goreyaagal	age-set relations (peer)	goreejo, gore
tokora	namesake	

for navigating processes of social and economic change. Indeed, many of the interactional routines I discuss in this chapter, such as joking relationships, were shared and exchanged across many languages. They are particularly useful to the study of southeastern Senegal, where populations have for centuries been politically recalcitrant and decentralized. As an example of a shatter zone (a term from political geography that often refers to contested borderland areas), Kédougou's diverse populations sought refuge in the region, located at the fringes of successive empires and states, all the while benefiting from trade and coalition as strategically as they could. Being able to cultivate selective relationships with allies while insulating oneself from the state apparatus has defined much of this region's history. By 2014, however, these verbal arts of mobility were happening on a social landscape that was increasingly inscribed by the Senegalese state. Along with the appearance of the state came a steady wave of bureaucratic efforts to identify and manage populations. This occurred in the form of mining ID cards, national ID documents, birth registries, and surveillance initiatives to monitor the border populations in the context of an Ebola epidemic. As such, the increased reach of the Senegalese state into the region of Kédougou has, in one sense, threatened to fix identities in place. These routines of relationality became increasingly entangled with bureaucratic modes of identification that included ID cards, land registries, and birth certificates.

In introducing these more interactional and textual forms of identification, I do not wish to posit the former relational routines like joking relationships as flexible and unconstrained and the latter bureaucratic forms of identification as utterly fixed. While a useful initial contrast, I add nuance to this distinction by showing how the textual technologies of statecraft such as ID cards were brought into more creative routines of negotiated social identification. As I have shown, forms of identity and self-presentation invoked in interactions are not merely controlled by an individual but rather emerge through the course of multiparty interactions, which is the topic of the next chapter.

The Pursuit of Relations

Keen observers of their own social worlds, my West African interlocutors understood the mediation of social relationships to be an inherently mobile process, often described as jokkere enɗaŋ, or the pursuit of relations—the social labor of building social relations with in-laws, kin, and neighbors.[2] Residents of the far-flung villages of the Fouta Djallon mountains recognized that the cultivation of relationships amid centripetal forces of cyclical migration required a significant investment in social visitations and the judicious balance of recognizing, teasing, and honoring others. These social and linguistic routines were not merely a question of categorical affiliation but also a strategic verbal art that both facilitated mobility and was brought into being through social visit reciprocities.

As explained to me by Taabe's village chief, jokkere enɗaŋ was achieved through "ko e ɗengal, newre, e jungo"—a linguistic, interactional labor entailing the itinerant cultivation of social ties through one's tongue and hands as well as feet. The chief of Taabe, who traveled from village to village along the Fouta Djallon plateau on regular trips, described the visitation of kin, affines, and collaborators as an embodied labor: tongues for speaking, hands for shaking, and feet for going the distance. In an area with limited cell phone reception, conducting business among villages in the area often required personal travel to friends and colleagues. Maintaining a strong social network thus entailed the linguistic and physical labor of social visitation and reciprocity.

Amid a deep history of cyclical migration, mobile West Africans have relied on interactional routines based in idioms like joking relationships to relate with other individuals and communities. One dimension of this history of migration has entailed a dense landlord-stranger network in which individuals from far away could often rely on the hospitality of autochthonous individuals through the payment of respect and patronage (Brooks 1993; Barry 1998). Hardly a place of discrete villages and ethnic homelands (Amselle 1985, 1990), West Africa has long been a place of movement enabled by performances of verbal creativity that link individuals to one another through various social idioms.

In this context of high cyclical mobility, maintaining a community of kin, neighbors, and friends necessitated significant social labor. Accordingly, farmers and itinerant laborers in southeastern Senegal invested in everyday routines of contact and exchange with neighbors and kin through reciprocal greeting and gift giving. These exchanges entailed the upkeep of visitation channels formed by long return trips to hometowns and regular visits to distant hamlets. The expected reciprocity of such trips also propelled a cyclical mobility of individuals who continually felt pressure to greet one another and attend the distant life cycle rituals or ceremonies of others in their network. This social labor could be felt through yearly cycles. While the rainy season drew people to and from agricultural fields, the cessation of the rains prompted a continual flow of visitations that dispersed residents across family compounds, neighboring villages, and urban centers in the region. Scholars viewing West and Central African histories with a broad lens have described this concern with cultivating diverse and wide-spread ties as "wealth in people" (Guyer 1993), a particular concern of African localities that are rich in land but low in population. Becoming a person of consequence in southeastern Senegal likewise entailed the continuous renewal of social relationships through the shrewd reciprocation of words and other objects.

Joking Relationships and Verbal Creativity

In what follows, I describe some of the routines that migrants drew on to interact with others across markets, overland trips, and hometown visits in Senegal. I begin by introducing the routine of joking relationships, which Duke partly feared his Pular customers might draw on to gain favorable terms with him in the previous example. Joking relationships are a very common form of verbal art performed on the basis of privileged relationships between particular last names (patronyms such as Diallo-Ba) and ethnic identifications (e.g., Pullo-Serer).[3] Although I refer to these routines as joking relationships for the sake of clarity, the local name for this routine was sanakuyaagal in Pular (or in Maninka, *senankuya*), where one's joking cousin was a *sanaku*. The French terms, *cousinage* or *parentés à plaisanteries*, were also commonly invoked to describe this practice in anthropological scholarship. In broad strokes, joking relationship routines involved the exchange of teases and jokes at the expense of individuals who were seen to be linked by a privileged relationship. The insults and relationships were often animated by historical relationships between individuals associated with different social groups based on ethnicity, patronym, or caste. Caste provides an important embodied dimension of social hierarchy that is prevalent throughout West Africa, though this became somewhat more fluid in the decentralized region of Kédougou (Tamari 1991, 1998). Early studies show how caste was partly enacted through particular linguistic practices that offered axes of differentiation between nobles and griots (the oral historians of West Africa), for instance (Irvine 1973; Irvine and Gal 2019). Joking relationships thus enabled West Africans to gain increased access to others in interactional contexts with an expanded range of conversational license. Not only limited to Kédougou, joking relationships can be found across the Sahelian region of West Africa and thus enable speakers from potentially distant places to formulate connections in the idiom of teasing. The origins of joking relationships are related in myths and historical accounts of West Africa. In the epics of old Mali told by griots, senanku joking relationships are often seen as the result of alliances of those clans who united in defense of Sundiata Keita, whose defeat of the Blacksmith sorcerer Sumanguru Keita gave rise to the Empire of Mali (Niane 1965). To this day, patronyms—last names passed along the male line—like Keita and Kante offer a well-known correspondence on which significant social bricolage is performed in face-to-face encounters. Table 2.2 gives some examples of observed correspondences in southeastern Senegal.

The following short example shows the social and spatial expansiveness that joking relationship connections could afford West Africans. I once witnessed a group of wandering Fulɓe merchants from over two thousand kilometers away in Niger be able to place individuals in Kédougou in an idiom of sanaku. I encountered these travelers as they set up a temporary encampment outside my friend Mamadou's house one evening. We managed basic exchanges across the Pular Fouta variety I had learned and their Fulfulde variety from farther east. Among those I met were individuals with the last names Diallo and Ba, just like many from the region of Kédougou. The merchants warmed up small pots of tea, using their flowing robes as blankets to protect themselves from dusty harmattan winds. Reclining on plastic mats on the ground beside the road, these traveling merchants soon showed me the wares they were selling across the region. They produced little vials of liquid and packets of powders from underneath their robes, touting their beneficial properties against insomnia and infertility as well as a product to enhance one's charisma: liquid clout.

Table 2.2. Attested Joking Relationship Correspondences

Patronymic Correspondences

Diallo	Ba
Barry	Sow
Keita	Kanté
Ndiaye	Diop
Camara	Dramé
Camara	Cissokho
Diaby	Danfakha
Diaby	Cissokho
Diallo	Kanté
Keita	Diaby
Diallo	Bindia
Ba	Boubane
Souaré	Keita
Souaré	Camara
Cisse	Dramé
Kante	Fofana
Diakhite	Diallo
Sidibé	Barry
Mballo	Diao

Ethnic Correspondences

Pullo/Fulɓe	Serer
Serer	Diola

As I returned to Mamadou's nearby house later in the evening, I asked him if he had seen these Fulɓe from Niger.[4] In a somewhat tongue-in-cheek way (that betrayed a previous joking performance with them), he assured me that while there were some sketchy Bas (his joking partners) out there to be watchful of, the Diallos among them (his people) would keep an eye on them. In saying this, Mamadou was drawing on the characters and dispositions from the narratives of joking relationship exchanges to build an initial understanding of who these individuals were.

Joking relationship routines thus afforded one possible frame through which interlocutors embodied characters and navigated relationships in their daily greetings and practices. Joking relationship routines ranged from lighthearted teasing between friends—for example, "yette Ba moy'y'aa!" (The Bas are no good!)—to what sounded like verbal abuse to the untrained ear.

Table 2.3. Example of Joking Relationships, "The Father of Them All"
Diallo: late twenties male Pular merchant from Guinea
Mar: early thirties male Serer merchant born in Kédougou

Pular

#	Speaker	Pular Speech
1	Diallo	Ko miŋ woni baaba maɓɓe fow! Ko miŋ soodani mo cafe Touba o yari mo.
2	Mar	Serer no waawi nangugol jungo Pullo o yeeya mo.
3	Diallo	Oo'o! Mi jaabataa ɗuŋ! Ko miŋ woni baaba Serer fop!

English

#	Speaker	English Translation
1	Diallo	I am the father of all of them! I'm the one who bought him Touba coffee, and he drank it.
2	Mar	A Serer can grab a Pullo by the hand and sell him.
3	Diallo	No way! I don't accept that. I'm the father of all Serers!

At times this could sound like bitter insults ("aŋ ko a maccuɗo aŋ" [you're my slave]), while at others it was expressed through more lighthearted-sounding critiques of diet: "a ñaamay ñebbe!" (you eat beans!) (Jones 2007). Table 2.3 transcribes an exchange between migrant sellers from Guinea in Kédougou City's downtown market that offers a simple example of this practice. This example demonstrates a common way that Serer merchants, who controlled much of the bulk trade in the Kédougou downtown market, related to the (mainly) Pular-speaking retail merchants.

Through the term *joking relationships*, ethnologists lumped together these practices with other similar routines of systematic license around the world (Lowie 1912; Radcliffe-Brown 1940; Brant 1948; Bradney 1957; Freedman 1977; de Vienne 2012). In earlier anthropological work, these relationships were frequently seen as forms of conjunction and disjunction that balanced social structures. When anthropologists like A. R. Radcliffe-Brown (1973) described things like joking relationships, they saw relatively static mechanisms of social structure. However, I have argued elsewhere that these practices function more as productive mechanisms of creative social negotiation than mere frameworks of social order (Sweet 2021a). This is possible in the first place, because individuals were creative in negotiating the relational grounds on which joking relationships were performed. For example, West

Africans often drew on poetic or conceptual equivalencies between particular names or ethnic groups to expand the list of individuals who might build such a relation with one another. Joking relationships have offered significant resources for regional and international migrants from West Africa. Bruce Whitehouse (2012), for instance, identified in his population study of West African migrants in Brazzaville, Congo, that these groups were held together partly through a shared understandings of joking relationships. As such, joking relationships offered these West African migrants a productive social idiom through which they could trace belonging and community.

Viewed more granularly, joking relationship routines offer more or less shared social principles—narrative settings in time and space—that make legible stereotypical characters and the kinds of appropriate actions they might take (Bakhtin 1981). These narrative frames thus allowed individuals from across West Africa to insert themselves into this performative social encounter. Joking relationship routines were successful partly because interlocutors understood that confrontations with their sanaku joking partners was a form of play. As such, anyone who encountered a purported sanaku relationships would often know how to enter into this interactional performance by drawing on existing understandings of the plots, settings, and characters (Sweet 2021a). These chronotopes often included established scenes like nighttime thefts that were purported to have been perpetrated by joking partners who are animated by characteristics like gluttony.

Although the principles for joking relationships were based on ethnic or patronymic identification, the possibilities for engaging in relational play in the idiom of joking relationships were not narrowly constrained. For instance, individuals from ethnic groups who do not originally figure into joking relationship correspondences have managed to implicate themselves into these routines by creatively building poetic bridges between names (Sweet 2021a). This was possible partly because of the existence of equivalencies in which particular last names were held to be the same, offering grounds for more expansive plays of relationality. In many cases equivalencies were motivated on the basis of a shared occupational niche, a perceived ethnic link, or a poetic similarity between names. This entextualized set of equivalencies meant that certain patronyms could "count" as the same. A group of Toucouleur vendors in the Kédougou market once explained it to me like this: "Ka et Diallo, fow ko gootuŋ" (Ka and Diallo are the same thing), such that they could be rendered equivalent in the performance of joking relationships. Even further, the Bassari (the autochthonous inhabitants of the Kédougou region) often inserted themselves into the game of joking relationships based on poetic parallelisms between their names and names that were strongly entextualized in joking relationship practice. Here Boubane might come to stand for Ba such that Boubanes (notice the poetic symmetry) might establish joking relationships with the Bas' joking cousins, the Diallos (Sweet 2021a).

Name Play

Not merely a question of joking relationships, the use of patronyms to evaluate the identity and provenance of individuals was extremely important throughout West Africa. Patronyms are some of the most salient social signs that are invoked throughout social encounters. In a context where given names were often perceived as disrespectful toward parents or elders, addressing one another with last names was often an early question that figured in routines of greeting. Patronyms were often assessed for a migrant's provenance and ethnic group ("Yette Souaré ko Pullo? Is a Souaré a Pular?"). Although Pular patronyms did not map neatly onto any clan membership and did not even unambiguously provide evidence of ethnic or regional origins, they were often the most significant first social index and term of address used by individuals meeting for the first time. In addition to being evaluated for potential joking partnership, patronyms were judged and interpreted with an eye to provenance, ethnicity, as well as a mismatch between name and language use. To discover that someone shared the same name as you (or even a parent or grandparent) was often a cherished connection that provided the grounds for important relational work in the context of mobility.

Two individuals found to be sharing the same last name could use this as a ground to purport some other shared grounds. For example, patronyms could be used to draw kinship connections in conversation as in the idiom of mussiɓe: "oo ɗoo ko Diallo, ko mussiɓe meŋ" ("This guy is a Diallo, he is our kin"), a migrant kola nut seller once said after hearing that someone shared his last name of Diallo. In this way, social actors routinely used patronyms to evaluate one another for social information. Knowing someone's patronym as well as hometown, for instance, could often provide a better indication of an individual's caste or lineage. While in many cases last names carried ethnic and other social information, reading identities from patronyms was in practice ambiguous.

Across West Africa, there was an indeterminate relationship between identity and patronymics, partly because individuals could change names in order to escape misfortune or death and posited equivalencies between names based on routines like joking relationships. In some cases, entire families or villages have changed their patronyms (often in favor of esteemed names like Diallo) in order to escape the less favorable connotations of certain names. Possibilities for social identification in the form of names was inherent to spatial mobility. Not far from Kédougou City, I once met a family whose father had given all of his male children female names. When I inquired about this, he told me of difficult times when he and his wives had lost son after son just weeks after birth. To confuse death and to throw it off the track, the man decided to give his male children female names. When he spoke to me, he talked of it in primarily spatial terms— that these new identities would prevent these children from being found. Notice here that identity and place are intimately entangled. Although this example concerns given names, similar strategies can be found concerning broader aspects of names, including patronyms. Across the region, naming children things akin to death or rubbish is a broader strategy of escaping misfortune. These fluid routines of naming and tracing connections among names provide mobile West African communities a greater range of possibilities for self-presentation. Mobility was thus an act of social transformation in which mobile West Africans built relational bridges with others in new places.

Sharing given names with others was thus a significant connection that could be activated to do social and interactional work. Names could be fleeting in certain interactions when interlocutors were momentarily rebaptized. For instance, face-to-face renamings, such as "hande aŋ ko Ba" (Today you're a Ba), were a common joking relationship tactic that attempted to voice grounds that might be drawn on in that interaction for hours to come. Indeed, rebaptizing one's joking partner often constituted a part of the joking cousin routine itself. For instance, I once visited a village chief who identified himself as my sanaku, playing on a correspondence between Kanté and Keita. Rather than call me by the name he knew me by (Kanté), however, he called me by his own last name (Keita) and used the rest of the encounter to compliment this name. I have observed similar strategies at other times. In this way, during joking relationship routines, joking partners frequently call one other not by their "actual" patronyms but rather by those of their joking partners.

As shown in this previous example, I was not immune to this relational name play. Although I was certain my name was simply Nikolas when I arrived in Senegal, by the end of my time in Senegal I wasn't too sure anymore. I was frequently loaned local names by the families who hosted me throughout my many years in Senegal working as a Peace Corps volunteer, experiential education instructor, and anthropologist. Newly arrived in Senegal in 2006, for instance, I had tried to convince people to simply call me "Nikolas," for which there was a common French pronunciation. I had even later met other Nicolas among the Bassari in Kédougou City. My first host family, the Barrys of Thiès, however, would have none of it. I was given the name Souleymane (and later known by the related nickname, Jules) in honor of my host father's own father. Moments of social rebirth happen across a person's lifetime.

The patronym I was known by in Senegal changed several times to reflect my connections to different people and households. For instance, while I served as a Peace Corps volunteer, I was known as a Kanté after living in a host family with this name. The Kantés were considered blacksmiths whose ancestors had emigrated from Mali. Later, as I spent more time in the Fouta Djallon borderlands, I slowly began to be known as Diallo like the family with whom I lived. Others were very keen to call me by these names and implicate me via these names into local joking relationship or namesake practices. Although this may seem exceptional given my position as an American expatriate in West Africa, the practice of extending names as way of implicating strangers as guests into Sahelian societies has a strong historical legacy (Brooks 1993; McGovern 2013).

Names were thus not merely something one acquired at birth but were lent, acquired, and lost throughout one's life. Being known in terms of the names of your children (like Neene Wury, "mother of Wury," often called teknonyms) was a rite of passage that marked individuals as vital life givers. Part of this pluralism in naming was a result of so many individuals sharing last names and given names. For instance, to share the real name of my close friend in this text—Mamadou Diallo—is not to risk revealing his identity in the slightest (and when I asked him, he told me to put his real name). Anyone looking for a Mamadou Diallo in the region of Kédougou will find an obfuscating abundance. Moreover, Mamadou is rarely what he is called. He was known by nicknames and kin terms, and as a result, he emerged as a somewhat different person through these different contexts in which he was defined in relation to others. One might even say that the preponderance of certain patronyms impelled a diversity in naming, in which individuals came to be known under different names in various contexts.

Patronyms were not the only grounds on which migrants might be able to find and evaluate a social link with others. *Tanagol*, routines of teasing based on generational distance, for instance, offered up interactional possibilities for those who might identify one another as honorary grandparents or grandchildren. In a context where respect to one's elders was often carefully policed and enforced, such practices were commonly expanded and invoked to give individuals a wider range of interactional keys through which they might relate to others. Like ethnic or patronymic correspondences, negotiating affinity (in-laws) also became a realm of play whose very existence was itself the subject of creative linguistic performances. Beyond furthering social reciprocities between families allied through marriage, affinity was a very productive connection used to negotiate interactional parameters between individuals in a diverse number of contexts. In chapter 3, I examine the hometown visit of a returning migrant, who found himself managing relationships with those who he had left behind in the idiom of in-lawship (*esiraaɓe*). The status of whether they were in-laws or not became an object of contention and a central axis along which they came to understood one another after periods of absence in the wake of immigration to Spain. Likewise in chapter 6, I examine how the creative negotiation of affinity provided a way for peripatetic merchants and laborers in Kédougou's downtown market to constitute the market as a domestic space from which they could share food and hospitality even as they were hundreds of miles from their hometowns.

Relational Identities and Techniques of the State

The first part of this chapter introduced some of the most important interactional routines of relational creativity that have provided a toolbox of mobility in West Africa. This relational creativity is not an apolitical, timeless social practice. Although many current practices likely trace origins back hundreds of years, West Africans have long used them to adapt to current social changes and contexts. More recently, these interactional routines helped locals navigate the contingencies of political, environmental, and economic change that Kédougou residents found themselves suspended in. Through steady incorporation into the Senegalese state, this mobile art of relationality was increasingly crosscut by political and bureaucratic changes. Principal among these were an increased enforcement of ID cards, birth certificates, surveillance initiatives, and a police presence that provided new stakes for identifying oneself and in a region undergoing social change.

Originally a shatter zone in which smaller scale, decentralized peoples strategically shielded themselves from political formations and oppressive tax regimes, the inhabitants of Kédougou were quickly becoming folded into the expanding Senegalese state. Beginning with the establishment of Kédougou as a region, this process led to a larger state apparatus and stronger connections to coastal Senegal that accelerated along the Dakar-Bamako international highway. Thus, while these more flexible forms of interactionally negotiated relations offered migrants tools for building relationships in diverse interactional contexts, new bureaucratic techniques of the state threatened to fix identities in place. As part of this process, administration initiatives aimed at counting and identifying residents of this region. Demographic knowledge of these borderland residents and their movement became increasingly scrutinized during the time of my research, as the Ebola epidemic in nearby Guinea raised the stakes of cross-border travel. As forms of biopower—knowledge as power over people as populations—bureaucratic technologies such as ID cards, birth certificates, land registries, and village rolls could regiment practices of identification and mobility (Foucault 1988).

At first glance, documents such as birth certificates and ID cards fixed into writing aspects of one's identity which might otherwise have been negotiated in more flexible routines of social transmission. At the same time, however, these documents also offered new opportunities for the negotiation of publicly visible identities. Not merely documents by which states accounted for their populations, birth registries and ID cards, among others, were also drawn on by individuals themselves to negotiate their identity and self-presentation in various contexts.

In the wake of these political pressures to rationalize governance, possessing a Senegalese ID card in the region of Kédougou increasingly impacted one's mobile pathways. In the context of the Ebola epidemic, having an ID card that identified oneself as a Senegalese citizen was critical in the borderlands around Taabe. Even in Kédougou City, not possessing an ID card significantly reduced one's ability to move about town in particular time spaces. Previously quite rare in the region of Kédougou, nighttime *ramsassages* (roundups) limited the mobility of those who could not produce an ID card. Ramassages were clandestine operations in which police established checkpoints at key intersections of a neighborhood. Stopping any pedestrians and vehicles, they would systematically seize those that could not produce official paperwork. In the case of vehicles, motorcycles that were found to be without papers (i.e., proof of legal purchase and registration) were confiscated by police and often sold at auction at later dates. In a town with many black-market Chinese motorcycles, these operations could be a windfall for police departments. Word got around quickly, however, and motorists leaving these intersections would frequently warn those approaching of the risk ahead.

Individuals who were caught in a ramsassage without an ID card were taken to the police station, where they were released only upon paying a fine. These individuals were often called *sans papiers*, or in Pular, *forodu*, which comes from the French, *fraude* (fraud). To be sans papiers thus was to find one's time-space opportunities significantly compressed. Even during the day, gendarmes were increasingly posted at the entrances of towns, where individuals would routinely be stopped. While there were often detours and side streets that sans papiers might take to avoid checkpoints, their status offered a more restricted set of pathways that they could inhabit at different times. By late 2015, I began to hear from individuals, particularly youth who wanted to circulate at night, that they increasingly felt afraid to go outside without an ID card. People living in rural parts of the region too began to feel these changes as well. Thinking in terms of language as infrastructure, the roads, borders, and other framework associated with mobility are built not only from their brute physical features but also out of routines of interaction. The lived experience of a border for an aspiring migrant is not the physical formation, such as a roadblock, alone. Mobilities are rendered possible through a discursive and material assemblage composed of interactional possibilities with officers and other mediators, physical border architecture, political and epidemiological discourses, and the pragmatics of proving one's identity through ID cards.

It is helpful to think about the category of forodu alongside other rites of passage in West Africa where one is to become a person. Beyond birth, the first ritual that people undergo in becoming social persons is a naming ceremony in the week or weeks after birth. Called a *denabo* in Pular, this naming ceremony is an extremely important moment throughout West Africa. It is at this moment that babies who were previously referred to as a generic type, *sanfa*, become people linked to others in the community through shared names and lineages. A second important moment in becoming a person is a coming-of-age ceremony—held separately for boys and girls—in which one earns status as an adult and a fuller social person. These rites of passage enable opportunities to speak with certain people, to attend certain events, and for the participant to be accounted for as a person. Not unlike the identities acquired through naming or coming of age, an ID card likewise transformed their bearers into ratified individuals who might have access to particular social spaces and opportunities—schools, international borders, or cities at night.

Despite these recent ID card drives, many in Kédougou remained sans papiers or forodus for various reasons. This was not only a precarious legal status, but it was also a category type that became productive in local discourses. For instance, Kédougou youth often teased one another for being a forodu. In so doing, power emerged not only from the top down, as a lack of recognition in the eye of the state, but also as a form of horizontal capillary power (Foucault 1977). In teasing one another, residents were characterizing one another in the frame of play, teasing those without an ID card as forodu or as yokels from the country with no official status. Umar, a young man from Mamadou's extended family who often lived with him in Kédougou, was often subject to such teasing. At several points, I came back to Mamadou's house to find him in deep conversation with some peers about his fear of the police. Being a forodu, he said, meant that he couldn't stay out late at night and go wherever he pleased. Worse yet, this status was starting to color the way his peers were thinking about him. As such, this designation put one in a precious position with both authorities, for legal reasons, and joking partners, for being the target of teasing and mockery. Even as he expressed his palpable fear, Umar nervously laughed alongside the lighthearted banter of his peers in a recognition of his liminal situation. Although a form of playful teasing among peers, these routines belied significant spatial limitations that confronted those who did not possess ID cards.

During the time of my fieldwork, ID card drives were being hosted all throughout the region. Many student and hometown groups hosted events like all-night dance parties that were dedicated to raising of awareness about ID cards. Yet even the acquisition of an official ID card was a process that entailed the effective navigation of social connections to administrative power brokers. In late 2014, I had scurried down the rocky hoore fello mountain path from Taabe to check out an ID card drive to be held in the village of Takkopellel. Men and women of all ages were lined up, dressed in vibrant wax fabrics. Everyday objects were often printed upon bright wax fabrics, and this year, oscillating fans figured prominently on the top and bottom matching *complets* of the patient crowd. If these individuals were going to have their likenesses rendered timeless on an ID card, they were going to look their best.

However, grumblings reverberated throughout the ranks of the side-lined Taabe residents, who criticized Takkopellel's nepotistic favoritism of their own residents to jump ahead in line. For many from dozens of kilometers away, waiting was a skill one honed as an adult—particularly in interactions with the state. Many had been there since 5:30 in the morning. The hope was that these individuals would have their pictures and birth documents processed into ID cards that they could pick up within three months. This seemingly simple process, however, entailed numerous bureaucratic steps. Applicants needed first to bring a *jibinande* (birth certificate). However, a new version of this document was required (one ostensibly more difficult to forge), which was to be found in the nearby administrative center for a fee. As James C. Scott, John Tehranian, and Jeremy Mathias (2002, 32) sardonically remind us, "[the birth certificate] is a remarkable and very recent innovation; even in the West, people managed, until quite recently, to be born and die without official notice!" In addition to being used for official purposes by the Senegalese state, birth certificates were being employed by local leaders to solidify their followers. During this time, the procurement of birth certificates for the residents of Taabe became an important concern for the village chief. In the wake of this move toward *regularization*, Taabe's chief frequently walked to the hamlets surrounding Taabe in an attempt to enroll individuals on the official register of Taabe, thereby boosting its official population. This also reflected a persistent concern to account for everyone. Yet in a context where many ostensible residents spent much of their time in Dakar, the Gambia, or Spain, it was not a straightforward task. Talk of where the borders between villages were to be officially recognized raised the stakes of these records and animated many nighttime conversations in the chief's compound.

To secure jibinande for residents in the register of Taabe was thus an act of strengthening political boundaries, which were slowly becoming more grounded in official documentation. This was not a passive act of recording an existing reality, however, but an active campaign to persuade individuals to join the registers of Taabe. Jom Wuro often spent time in neighboring compounds, explaining the importance of birth registers and the prerogatives it would afford Taabe's sons and daughters. This included the ability to own land in an official capacity, to secure loans, and to travel in security without fear of being arrested by police at travel checkpoints.

In the first part of this chapter, I argued that routines of social idioms like joking relationships have offered relatively flexible systems for self-presentation among West Africans in interactional contexts who would have occasion to travel and embed themselves in different communities. While last names might give the impression of fixed objects of reference through which individuals could be separated and identified, names frequently became affordances for building relationships and connections with others amid a rich poetic tradition that relied on forms of conversion and association. These combinatory principles allowed for the creative building of relationships with others based on affinity, joking relationships, or generational distance. This pluralism of naming includes teknonyms (e.g., "mother of Mamadou"), nicknames, birth order names, Saint's names, or *jammoore* taboo names based on migratory experiences.

This diversity of names poses a problem for states who are in the business of identifying unique individuals in the context of law enforcement, taxation, or resettlement. The issuance of state identification cards and numbers has often served to monitor and control populations. To be able to identify a biographical individual with a set of information, including names, addresses, and social history, is an act of power that enables taxation and conscription. As biopower in a Foucauldian sense, these offer systems of recording, monitoring, and legislating human life through bureaucratic means (Foucault 1988). Scott, Tehranian, and Mathias (2002) have examined how naming practices fit into the state's desire to identify individuals under its control in a systematic way, terming the process the *conquest of intelligibility.* Indeed, many of the villages founded in this part of the Fouta Djallon plateau came here to escape the *sagalle*, cattle taxes, as well as quotas for rubber collection in Guinean territories to the south. For many adults who had long traveled to and from Kédougou, Dakar, and mining centers, having an ID card was novel. Many villages on top of the hoore fello plateau, in fact, had changed from the Guinean to the Senegalese side and back. Some, in fact, had multiple ID cards. For most borderland dwellers, to become Senegalese or Guinean was not primarily a locus of identity but rather a strategic move to take advantage of a more favorable tax regime. Mining ID cards, which had been initiated since Macky Sall's presidency, also provided a state-sanctioned form of identity that could facilitate admittance into mining areas.

At first glance, it is tempting to see these power imbalances between state agents and individuals as antithetical to the more flexible ways in which mobile Kédovins have traditionally managed relationships. In the former, state agents unilaterally determine the criteria through which individuals are to be identified that is evaluated through a fixed name entextualized on a physical ID card. However, these bureaucratic forms of identification were not merely a domain of the state. ID cards themselves became a textual part of these broader repertoires of self-presentation that too were taken up in creative routines of relation building.[5] Taking these bureaucratic texts into creative interactions took many forms. For instance, ID cards were often traded among individuals of the same approximate generation, likeness, or origins to help them gain access to particular social domains. I knew many youths who commonly borrowed one another's ID cards as a way to gain access to a football tournament, to register for an exam, or to guarantee safety during long-distance travels. Joking relationships of a kind also flourished between those individuals with ID cards and forodus, who were now freely mockable due to their liminal position. I also witnessed the strategic brandishing of ID cards during debates about relative age as proof of one's status as elder—a distinction of utmost importance.

To be sure, the relationship between official modes of identification like censuses and ID cards on one side and lived forms of identification on the other are complex and multidirectional. However, it is important to consider the ID card as another potential mode of relational negotiation rather than a stable representation. Rather than definitive markers, the information on cards, such as birth dates, were subject to further discussions of whether they reflected the true date or were altered, as was common practice. Often names listed on ID cards smoothed over more complex dimensions of an individual's social markers. For instance, Taabe's village chief often had long conversations with individuals before he officially registered their information in which they mutually agreed on the simplest versions of names to be entered. Similarly, accounts of where individuals were from could be adjudicated through verbal rhetoric as well as the timely demonstration of an ID card (e.g., were they a true Kédovin?). Moreover, many birth registers and ID cards were produced from information that was collected years after individuals were born or married—as people could best remember. Identity cards were also not fixed in stone. For so many students who had lost years to farming or home labor, reducing their age on ID cards (*jugement*) was a strategic play to ensure they could continue along with their education.[6]

In the first part of this chapter, I endeavor to provide a sketch of the verbal creativity through which mobile individuals manage to present different "versions" of themselves in different contexts. They partly do this by juggling different names, identifiers, and categorical memberships through which they emerge as slightly different individuals in distinct times in places. Scholarship on mobility has primarily emphasized kinship structures as stifling or constraining for migrants who pursue mobile adventures to escape them (Diggins 2015). And while kinship, caste, and affinity do loom large in the social lives of West Africans, interactional perspectives offer a corrective view to what have often been viewed as constraining social structures. This chapter has explored how routines and idioms grounded in kinship, affinity, and mutuality also offer resources for navigating precarious contexts. Although West Africa witnesses a strong verbal tradition of creativity based on shared idioms like joking relationships, this is not a process that occurs outside of history, politics, or landscape. In discussing issues of birth certificates and ID cards, I sought to give a fuller texture to the modalities through which mobile individuals give evidence of themselves and their relationships with others.

Rather than a strict division between fixed, written forms of identification, such as ID cards, on one hand and creative, oral forms of relation making on the other, I have shown how ID cards are themselves brought into creative routines of self-presentation. However, establishing oneself in relation to others through an idiom of joking relationships or affinity is not the achievement of individual actors, but a process constrained by the interactional dynamics of multi-party encounters. The following chapter examines these interactional processes. Although the first and second half of this chapter might initially appear to be phenomena of a different order, they show that being mobile is enabled by forms of negotiated identity and relationships and, likewise, that social relations are built out of the labor of being mobile. Names—written on ID cards or spoken out in interactions—are affordances for being mobile and making new places your own by relating yourself to others.

Notes

1. Like many other languages in the area, Pular uses a base-five system for counting money but a base-ten system for counting objects or individuals. As such, "bu sappo" (ten) means fifty francs CFA (five times ten) but "na'i sappo" (ten cows) refers to only ten cows.

2. In this book I translate *jokkere endaŋ* as the "pursuit of relations," drawing on the meaning of *jokkere*, which can mean "pursuit." *Jokkere*, or *jokkal*, can also refer to a joint, or articulation, and thus might be thought of as the articulation of sociality. Although I only infrequently heard this interpretation, *endaŋ* also means "sap." Other possible translations of *jokkere endaŋ* include "social ties," "solidarity," or, in some cases, "kinship relations."

3. It is useful to distinguish between two different levels of the term *joking relationship*. First, *joking relationship* can refer to the sociopoetic correspondence of patronyms that is posited between individuals across the Sahel. In a second sense, we can examine a joking relationship as the instantiation of such a correspondence in a face-to-face interaction (see Canut 2006). A takeaway from a performative approach to joking relationships is that the mere existence of such a correspondence does not guarantee its success in interaction. Part of the verbal art was indeed to deny, expand, or subtly shift these relationships in ways that suited the interactional goals of interlocutors.

4. *Fulɓe* is the plural ethnonym, while *pullo* refers to the singular, which is associated with the language spoken, Pular or Fula.

5. These new ID card drives were intended to provide biometric documentation to Senegalese residents, which was a broader strategy of the countries of the Economic Community of West African States. Whether or not this affects the ways in which individuals are able to bring them into routines of more flexible relationality remains to be seen.

6. For instance, much is made of African football's tendency to reduce the age of its players such that much older players might lead their countries to victory in the under-seventeen championships. Nigeria, Ghana, Cote d'Ivoire, and Senegal often stand out in the headlines. While a cynical perspective might merely view this as a form of blatant cheating, it is useful to see this alongside the other myriad ways in which West Africans have creatively performed themselves through the bureaucratic materiality of the state-issued ID card.

3

ARTICULATING MOBILITY

Migration in Interaction

From Representing to Articulating Mobility

Abdou, a slender young man from Guinea, had made his way to Kédougou from his hometown in the highlands of the Fouta Djallon mountains. Here, he worked odd jobs at the downtown market, offloading lorries and selling small Chinese electronics from a makeshift table. In Kédougou, he was surrounded by many other regional migrants who, likewise, worked as porters and merchants in this thriving road town. But while his commercial activities were enabled by these networks, he hadn't yet managed to leverage his time there into a commercial success. In 2011, Abdou struck out for Nouakchott, the capital of Mauritania, in the hopes of making it in a new place. He spent four years there before returning to Kédougou. When he returned in 2015, however, he had little more than he left with. His fellow Guinean colleagues in many respects treated him as though he had never left. This chapter draws on this case study and three other examples to explore how mobility is constituted through interactions between migrants and those they left behind. In so doing, it offers a toolkit for studying mobilities interactionally and not merely as individual narratives held to represent experiences of migration.

In reading this chapter, consider the following question: Can an individual leave their home, spend four years abroad before returning, and not be considered a migrant? This might initially appear to sound like an implausible state of events. However, looking at mobility as coming into being through linguistic exchanges and not merely as a preexisting, represented experience helps resolve this apparent conundrum. That is, the perspective of mobilities is not merely one of tracing how people and things move around the world and then using language to report on this movement. Linguistic practice in interaction brings mobility into being and provides an embodied encounter through which concepts, connections, and people can be articulated across space and time.

Throughout this chapter, I analyze a series of encounters between returning migrants and those they left behind in order to examine how mobilities become instantiated through multiparty interactions. Traditionally, migrant experiences have been represented largely through short narrative texts obtained through interviews that provide readers with a summary of a migrant's itinerant experiences. In contrast to the textual representation of this monologic individual interview as the method through which we might explore mobilities and migrations, contested encounters of social interaction show how mobilities and emergent meanings come into being. By examining language as the site of social action rather than a mere representation of preexisting experiences (of mobility), this chapter sheds light on how we can understand language and social interaction in the context of mobility studies. Most work on mobilities has tended to focus on physical movement and the geographically bounded experiences migrants had while they were away. Basing our knowledge of migration primarily on individual interviews often leads to an individualist, univocal perspective to mobility. When language does enter into studies of mobility, it is often tacked on at the end to investigate how the meanings of these mobilities as experiences are represented (Cresswell 2006). Such approaches to mobility often use terms such as *imaginaries, fantasy,* and *representation* (Salazar 2011). While such terms can be useful, they eschew the central ways in which mobility comes into being through language and mediated interactions.

As migrants return to their hometowns and talk of their time abroad with those they left behind, social interactions offer sites through which meanings are mutually negotiated. One way of understanding this constitutive role of language is to recognize that communicative acts bring things into being at the same time that they represent experiences. In this book, I therefore use the term *articulating* rather than *representing* in order to draw on the dual meaning of expressing a proposition and making linkages. Articulating mobilities entails a social practice that can shape relationships, mediate the formation of collectivities, and enable the movement of people, bodies, and ideas. While linguistic representations of mobilities might first appear to be a communicative act of reporting on existing "events" or "experiences," these encounters demonstrate social action—a practice of mobility itself.

Thinking in terms of articulations instead of representations emphasizes the relation-making aspects of mobilities. Tracking the meaning of mobility requires more than an attention to how experiences abroad are represented as if these were answers that a single individual could simply give an answer to. Returning migrants were often thrust into encounters in which the meaning and impacts of mobility were mutually negotiated. These all happened during a series of seemingly mundane interactions in which individuals offered up and contested understandings of themselves and their experiences. These were not only opportunities for returning migrants to offer new understandings of themselves but also occasions for those who stayed behind to redefine themselves in response. Looking at the creative verbal interactions that result out of return trips like these can help us better understand how mobility affects social relationships in such communities. Tracking the central role of language in constituting mobility therefore entails an analysis of how language becomes negotiated in multiparty encounters. Not merely a narrative about faraway travels, linguistic articulations of mobility were negotiated in the action of everyday conversations. These meanings were contested and negotiated and thus out of the singular control of storytellers. Tracking this action entails a close attention to how conversations happen—how they are spatially constructed, how interlocutors draw on different linguistic stylistic features, and how individuals evaluate one another's speech through different language ideologies. Although tracking this social action is often messier than the simple translation of a story, these approaches are critical tools in understanding the lives of migrants.

The act of becoming a migrant or refugee thus requires not only a lived experience of precarity or even oppression but also the ability to articulate oneself socially in specific contexts through the mastery of appropriate linguistic routines and embodied signs. To be mobile is to enact a reconceptualization of oneself—a kind of multiparty storytelling in practice. West African migrants achieved this through the deployment of institutionalized joking relationships, host-stranger idioms, kinship relationships, greetings, and other forms of verbal creativity I examine in chapter 2. I suggest that we think beyond abstract terms like *representations* or *imagination* and pay close attention to the embodied, performative acts that bring mobility into being. The craft of negotiating social capital (Bourdieu 1991)—the ability to successfully articulate oneself and render oneself legible in social networks—is much harder to track and to appreciate.

Conceptually separating acts of mobility and their representations also results in unintended spatial assumptions about how to map out and study mobility. Frequently, migrant experiences abroad (often an urban site) offer the subject of interviews that are reported on at home (often a rural site) in discursive form—a story told at home about faraway travels, so to speak. Yet articulating experiences of migration was not merely something done when one "returned home" and told stories of distant lands. Positing these distinct realms—one in which the act of mobility occurs and another where it is represented—sets up a priori distinctions about the sites in which mobility supposedly happens. Instead, I suggest that we track how migrants themselves constitute relations between places. (I explore these processes of distinguishing sites in more detail in chapter 5.)

Much scholarship in mobility employs short narrative descriptions to introduce migrants and exhibit migration. Instead, I emphasize interactional encounters. When scholars present these narratives, migrants' names, origins, and short bios are usually included in their own words as a representation of their experiences. While these narratives in the words of the migrants are important, they do not fully demonstrate how language is actually used and interpreted in contexts of mobility. These representational approaches occlude the fact that "meanings" are intersubjective outcomes between people rather than the unchanging property of individuals. The meaning of migrations is thus a complex question of iterative interactions in which migrants articulate mobility at the same time that they are performing social action (such as building relationships with colleagues, hiding wealth from kin, or requesting support). In drawing attention to this dimension of linguistic practice, my work complements scholarship in mobilities that has emphasized trajectories and in-betweenness rather than merely attending to migratory points of origin and end points (Schapendonk, Bolay, and Dahinden 2020). As such, language works as a connective form of labor whose work is yet unfinished rather than a representation of mobile experiences whose arcs and endpoints have been anticipated a priori.

Cyclical mobility was not merely something that a few individuals experienced; instead, it was a social process that mediated the social constitution of transnational communities. As other ethnographers of mobility in West Africa have pointed out, a critical dimension of mobility is coming full circle and reintegrating one's experiences, belongings, and knowledge with one's home community—a path that often ends at home (Jonsson 2012; Whitehouse 2012; Chappatte 2022). While some might be able to return several times a year for important life cycle rituals, others only managed to return every few years. At these moments of reentry, migrants must articulate years of mobility to kin, colleagues, and strangers. This chapter captures the interactional negotiation of mobilities in the social encounters of returning migrants.

Previous research on social mobilities has usefully conceptualized the goods brought back by migrants as more than material items like money, technologies, or clothes.[1] They might include ways of speaking, social perspectives, religious practices, and other cultural products, which some scholars have examined as social remittances. Scholars have reframed such transnational flows through the frame of such remittances, thereby eschewing a narrowly economic approaches (Levitt and Lamba-Nieves 2011). "Things" brought back home, such as social remittances, are not unchanged objects transported to a new setting. Instead, returning migrants embed these new norms, ideas, or representations within existing social and linguistic practices that shape their uptake. The Malian aventuriers in the work of André Chappatte (2022, 7), for instance, viewed *tunga*, (migration to a foreign place), as a school that "widens people's horizons and opens their minds." When representations of new places and experiences are brought to hometowns, these experiences must first be translated through the bodies and mouths of migrants in particular places and amid specific social relationships. Language as articulation helps account for how individuals come to be migrants and engage in creative social action as they negotiate their lives across space. The social and cultural capital enjoyed by migrants coming back to places like Taabe after time abroad or in capital cities did not happen by a matter of course. This time abroad was rendered meaningful as mobility in the ongoing communication with hometowns and during precious return trips.

Hometown community members often had strong feelings about how migration changed a person. Kédovins often said that they could immediately tell what countries returning migrants had been living in based on patterns of behavior. France and the United States as migration destinations, in particular, offered a paradigmatic distinction that brought out strong opinions. Those who were returning from France, I often heard, would often put their wealth and experiences abroad on display. They demanded to be chauffeured in cars rather than walking about and curated their dress to make their time abroad abundantly clear. In contrast, those returning from America could not be distinguished from those who had not been abroad at all. They walked rather than insisting on a car for transportation and tended to wear things that didn't make them stand out. I often wondered whether these assessments were impacted by a long-standing familiarity with American Peace Corps volunteers who walked and rode bikes rather than using cars and put little effort into what they were wearing. While these categorical explanations clearly did not always conform to reality, they demonstrate that migrants carefully curated embodied signs of mobility and reflected on these typified styles of self-presentation.

Negotiating Mobilities through Teasing Nicknames

In the following, I discuss a genre of teasing nicknames that demonstrates how migrants in Kédougou's downtown market came to articulate their mobilities through their complex, multiparty interactions. When I returned to the Kédougou market in 2014 to begin anthropological fieldwork, it was as though I was encountering a new place. However, I still knew a few kola nut sellers from my time in the Peace Corps. The market was now a place of linguistic and social effervescence. Amid this new din, I began to pick out unexpected names: monikers like *pillow*, *avocado*, and *ten o'clock*. I soon learned that the migrant merchants and laborers of the downtown market came to know one another through the exchange of nicknames. Known locally as *jammooje*, these nicknames harkened most frequently to moments of migratory precarity. For instance, France's nickname alluded to numerous failed attempts to cross the Mediterranean and Avocado was so named after one of his large shipments of fruit spoiled while it was waylaid along the contentious Senegal-Guinea border.

However, these teasing nicknames could not be used by just anyone. In order to be ratified to use a jammoore, you had to acquire usage rights in one of two ways. Firstly, you could have been present at the baptismal moment of folly that led to the nickname. This means that you had to either be present at the original moment of crisis or when the *jammoore* nickname first materialized through a telling of this hardship (I will discuss such a case shortly). Secondly, as a kind of "pay-to-say" principle, you could become ratified to use a nickname by offering money or food to the owner of the nickname or to others who were already ratified users.[2] To become known by such a nickname could be a painful experience for some migrants, but it was to be in good company. Having one's migratory misadventures narrated through the routine of jammoore was to become wrapped up in a social network through the reciprocity of shared stories. Coming to terms with migratory struggles through this genre resonates with the experiences of migrants across West Africa. André Chappatte, for instance, notes that suffering and a shared intimacy are key aspects of Malian migrants in search of adventure abroad (Chappatte 2022). Such stories of success and failure abroad were common discussion in the downtown market. In many cases, particular parts of these narratives became *entextualized*—that is, cut off from surrounding text to be cited in new contexts—such that they carried along associations from these past stories (Bauman and Briggs 1990; Spitulnik 1996). It is in this way that jammoore nicknames, which were once part of larger narratives, could be lifted out of context and come to encapsulate a stance on migration.

Constructing taboo nicknames and navigating their meanings demanded feats of linguistic creativity. This entailed acts of presenting oneself, managing one's clout, and building a social network as central to one's status as a successful migrant. While most migrants of the downtown market readily exchanged jammooje, only some developed it into a verbal art and could truly make a name stick. Sadio was a charismatic young electronics seller from Guinea who had mastered this art. He had built his strong reputation partly from his success in selling clothes and small electronics in the downtown market. However, he was also an engaging storyteller who found an accomplice in the sweet green tea that he routinely shared in the market. It was this liquid form of sociality that brought in clients and other merchants to him in rapt circles of attention. Early one morning during his first pot, Sadio, was joined by nearby merchants Abdou, a slight young Guinean seller, and Leye, a middle-aged, Wolof-speaking merchant from coastal Senegal. The merchants were exchanging stories of adventure when discussion soon turned to the importance of learning the local languages of migration destinations. Sadio ventured that Abdou, for all his time in Mauritania, never even learned any basic greetings. After a short rebuttal, Abdou concluded, "Mauritanians are hell; why don't you get it." In response, Sadio launched into a story of Abdou's time in Mauritania; he leaned over to Leye and exclaimed, "*Four years* in Mauritania! He was in Mauritania for *four years* in a towel!" This phrase would punctuate an emerging narrative about Abdou's adventures in Mauritania.

The story of Abdou emerged in bits and pieces. It was told again and again over the course of two hours by Sadio, who found in every new inter-locutor an opportunity to refine its telling. The refrain, repeated continually, was clear from the beginning: "quatre ans, sarvet!" (four years in a towel!). Abdou, who had traveled to Nouakchott, Mauritania, was "taken in" by a Mauritanian family soon after arriving in the bus station. In search of com-mercial opportunities, he instead found himself entrapped in the courtyard of this family where he was paid next to nothing for menial domestic work. As Sadio tells it, Abdou was clothed in nothing more than a towel (*sarvet*) for four years since he (ostensibly) never left the compound. Abdou's big op-portunity had turned into a tragic tale of exploitation.[3] Sadio's telling insists on the fact that for all the time Abdou spent there, he had gained nothing new. He came back after four years with only two sacks of old clothes and no more than CFA\$40,000 (approximately US\$70). Moreover, Abdou didn't learn any new languages, lacked an insider's understanding of Nouakchott's neighborhoods, and hadn't returned with any linguistic fluency. As I show in the following discussion, Abdou was ultimately denied migratory status, for although he had traveled somewhere, he neither changed nor gained anything in the process.

Though told in a key of conviviality, it was at times a painful story that Abdou might have covered up and carried as a secret burden. In the context of this market, however, the story of Abdou's time was repeated alongside a host of other migratory misadventures, marking him with a badge of be-longing in the idiom of a jammoore. Not merely a representation of ex-periences as they happened however, these linguistic practices articulated community belonging and provided a site through which individuals ne-gotiated one another's status as migrants. Through language, mobility was something that happened not only *away* in Mauritania but also *here* at the market.

The transcript given in table 3.1 offers some more detailed perspectives on how this emerged in interaction. Though early in its telling, lines 3 and 5 show the repetition of "quatre ans" (four years) and on line 6 we hear the refrain "sarvet rekk" (only in a towel). On line 7, Sadio begins to talk about the frail constitution that Abdou returned in—not at all the embod-ied figure of a successful migrant. Told in both Wolof and Pular (at times for the sake of fellow participant Leye, who spoke little Pular), Sadio's tell-ing embodied migratory success, partly through his facility with multiple languages. Though code-switching between Pular, Wolof, and French is not

Table 3.1. "Four Years in a Towel" Encounter
Bold = Wolof; normal = Pular; italics = French
Abdou: young migrant who had gone to Mauritania; speaks only Pular and a little Wolof
Leye: middle-aged trader from the coast; speaks primarily Wolof and a little Pular
Sadio: young successful migrant; speaks Pular and conversational Wolof

#	Speaker	Speech	English Gloss
1	Abdou	naar noŋ ko yiite faamu aŋ kaɗi	Mauritanians are hell; why don't you get it
2	Abdou	kaa a yaraali de lakka oŋ	Or have you not drunk the swill?
3	Sadio	*quatre ans* Mauritanie *depuis* dem na Mauritanie *quatre ans* bi- *sarvet*	Four years in Mauritania. Since he went to Mauritania, for four years.
4	Sadio	**dem na** *cour* ( )	Went to a courtyard (unintelligible)
5	Sadio	*quatre ans* **dem na benn** *cour*	Four years in one courtyard
6	Sadio	*sarvet* **rekk**	Only a towel
7	Sadio	**amul** *force*	He has withered away

uncommon, this linguistic feat became significant here because of their earlier discussion about the importance of learning local languages as a migrant. As such, this was not only a story of Abdou's time in Mauritania but also an opportunity for Sadio to articulate himself as a successful migrant who could perform knowledge of the world. Surrounded by other merchants from Guinea, the Gambia, and Senegal, Sadio comported himself with the demeanor of a migrant who had made it. By this time, he had almost saved up enough money to buy passage to Angola and had already learned Wolof quickly from doing business in Dakar. In fact, soon after this encounter, Sadio made it to Angola, a place of significant commercial opportunities.

Abdou's more limited opportunities as a migrant were rendered palpable by his concomitant linguistic constraints—he could only speak Pular. His unfamiliarity with Wolof or Hassaniya (a common language of Mauritania) soon became an embodied sign of his failure as a migrant. Building on a critique of Abdou's language skills, Sadio and other interlocutors continued to evaluate the extent to which Abdou was shaped by his time abroad. At one point, they questioned Abdou's knowledge of Nouakchott's neighborhoods and dismissed the faltering list he offers up. Along these lines, Sadio assessed the goods and material traces that Abdou was able to

Table 3.2. Old Clothes

#	Speaker	Speech	English Gloss
		. . . ((does not follow directly from previous table))	. . .
8	Sadio	si a co- haala mo conci makko ko kiɗɗo rekk eh	if you cl- tell him his clothes were just old
9	Mansa	**yere yu màggat rekk la fii indaale**	he only brought back old clothes
10	Mansa	**ñaari sak la woon**	it was two bags
11	Sadio	**ñew na fii**	he came here
12		((laughter all around))	

bring back as evidence of true mobility. "His clothes were all old!" Sadio explained at different points, adding that Abdou had brought less than one hundred dollars over the course of four years. In transcript provided in table 3.2, Sadio urged another migrant peer, Mansa, to talk about Abdou's clothes. As others, such as Mansa, are drawn into this encounter, more and more passersby learn of Abdou's fate. This provides a first cast of individuals who feel ratified to use "quatre ans, sarvet" (four years in a towel) as a nickname. This example demonstrates the importance of tracking not only who is speaking but also who is performing their involvement through backchannel cues. These old clothes and two old bags were a far cry from the ideal of "ostentatious [leather] bags" that successful migrants were expected to return with (Chappatte 2022, 9). In so doing, the storytellers collectively establish that Abdou acquired nothing new in Mauritania. This was a significant charge in a context where mobility was expected to offer opportunities for wealth accumulation, often away from familial networks that might have exerted pressures on one's resources.

In sum, over the course of these dialogic articulations, Abdou is denied any lasting experience of Mauritania. Despite four long years, he could not successfully channel any signs of his time abroad. Although Abdou had physically traveled to Mauritania, the status of migrant was effectively denied to him as evidenced by his lack of new language skills, acquired goods, local knowledge, and clothing. Ultimately, the one thing Abdou did share with many of his peers, however, was this shared experience of failure. "Aventure no muusi" (Adventure [traveling] is painful), offered a member of the audience. His relationship with this emergent community was a nuanced one, however. On one hand, his status as migrant was cast into doubt through collaborative articulations of his failure. On the other hand, his precarity also situated him alongside many other struggling migrants whose fates were remembered through jammoore names.

It might be tempting to see this dialogic storytelling session as an act of representing through language the experiences Abdou had as a migrant. However, rather than positing ostensibly transparent experiences of mobility that are subsequently put into words, this episode shows how migrants and mobilities are constituted through language-in-interaction. Telling a story was thus not to narrowly represent an experience but to enact mobility and to mediate relationships within a community of migrants. By articulating the story, Sadio was revealing a difficult moment in Abdou's life; Abdou was also becoming someone. In so doing, Sadio was also cultivating his status as a charismatic storyteller—a kind of person who tells it like it is. Although his voice is dominant, Sadio does not singlehandedly define Abdou's fate. At times these stories are channeled through other interlocutors, who soak up the tale and further interpret Abdou's travels as they translate it into other languages and perspectives. These contested meanings emerge through repeated rebuttals and retellings, which are offered to passersby who themselves interpret and pass on these stories. The dialogic nature of this story shows the significance of such articulations to be emergent and not predetermined.

Told by his own mouth, Abdou's plight might have become a story of ethnic disdain of Mauritanians. However, the existence of jammooje as a genre of migratory suffering presented opportunities to reframe the encounter: "four years in a towel!" It is this image of a laughable and frail Abdou wearing a towel that came front and center, the figure of someone who had perhaps moved about some but not really been mobile. As articulations, routines of jammoore teasing disabuse notions that mobility constitutes experience which is merely captured by language as representation. Articulating the trauma of mobility through taboo, jammoore reveals this to be a central site of social action in which individuals came into being as migrants.

This chapter thereby illustrates the dialogic and performative work of articulating mobilities. Sadio's tales of Abdou's time in Mauritania were not individual verbal feats. Rather, they emerged in collaboration with listeners who ratified and shaped the story. Even if articulations of mobility do appear to take the form of stories, these narratives are told in particular times and often have a part to play in the broader interactional goals of the moment. These may include impressing one's peers, dissuading others, or engaging in cultural critique that compares styles of living in different places. These considerations carry important implications for how we conduct research on mobilities. An interview with migrants, for instance, is not a transparent window on their experiences. Instead, it is a negotiated encounter in which different actors bring different expectations and understandings of what is happening (Briggs 1986). The kinds of stories elicited thus are shaped by the broader interactional goals, power dynamics, and social roles of those involved.

Viewing mobility as dialogic articulations shapes the conclusions that we can draw about qualitative data gathered from respondents in the context of mobility. For instance, in a recent article on mobility that encounters seemingly irrational behavior by artisanal miners, the authors note that "people looking for wealth-enhancing opportunities are enticed by overstated narratives, which in this case were 'gold-gilded'" (Fahy Bryceson, Bosse Jønsson, and Clarke Shand 2020, 459). These are the kinds of pronouncements that we as scholars on mobility frequently encounter. Not merely narratives of success in mobility, these were forms of action that did social work. The ways in which migrant miners articulate their mining activities is a complex question that requires a look beyond the referential elements to the interactional context surrounding these responses. Complaining, bragging, and other talk about one's successes (Fahy Bryceson, Bosse Jønsson, and Clarke Shand 2020, 459) can be understood as articulations of migratory mining practices: forms of social action that build a person's status and situate them in relation to others. These verbal strategies can even influence one's luck in mining. On one hand, bragging and performing largesse from small successes often form the part of a larger strategies of status negotiation or interactional one-upmanship that have the potential to mobilize clout and resources (Walsh 2003; Newell 2012). In other cases, however, West African migrants also avoid flaunting their wealth or representing their success, for fear of attracting jealous gazes and evil eyes that might make demands on their resources. Becoming a successful miner in West Africa entails the capacity to manage relationships with spirits of the earth (d'Avignon 2022), which is itself contingent on one's ability to articulate oneself or one's hosts as autochthonous parties who have rights to the land. Miners thus balance the cultivation of good fortune through ritual activity with the deflection bad luck and jealous eyes through the tempering of apparent successes. In the case of migrant West African miners, thinking of articulations of mobility as forms of social action in their own right rather than correct or incorrect representations helps account for language as a performative medium.

Evaluating Migrancy: Connecting Places through Language

The remainder of this chapter expands on the perspective of articulation by examining three further encounters between migrants and home communities. They explore the linguistic and relational dynamics in interaction through which migrants' connections with places and cultural formations is evaluated. To come back to one's hometown village, then, was to enter an arena in which traces of one's mobility were scrutinized. Abdou's story provides an initial case study of how this happened in the downtown Kédougou market. As such, certain linguistic performances could sediment one's status as a successful aventurier, while others risked mockery as evidence of backwardness and migratory incompetence. These kinds of interactions were also common in Taabe. One afternoon I was listening to the radio in front of a village store when a young man I knew as Boubs showed up to greet the lot of us sitting around on rattan chairs. I soon learned that he had been away for several weeks, and various stories had been circulating about his activities. After some brief introductions, he turned to me and said, "A wallay laŋ e kele. Meŋ hawtay kele" (You will help me get a "girlfriend." We will share a "girlfriend"). Bursts of sardonic laughter sputtered out from the mouths of my fellow companions and dislodged many from their seats. Whereas he was actually asking about a USB key, his pronunciation of this word sounded like the Pular word for girlfriend, *kele* (see table 3.3).

The context of this request was that I had just given to the members of the local youth soccer league several USB keys filled with video footage of their recent soccer tournament. Not interested in a girlfriend, Boubs was instead asking me whether I would help him get a hold of a USB with a video of the match on it. To Daouda and his companions, however, he had (mis)pronounced a word borrowed from French, *clé* (as in USB key), as *kele*, which means "girlfriend" in Pular. Based on Pular phonology, speakers often insert vowels between consonants, implicitly following a linguistic sound pattern that avoids consonant clusters. The loan word *clé* from French was thus pronounced by a rural Pular speaker as "kele" to avoid what would otherwise be for monolingual Pular speakers an awkward consonant cluster. For those mobile youth who had acquired a facility with

Table 3.3. "We'll Share a Girlfriend"

#	Speaker	Speech	English Gloss
1	Boubs	a wallay laŋ e kele	You will help me get a "girlfriend" ((i.e., USB key))
2	Boubs	meŋ hawtay kele	We will share a "girlfriend"
3	Daouda	meŋ hawtay kle USB	We will share a USB key!
4	Daouda	kle, Boubs, a he6i kle	Key, Boubs, you got a key!

style shifting through previous migratory experiences, to pronounce the word in this way betrayed the voice of a country bumpkin whose linguistic horizons did not stretch far out of the Fouta Djallon mountains.

Such potential missteps were often widely discussed among peer groups and could provide ammunition for teasing for weeks. Among youth who were often traveling to coastal Senegal for economic opportunities, interpretations of such linguistic displays revealed an individual's connections to wider social worlds. Those who wielded these linguistic insights often made a showing of their broader knowledge as marks of mobility and experience of the world. In the eyes of his peers, his potential misstep demonstrated a lack of cosmopolitanism, extrapolated from his inability to produce the loan word within the flow of spoken Pular. Articulating sounds even on a phonological level thus indexes contact with broader cultural spheres. Not merely a question of communication, these sounds spoke volumes about migration histories.

Although seemingly minor, the steady repetition of these kinds of assessments could significantly alter the way in which individuals were positioned within a community. They furthermore show that it was not merely a question of accumulating "experience" as a migrant abroad. Mobilities and concomitant connections with other places and cultural forms were assessed and constituted through everyday encounters.

To offer a second example, just a few weeks before my encounter with Boubs, a young man known locally as Drogba from a nearby village began hanging out in Taabe. Drogba often played on the Taabe football team, where he received his nickname in honor of the famous African footballer. After a longer absence from the village, Drogba began to spend more and more time in the village. I often spotted him making the rounds, dropping in on various acquaintances throughout the village. In talking with his peers in the village, we soon gathered that Drogba was interested in finding

Figure 3.1. Hanging out in Taabe.

a wife. Like Boubs, he had spent several months at a mining zone, where he expressed hopes of soon striking it big. I was out with a young man named Yoro when we crossed Drogba hanging out under a small baobab tree. Like the mountain path from Takkopellel to Taabe, this tree was a space of dense sociality partly because of the rare bars of cell reception one could often find there. On a plateau where the cellular network was extremely patchy, this was the most reliable place near the village center to receive signal. As such, it was a place where people were accustomed to encountering others and being overheard. When we arrived, Drogba looked at us and said, "Lu kew?" a short greeting in Wolof, Senegal's lingua franca that is so commonly spoken in Kédougou. Table 3.4 captures our short exchange.

A common acquisition "error" among Pular speakers is to pronounce the Wolof velar fricative [x] (as in Ba<u>ch</u>) as the velar stop [k] (as in <u>k</u>ettle), as Drogba had in saying "ku kew." A Wolof greeting that could have displayed Drogba's broader experiences had hopelessly backfired, marking him as a West African hillbilly through his Pular *villageois* pronunciation. After Yoro first points out Drogba's mistake, I mindlessly repeat these two potential pronunciations to myself. Yoro, who had spent years working as a tailor in nearby villages, felt at ease speaking Wolof, which was the language of instruction in his workshop. Yoro's intonation had made it clear

Table 3.4. Interpreting Awkward Greetings

#	Speaker	Speech	Gloss
1	Drogba	lu kew	what's *up
2	Yoro	hein lu kew	what? what's *up
3	Me	lu kew lu xew	what's *up, what's up
4	Yoro	((to Drogba)) danga ma wax lu kew wala lu xew	you asked me what's *up or what's up

Note: An asterisk (*) indicates the relative placement of a pronunciation of the Pular velar stop [k], as in "kettle," rather than the Wolof velar fricative [x], as in "Bach."

that he heard Drogba's greeting as a novice mistake. Chuckling about this confrontation, Yoro soon spread word of Drogba's blunder. Youths could be ruthless in monitoring each other's attempts to deploy these resources. And Drogba's mistake was not just a meaningless error, for at this time, he was actively searching for a spouse; such missteps had the potential to incisively undermine his strategy of self-presentation. Although this example presents but one instance of an interaction between returning migrants and those in the village, the cumulative effect of these kinds of evaluations impacted the social standings and trajectories of individuals.

Examining this short encounter alongside that of the conflated girlfriend/key, we can see how mobile connections to coastal Senegal or mining regions were interpreted through everyday linguistic features. To be a mobile migrant was thus a status that one earned not through the mere accumulation of time abroad but—as with the case of Abdou in Mauritania—through the instantiation of that experience in everyday social evaluations. It was not enough to have spent time away in a number of different places. Signs of your connection to faraway places were negotiated with others in interactions that you never completely controlled. Taken together, these encounters could cumulatively articulate your connection with other people and places.

Usu Returns to Taabe: Articulating Mobility, Articulating Relationships

Return trips for migrants often became fraught encounters where interactions or gifts were highly scrutinized as evidence of success abroad. Though these trips were joyous occasions, migrants were also often compelled to navigate relationships with hometown residents with whom they held complex, crosscutting relations. The return of one villager, Usu, from the south of Spain offers a third example of these dynamics of mutual recognition. Usu was from a nearby village but had married a woman from Taabe and thus held ties of kinship and affinity with many in Taabe. Across the hoore fello plateau, anxious talk of Usu's return from Spain circulated for many weeks. Was he really interested in separating from his wife despite the recent birth of their child? What would he bring back, and how long would he stay?

Luckily, Usu had managed to regularize his status in Spain and thus could travel back and forth between there and Senegal. Despite this, he had come back only infrequently over the past five years. He had been back in the past year, and his return was partly to baptize his new daughter, who had been born in the nearby village of Mariwuro. The draw of this life cycle ritual was strong. "Eŋ heɓay haaju" I heard repeated over and over: "We're having an event!" In the days before this event, Usu visited the surrounding villages like Taabe, greeting his friends and kin across the plateau. Although it is not explicitly a story of Usu's travels, the exchanges between Usu and Rune (Mamadou's younger brother) during a hometown visit also exemplify articulations of mobility. His return exemplifies how tracking the meaning of mobilities was not merely a question of representing preexisting experiences into language. Articulations of his mobility occurred amid multiparty encounters in which acts of storytelling served as platforms for negotiating the relative statuses and relationships of those involved.

In anticipating these kinds of return encounters, I imagined that migrants would regale each other in stories of migration: the struggles they faced, their living and work conditions, or their harrowing journey abroad. What I found, however, was that such explicit stories were infrequently offered to people back home unprompted. At first, I thought this reticence might be conditioned by my positionality. However, the lack of detailed knowledge of many migrants' everyday activities—even by close relatives—hinted that this was a broader phenomenon. As an ethnographer, I was still in the mindset of representation—thinking that these experiences would be expressed neatly in story form for me to capture. What I found instead was that articulations of migrations were slowly built up through lived encounters with people back home. Mobilities were articulated through the money sent back home, clothes worn back, gifts offered to family and friends, migrants' demeanor during visitations, marriage opportunities, and financial investments back home (processes other anthropologists of transnational West Africa have tracked [Buggenhagen 2012; Yount-André 2018; Hannaford 2017]). The "meaning" of mobility was thus not merely something that was told in a narrow sense but something that was done. Mobility was rendered intelligible to people through these various modalities and not merely through narrative quips.

Days after returning from Spain, Usu finally made it to the village Taabe to pay his respects. His wife was in the lineage of Taabe's chief, and as such, many in the village were his in-laws. Like others, he felt pressure to make numerous trips to surrounding in-laws, kin, and colleagues, thereby paying respect through time spent together. In Taabe, Usu was welcomed for a midmorning tea under a shade structure, surrounded by six other local youths, including Rune, who was a longtime acquaintance. Because of Usu's endogamous marriage, Rune and Usu can trace connections with one another based on affinity and kinship. As I go on to discuss, they are ultimately impelled to negotiate this connection by the provocation of a fellow youth, whose remark stands as a challenge for them to negotiate their mutual status.

The status of in-law was an important one that drove many interpersonal relationships in this region of West Africa. In principle, among these communities of Fulɓe, there were two categories of in-laws. *Esiraaɓe* were senior in-laws, older than one's spouse, to whom one owed deference. In contrast, one could cultivate more casual relationships with one's *keyniraaɓe*, those younger than one's spouse. At other times, however, individuals might try to base these relationships on their relative ages. While the status of such relationships should be clear in theory, in practice that status of who was an esiraaɓe and who was a keyniraawo could be a contested affair.

The flexible nature of these relationships contradicts much received wisdom that questions of affinity and kinship present unchanging principles of social constitution. As I describe in chapter 6, in-law customs not only are a narrowly rural concern but also provide a frame for individuals to creatively negotiate relationships. These considerations cast doubt on the utility of creating distinctions between kinship and fictive kinship; attempting to maintain strict, categorical separations is a practice that is difficult to square with the expansive ways in which individuals employ kinship idioms to build very real connections with a wide range of individuals (Agha 2007; McGovern 2012).

As they were sitting under a shade structure, Rune (who had never been to Spain) glanced up at Usu and said, "Hombre," using a familiar Spanish greeting that invoked Usu's time in the south of Spain. After a long pause, Usu replied, "C'est bon, c'est bon" (it's good, it's good). The presence of returning migrants like Usu conditioned others—many of whom had never migrated—to employ the linguistic and cultural capital of places abroad. As Rune and Usu began to chat, they collectively imagined a possible trip they might take together to Usu's nearby hometown village of Mariwuro (see line 5 of table 3.5). Note that even such stories that don't seem to describe real events nonetheless carry significant meaning. In this exchange, Rune proposes dropping off Usu at his town, situating himself as the giver of rides and the owner of a motorcycle. While it is Usu who can afford new motorcycles, Rune can articulate a reality in which he is the giver of hospitality in this friendly interaction. During these exchanges, Rune and Usu addressed each other familiarly, using *a* (you, singular) pronouns rather than pronouns of respect, *oŋ* (you, plural). For the sake of simplicity, I have omitted most conventions for marking pauses and timing between speech, which can often tell useful stories about interactions.

This imagined story offers a stage on which Rune and Usu negotiate one another's relationship. In a state of lighthearted contention over who might front gas money for their motorcycle trip, the terms of Usu and Rune's relationship remain implicit until the question of in-law status was raised by Baylo on line 1 in Table 3.6 Uttering, "Ah he's your in-law too man," Baylo's instigation defined much of the remaining interaction by placing Usu and Rune at odds over their relative status. What had been a more egalitarian interaction among peers suddenly became an intense discussion of their affinal status. Rune vehemently disputed the fact that Usu is his senior in-law (who is to be respected) and instead invoked his own status as Usu's senior in-law based on his kinship relationships with Usu's wife (see line 3 in Table 3.6). The other interlocutors present did not end up buying this characterization, however, and Rune found himself unable to make his case. Rather than outright refusal, this lack of support emerged more subtly when they eschewed Rune's eye contact and any attempts at addressing them.

Not just a dyadic affair, however, once the terms of this interaction were set, all other copresent participants provided potential resources through which Rune and Usu voiced their positions, eschewed challenges, and garnered support. Viewed merely as stories or as descriptions of relationships or states of affairs, these interactions wouldn't make much sense. Looking at

Figure 3.2. Usu's return visit. Captured at the moment line 17 is uttered below. Rune is in blue at the back of the right bench, and Usu is in white in the front left. I am sitting in the middle right, and Baylo, sits in white at the front of the right bench.

Table 3.5. Imagining Travels Together

#	Speaker	Speech	Translation
1.	Usu	si mi arti noŋ	If I come
2.	Rune	si a arti ((sniff))	If you come back
3.		a ẙettay mille francs	You'll take a thousand francs
4.		jonna Gigol waɗeŋ essence	Give it to Gigol and we'll get some gas
5.		mi deposay maa Mariwuro	I'll drop you off in Mariwuro
6.	Usu	eeee jaka eŋ hootay Mariwuro	Eee well then we'll return to Mariwuro
7.		haray noŋ a jaaraama mawɗo	If it's like that thanks brother
8.	Rune	mi deposay maa Mariwuro	I'll drop you off in Mariwuro
9.	Usu	haray a waɗi ko moẙẙi	Then you will have done me a solid

their interactional dynamics helps us understand how a migrant's conception of self is articulated in home communities and how people make sense of such migration experiences collectively. This encounter shows several important dimensions of how mobilities are articulated between individuals who have a range of local and transnational commitments. First, such interactions can be described as dialogic in that they are the product of

Table 3.6. "Ah but He's Your In-Law"

#	Speaker	Speech	Translation
		((. . . some speech omitted))	
1.	Bay	ah- ko esiraawo ma nii kaɗi goy	Ah but he's your in-law
2.	Usu	mi-mi haali (haa-)	I- I- spoke
3.	Rune	oo ko min okki mo debbo	Him I'm the one who gave him a wife
4.		ko kanko fotti laŋ respektude	He's the one who should respect me
5.		wonaa miŋ fotti mo respektude	I'm not the one who should respect him
6.		oo miŋ ko mi esiraawo makko	no, me, I'm his in-law
7.		onoŋ fow ko mi esiraawo moŋ	I'm all y'all's in-law
8.		-ta yawu laŋ	Don't mock me

multiple parties. This means that representations are not merely presented but are evaluated, contested, and shaped in interactional contexts. This can be seen most clearly in the contributions of Baylo, who explicitly brings up the question of in-law relation. Any significance or resulting consequences must be negotiated through this multiparty interactional matrix.

Second, much of the action of these articulations can be tracked only by attuning to the multimodal dimensions of interaction (Stivers and Sidnell 2005). By the term *multimodal*, I mean embodied, complementary aspects of communication, such as gaze, gesture, and bodily alignment, through which individuals recruit addressees and contextualize meaning. In this interaction, Rune attempted to recruit the others in supporting his position of senior in-law, but he was unable to do so partly because they evaded his gaze and body alignment. Attunement to a conversation here reveals itself to be more of an achievement than a given. Finally, as sites for social action, these articulations were encounters through which individuals affected changes in one another's relative status, moving them from being a mere representation of affairs to being the work of relationship negotiation.

Usu's return from Spain moreover shows the importance of accounting for mobility in terms of temporality in addition to spatiality and movement. In such cases, social links lost and forgotten in one place offer opportunities for self-fashioning in another. In the greetings and exchanges of the everyday, for instance, individuals often develop habits of interaction—an interactional inertia of placing one another as particular kin or of adopting certain keys of interaction. Given these interactional ruptures, the length of time between encounters granted migrants and those they left behind a greater latitude to redefine relationships. This expansion of time intervals along with travel to distant lands thus entailed numerous implications for social relationships. It meant that news of migrants abroad was delayed, offering kin back home an opportunity to debate these missives for days, weeks, or years before they could confront the individuals about them directly.

While it is tempting to capture the meaning of mobilities in the form of individual narratives, this chapter has shown how meaning making in mobilities should also be examined through interactional encounters. Rather than *representation*, I have been using the term *articulation* to emphasize the negotiated linkages that emerge during the course of these encounters. Thinking of mobilities in terms of articulations that further social action rather than mere representation helps eschew inherited theories of meaning making in which ideas are brought unaltered to new places. As such, migration offers opportunities for broader social transformations as individuals navigate their relations between distant sites and hometowns. Attuning to the broader interactional dynamics shows how mobilities are articulated in the everyday. Moments of homecoming, such as the ones discussed in this chapter, offer rich contexts in which these dramas can unfold. Tracking these linguistic practices requires attention to the interaction as a whole rather than accounting for individual speakers and their narratives alone. To study language intersubjectively is therefore to recognize that a migrant's ability to self-identify and present themselves is contingent on the evaluations and diversions that happen during the course of multiparty interactions. As migrants move, they also move between different, overlapping fields of evaluations and associations through which their linguistic practices come to make sense.

Notes

This chapter is derived, in part, from an article published in the *Journal of Ethnic and Migration Studies* on May 31, 2021, available online at https://www.tandfonline.com/doi/10.1080/1369183X.2021.1924050.

1. Moreover, a long-standing anthropological insight is that the exchange of things are often as much about relationships between people and groups as they are about the things themselves (Mauss 1925; Malinowski 1984; Buggenhagen 2012).

2. With no fixed amounts, payment for access to nicknames is negotiated through a group-ratified acceptance of the amount paid. These negotiations often occurred immediately after the climatic utterance of the taboo name in front of the concerned individual, in which a payment was often demanded to remedy the transgression. In many cases, a third party who was ratified to say a particular taboo name would act as an instigator. They would bait individuals into saying a taboo name and subsequently attempt to extract a monetary fine for its violation. Once money is out on the table, all present participants and not only the taboo namesake could motivate a claim to the extracted payment, and thus, all present had an interest in encouraging taboo diffusion and transgression. Fine money would often be used to buy water, peanuts, or other snacks that would be distributed to all present.

3. The experiences of Abdou in Mauritania resonate with broader regional histories in which white baydân Mauritanians commonly exploited or even enslaved Black Mauritanians who lived south of the Senegal River (Bonte 2002). Slavery as a local institution has often been understood as affording different kinds of rights to distinct groups rather than absolute ownership (Miers and Kopytoff 1977). In Mauritania, the legal institution of slavery was only abolished in 1980. The legacy of this exploitation and later ethnic tensions could lead to alternative interpretations of Abdou's exploitation.

4

KOLA, SALT, AND STONE

Forging Pathways of Belonging through the
Materiality of Language

T HE PREVIOUS CHAPTER EXAMINED HOW MIGRANTS AND THOSE they
left behind engage in complex negotiations of evaluating and performing
traces of mobility during the course of social interactions and homecom-
ings. This chapter explores how language can trace enduring connections between dispersed people who come to be connected through webs
of exchange. Ethnographers of West African migration such as Paolo
Gaibazzi (2015) have shown that while movement and mobility have captured significant scholarly attention, an exploration of staying put and stasis
is also necessary. This chapter builds on these understandings to capture how people stand in and account for nonpresent others. Capturing
mobilities entails not only the analysis of travel to destinations away but
also how mobile individuals managed their oftentimes intermittent pres-
ences at home. By drawing attention to how language can mediate connections amid distance, I show how migrants use language creatively to remain
interwoven with dispersed communities despite their frequent absences.
This requires a consideration of language as a material substance, which
helps coalesce participation, domestic space, and social standing.

To do this, chapter 4 draws on two extended examples of how mobile
individuals negotiated their rootedness in communities through linguistic
exchanges in a ritual context. The first, a story of ritual teasing and kola nuts,
concerns a mobile female trader who must resort to creative verbal arts to
maintain her belonging in a local village during a naming ceremony. The
second example demonstrates the infrastructural properties of language as

demonstrated by my attempts to found a field station in conjunction with local partners in the outskirts of Kédougou City. Both stories show how individuals in mobile contexts navigate contingent connections with distributed communities through the exchange of words and gifts. While the analysis of naming ceremonies and the rituals of blessing homes appear to be the purview of structural anthropologists interested in the reproduction of societies, they are key sites through which increasingly dispersed communities navigate mobilities.

An expanded attention to language use helps account for how members of frequently overlooked categories of migrants, such as women, navigate mobility. As such, this chapter tracks how foreigners (like myself), tourist guides, and women traders were able to ground themselves in places where they couldn't always maintain their physical presence. Looking at language as a material technology helps uncover its power to mediate extreme distances in the context of mobility. Language was particularly efficacious when it was imbued with power through ritual context or connected to the circulation of material objects. Such strategies were essential components of the social lives of traders and migrants, who regularly faced the challenges of negotiating their connections to multiple social spheres. In both examples in this chapter, it helps to understand language as infrastructure—a material technology that not only floats on and represents the world through narrative but also shapes the material pathways across which migrants build their lives.

Of Trash Owls and Kola Nuts

The infant granddaughter of Taabe's village chief had just been given a name at a naming ceremony. The ceremony's hosts had distributed gifts of kola nuts to those in attendance as a mark of witnessing this important event. As they left the event, many attendees noticed a figure at the edge of the compound. With their face obscured by a long, flowing scarf, the cloaked figure emerged from beyond a bamboo fence and slowly approached a group of elders standing in the compound. The figure's reliance on a long staff betrayed the stride of an elder. In cascading moments of recognition, cries of shock and laughter rebounded inside the small walled compound as the figure drew nigh. Shrugging off any hands that attempted to impede their advance, the cloaked figure thrust a staff into the earth, planted two feet beside it, and bellowed, "The name of this child has come, and it is Trash Owl!" The people standing about erupted in peals of laughter at this odd pronouncement that mimicked the austere naming ceremony of an infant.

The cloaked figure revealed herself to be Aunt Aissatou, the sister of the village chief who had narrowly missed out on the naming of her brother's granddaughter. As I describe later in this chapter, Aissatou's moment of performative reinterpretation was in defiance of her exclusion at a naming ceremony. Just moments before Aunt Aissatou's satirical entry, the infant had been named Aissatou, or, as she was more commonly called, Aissa. As such, she shared a name with her "great-aunt" Aissatou, sister of the village chief. Baby Aissa occupied an important position within the village of Taabe. Each side of baby Aissa's family represented one half of its leadership—the lineage of imams on one side and the lineage of chiefs on the other. Together, these two branches encompassed the village's political life. A naming ceremony was a big deal among these predominately Pular-speaking villages along the Guinean border because, in addition to being the ritual through which infants become people, the naming ceremony brings together the father's family, the *takanɓe* hosts, and the mother's family, the *futuuɓe* in-laws.

Crossing paths with the chief and other authorities after the ceremony, Aissatou disguised herself as an imam and performed a parodic renaming in which she teased the infant, renaming her "Buubu Ñooge" (Trash Owl). The name Trash Owl referenced the bird form that witches adopt at night as they prowl the outskirts of human settlements. Allusions to witches were not often taken lightly. Aissatou had not received kola nuts—in effect a denial of participation in the ritual—and she was making an issue of it. This striking performance highlighted fissures between those who had been included in and those who had been excluded from the naming ceremony. In the following days, Buubu Ñooge was taken up by women, like Aissatou, who felt they had not received an adequate part in or invitation to the ceremony. Participation in the naming emerged not only from one's bodily presence at the event but also through the giving and receiving of kola nuts, which were distributed to witnesses in the aftermath of a naming. Those who considered themselves shut out from the ceremony mobilized the practice of teasing the child's family with this parodic name as a way to playfully extort kola from ritual organizers and thereby gaining greater representation in the event.

This encounter tells us an important lesson about mobility and how migrants and traders who were often absent maintained ties to communities distributed in space. Even more, it shows how we should conceive of community in the first place—not a clearly bounded entity but rather an articulated network of exchange that mediates participation across space. Moments of verbal art such as these show how increasingly mobile individuals like Aunt Aissatou could maintain a presence in the community despite being physically absent for much of the ceremony. Across West Africa, the exchange of gift objects such as kola nuts enables mobile individuals to insert themselves into hometown action despite their absence. Given her increased absence from Taabe, Aissatou's satiric performances helped her maintain a strong presence in the community despite her periodic exclusion. This offers an unconventional example of what constituted broader repertoires of value creation by Senegalese women at naming ceremonies and similar ritual contexts. As Beth Buggenhagen (2011, 718) has demonstrated elsewhere in Senegal with the analogous example of fabric, "displaying and distributing cloth . . . were not forms of conspicuous consumption. Rather they were about seizing the occasion to make visible the strength of their social networks." This chapter builds on these insights by tracking the ways in which language can mediate material exchanges as a particularly useful resource for dealing with systemic distance. Language as infrastructure thus offers a framework for better understanding the linguistic dimensions of promising future gifts, words standing in for material objects, or using creative linguistic performances to attract gifts themselves as strategies of mobility.

Aissatou was the wife of a fonio farmer and often traveled to and from Taabe to sell products across the region. Although her mobility is less frequently recognized in relation to those of her male counterparts, Aissatou was part of an increasingly active community of traders on top of the plateau. Sayings such as "goor dekkul fenn" (a man doesn't live anywhere) were often passed as common knowledge in West Africa, where migrancy and travel often appeared to be a male-dominated sphere. However, these proverbs belie the significant mobility of women, who often worked as successful entrepreneurs across much of the region. Together, this chapter and other recent work demonstrate the capacity of Senegalese women to react to processes of social change and global economic volatilities through creative social labor (Babou 2008; Buggenhagen 2012; Hannaford 2017; Riley 2019). Aunt Aissatou had been actively participating in a regional trade network of fonio, a local grain that was increasingly becoming a cash crop instead of being domestically consumed. Aissatou's husband was a respected farmer, and she had been visiting regional markets and those in the regional capital. Increasingly, a flourishing gold mining economy and the construction of a new international highway provided opportunities for aspiring traders. Being included in such life cycle rituals constituted a central concern for those, like Aissatou, who increasingly had opportunities to travel throughout the region.

Negotiating Participation through Gift Giving

On the part of guests, the roll call of those who made it back to hometowns for such events was intensely anticipated, whereas hosts were scrutinized for the status of their invitations, spread across capillary social networks through word of mouth, telephone, and text. Many events were put on hold so that certain key members living at a distance might be able to attend. During these naming rituals and other ceremonies, absent relatives would manage their inclusion through return visits, telephone calls, familial representatives, and gifts. Over the course of naming ceremonies, the arrival of in-laws and other guests was keenly anticipated. Kédougou was a region with an inconsistent cell network and challenging travel conditions; the steep mountain roads made auto travel near impossible. The need to account for distant relatives as well as alert kin and neighbors across the region therefore set a scene of high social drama for such events as naming ceremonies. As guests arrived from surrounding villages and neighborhoods, they brought along with them offerings of bars of peanut soap, onions, liters of oil, corn, and wax cloth, all carried in calabash dishes on the tops of women's heads. The giving of gifts was a very important aspect of the naming ceremony, and it was customary for takanɓe hosts to offer return gifts to departing futuuɓe guests. In many cases, the farther guests traveled, the more they were feted at such events. Hosts were careful to not simply return the same kinds of gifts in what one man jokingly explained to me as *okkindirgol*, "giving the same stuff back and forth."

At such events, kola nuts (along with cloth) were some of the most significant gift objects that could facilitate connections with new people. The shape of the nut, composed of two halves that join along a perfect seam, was often held to be iconic of social conjunction. Across West Africa, for instance, kola nuts were offered to the family of a woman as overtures to marriage. As social lubricant, kola were likewise a tool for the traveler in unknown lands. They were often presented to village chiefs as an offering of peace and respect upon a new visitor's arrival—a material gift that provided an opening for introductions and future relations. More broadly, their trade demonstrates the mobility of West Africa at a regional level. Grown in forested regions such as Guinea-Conakry, kola nuts provide an important and long-standing trade product between the savanna and forest regions of West Africa. As I discuss in chapter 6, kola nut sellers also occupied a special place within West African markets. Trading in this ritually significant object, their privileged position often insulated them from the vagaries of the state's intervention into local trade.

During a naming ceremony in rural areas like Taabe, a central concern for village chiefs and ritual organizers was to ensure a fair and representative distribution of gift objects, such as kola nuts, so that all social segments were represented. In the context of mobility, this often meant that migrants were accounted for amid established webs of kinship and domestic relationships. Hosts were careful to offer enough gifts and food since these redistributive rituals were centers of social gravity that could bring in far-flung friends and relatives. Connections between distant communities were thus forged through invitations passed from mouth to mouth and through the webs of reciprocity. Mobility was thus facilitated through these linked series of interactions formed through the exchange of words and gifts. Days after life cycle events, attendees reflected on ritual events based on the gifts and food they received. They often teased the hosts about the success of the event on the grounds of gifts given as markers of participation. Those events that were held to be successful and good (*weelugol*) were often ones from which attendees walked away with hands full of gifts and bellies full of rice. Because of this preoccupation with representation and subsequent reports of success grounded in the receiving of gifts, the distribution of kola nuts at naming ceremonies was keenly monitored. Given this broader context, it was consequential that Aunt Aissatou had not received a share of kola nuts.

Certain organizers, such as the village chief, often felt intensely responsible for making sure that appropriate parties got their share. These elders had to make calculations about how to appropriately distribute the kola in such a way that those who received gifts would "count for" nonpresent migrants and other kin. This could happen in one of a few ways. In some cases, those away from Taabe could be accounted for in ritual events when their remaining kin accepted kola or gifts on their behalf. Such calculations often happened along the lines of kinship and lineage, in which certain people fell under larger social entities. In a second sense, these moments also offered

Figure 4.1. Distributions at the naming ceremony.

opportunities for individuals to evaluate whether a particular individual was in fact a steady resident or not. Was their absence more or less temporary, or was their primary residence now in a distant economic center? Amid cyclical migration patterns and a mobile populous, these calculations were not always evident. The pressures of redistribution were central to the social context of mobility in which individuals could be made to "count" as part of the community through the exchange of language and gifts.

Collective negotiations of presence and belonging were thus particularly significant in communities such as Taabe, where at any given time, much of the community was absent or dispersed across the region. While those present often had a claim to distributed gifts, those performing the distribution (*sendugol*) always had an eye on those migrants away from home who needed to be accounted for. As such, the distribution of gifts like kola functioned as a form of reciprocation for those present at community rituals as well as an extension of participation to those who might not have been originally present at the ritual action. Although a naming ceremony might appear to be local, it accounted for and traced out the mobilities of a broader diasporic community. Oftentimes, they were even financed and organized from abroad.

For instance, at another naming ceremony I attended several weeks before baby Aissa's, kola nuts were put aside and entrusted to a third party, to be given to the imam for whom they were intended at a later date. In addition to being a sign of deference, this gift of kola also forged a material channel that allowed those present to enlarge the framework of participation to those who were absent. The kola nuts subsequently followed along intermediaries, from those present at the original naming ceremony, to the imam's wife, and ultimately on to the imam himself. As such, they provided a material, linguistic mediation of his ratification as a witness for the naming ritual. Reports of what happened during the naming rituals traveled alongside the kola nuts, thereby positioning the imam as an individual who could authoritatively talk about the naming ceremony. In the days after the event, the imam invoked the chosen name and remarked on the occasion as a ratified witness instead of asking others for news of the event. In this way, kola exchange across time and space can be seen as a mediator of participant frameworks, bringing in and including individuals beyond the otherwise limited here and now of ritual action.

The Ritual Shaving

Baby Aissa's naming ceremony, which began with a ritual shaving and then continued with the imam's official naming was a site for these negotiations of inclusion. In the following section, I offer a more detailed analysis of this naming ceremony that Aissatou parodied with her cloaked performance. Shortly before acquiring her name (the part in which Aunt Aissatou had been excluded), baby Aissa's head had been shaved by the women in her kin group as dozens of men and women crowded in anticipation. They attuned to the action by sitting on mats or standing on the outskirts. The management of seating arrangements occupied many of the participants, where prime locations were often reserved for honored guests and in-laws. Amid the audience, who sat in a semicircle around the ritual space, some played the roles of playful suitors who teased each other, the newborn, and her family on marriage prospects. Older adult men jokingly remarked on the baby's beauty, wondering if they would have a chance to marry her. "Meneŋ ko paykuŋ meŋ faalaa" (We want the little girl [as a wife]) one man belted out to Rune's brother, my dear friend Mamadou. Guests and neighbors bandied about in the space around the location where Rune's baby was being prepared. Finding one's place entailed not only determining a physical spot to sit among one's social peers but also navigating status, with more honored guests provided chairs and benches.

While the name of the baby, Aissatou, was chosen over the course of discussions between elders before the ceremony, the imam announced the name of the newborn after her ritual shaving. Facing east with a wooden pole in two hands, he began with an Arabic incantation of blessings on the master Muhammad and declared the name of the child to be Aissatou in successive rounds of potent oration.

Blessings of the master:

Arabic in italics
Pular in standard font

> *Bismillahi al rahmani al rahimi.*
> *Allah humma salli ala sayyidina Muhammad wa sallim.*
> *Allah humma salli ala sayyidina Muhammad wa sallim.*
> *Allah humma salli ala sayyidina Muhammad wa sallim.*
> Innde boobo no seeni ɗo yumma makko e ɓeŋ makko ko inni mo ko Aissatou.
> Innde boobo no seeni ɗo yumma makko e ɓeŋ makko ko inni mo ko Aissatou.
> Ko ɗuŋ windino ka alluwal Allahu.
> Yo alla wurnumo barkina.

English Translation:

> In the name of God, the gracious and the compassionate.
> O Allah, send blessings on our master Muhammad.
> O Allah, send blessings on our master Muhammad.
> O Allah, send blessings on our master Muhammad.
> The name of the child has come here, her mother and her father have named her Aissatou.
> The name of the child has come here, her mother and her father have named her Aissatou.
> This is what was written in on the tablet of Allah.
> May God grant her blessings.

This text, originating from 33:56 in the Koran, is a traditional "blessings on the master" that is commonly cited throughout West Africa. In it, God and his angels send blessings upon the prophet: "oh you who believe, greet him in peace." This invocation is particularly efficacious since blessings offered in this way are multiplied by ten based on hadith (sayings attributed to the Prophet Muhammad). As the imam concluded, several members of the father's family pressed bills into his hands in exchange for his linguistic labor. Rune's elder brother began to hand out kola nuts to those attendees closest to him, and soon kola nuts filtered their way through the grasping hands of those in attendance until all those present had received a share.

Just after the imam's proclamation had been concluded, Rune's paternal aunt (*yaaye*) Aissatou rushed into the compound where the naming had just occurred.[1] There, Aunt Aissatou, the youngest sister of the village chief and aunt of baby Aissa's father, found out that she had missed out on some of the most important part of the naming ceremony: the shaving, the ritual naming, and just afterwards, the distribution of kola nuts and biscuits. Even though she lived just on the other side of town, no one had alerted her in time. In places like Taabe, events don't begin at a given time; they get going when those necessary participants and preparations fall into place. Aissatou's relation to baby Aissa should have positioned her as a significant member of the takanɓe hosts, so the fact that they had gone ahead without her presence was striking to her. Aunt Aissatou's absence was also significant because she shared names with baby Aissatou. Being a namesake (or *tokora* in Pular) is a special bond that is often broadly invoked and remarked on by Senegalese and West Africans. Newborns are often named after respected individuals in the family lineage, such as a grandparent, to connect new generations with forbearers.

After the main naming event, Aissatou redressed her exclusion with the elders. As a first wave of participants (including me) left the main naming site, we ran into Aunt Aissatou and another woman, Maty, the first wife of the village chief. Maty began to make an issue of her and Aissatou's exclusion from the ceremony and slowly emerged as an instigator and ally to Aunt Aissatou. Intercepting the village chief as he came through the compound, Aunt Aissatou demanded to know if they had named the child already. She further insisted on her and Maty's important roles in naming the child and made an issue of her absence from the ceremony. The chief, however, rebuffed these accusations and made it clear that he interpreted their comments as an overture for kola nuts: "Ah lanni hino geɓal moŋ ngal ka innde moŋ" (You already got your share, in your name [Aissatou]). In other words, Aissatou should be contented with this shared namesake connection alone. Not only an incidental gift, however, kola nuts could ratify individuals as socially sanctioned witnesses.

Aunt Aissatou and Maty grumbled about their exclusion from this naming with palpable frustration. In fact, it was Maty who first dropped the teasing name for the baby: Buubu Ñooge (Trash Owl). This was an effective jibe, partly because the name had poetic allusions to other common first names, such as Dudu. *Buubu* here refers to an owl (*buubuuru*), the reviled nocturnal bird that in the area's folklore is believed to be witches' animal form, while *ñooge* refers to rubbish, or trash.[2] During this first encounter with the chief, Maty and Aissatou continued to use Trash Owl to refer to baby Aissa. At first, the name did not inflict any enduring ritual disturbance, and the elders were not swayed by their protestations. They continued to offer a stout defense for Aissatou and Maty's exclusion. Aissatou soon left, appearing frustrated with her exclusion from the main naming event.

A Teasing Reenactment

The following encounter picks up at the opening scene of this chapter with the cloaked figure of Aunt Aissatou. After Maty and Aissatou had unsuccessfully teased baby Aissa, Aunt Aissatou returned only minutes later, bedecked in a long headscarf in the style of a devout elder with the very staff that had been used in Aissa's naming ceremony. Her arrival on the scene ignited laughter and cries of surprise among those standing by. Planting first her feet and then the ritual staff onto the gravel courtyard, Aissatou lifted her head from underneath the flowing scarf and, facing east, recited the blessings of the prophet. She bellowed out the proclamation over and over again as overhearers protested, laughed, and half-heartedly attempted to stop her. Left out of the ritual proceedings, Aissatou had come to reclaim her place.

The imam's original blessing had been performed in a quick, almost methodical recitation in which the boundaries between phrases were nearly imperceptible. In contrast, Aissatou's performance drew emphasis to parts of the text by her pausing frequently and extending the final vowels in emphasis (for instance, "salli:m"). Whereas the imam's tight oratory clusters appeared to be impenetrable to contestation, Aunt Aissatou's blessings were interspersed with calls to stop, affective protestations, and chaotic laughter. As such, Aunt Aissatou's performance was produced in concert with her interlocutors and almost invited interactions from others.

In the transcript shown in table 4.1, Aissatou's recitation is interspersed by calls to stop from three separate elder men. She occasionally addressed the protestations directly, uttering "no" ("o'oo") on line 15. In fact, the power of her performance lies not in her individual act but rather in the way in

Table 4.1. A Performative Renaming
BD = Mamadou; SD = the village chief; GD = a friend and neighbor of Rune and Mamadou;
AD = Aunt Aissatou

#	Spk	Pular	Translation
1	BD	eh eh no- no-	eh eh no no
2	AD	Allah huma salli al a seydina: Muhammad wa salli:m	((recites blessings on the master))
3	SD	hey he:	hey hey
4	GD	nangee ɓe taw nangee ɓe taw doŋ	grab her already grab her there
5	SD	a yi'ii onoŋ (wano) godɗuŋ faaledoŋ oŋ wi'ay	you see if it's something you want you speak
6	BD	nangee	grab
7	AD	((continues)) . . . Muhammad wa salli:m	((continues blessings of the master))
8	BD	uh uh accee ɗuŋ ɗoo de	eh eh stop that there
9	GD	nangee ɓe ɗoŋ taw	grab her there already
10	AD	innde boobo no seeni ɗoo:	the name of the child has come here
11	AD	ko Buubu Ñooge	it is Trash Owl
12		((laughter))	
13	SD	innde boobo no seeni ɗoo ko Aissa o wi'ete	the name of the child has come here, her name is Aissa
14	SD	ko Aissa o wi'ete	her name is Aissa
15	AD	o'oo	nope
16	SD	ko Aissa o wi'ete	her name is Aissa
17	AD	boobo no seeni ɗoo ko buubu ñooge o innetee	a child has come here she is called Trash Owl

which it was protested and reacted to by the elders. Though humorous, their actions gave weight to the satirical performance of Aissatou. Rather than a mere representation of a text, her performance emerged in concert with her surrounding interlocutors. This embodied inhabitation of the figure of the imam—achieved through staff, scarf, and body posture, along with mastery of the honorific Pular and Arabic text—went well beyond the casual reference to Buubu Ñooge some moments before. Drawing on Erving Goffman's (1990) wry terminology, I suggest that Aissatou had now *created a scene*, performing an over-the-top reenactment that offered a provocative alternative name for baby Aissa. This was a scene in every sense—not only as an interruption of the ritual action through a teasing performance but also as a performative infrastructure that encircled her audience. Though interspersing their interjections with bouts of laughter, the men in attendance successively called for her to be stopped and playfully grabbed for her. Amid these protests, Aunt Aissatou remained in character and repeated key parts of the text over the exhortations and shrieks of her audience.

The Stakes of Distribution

The name Buubu Ñooge emerged as a popular topic of conversation in the village of Taabe for days to come. Its utterance came to represent the dissatisfaction of those who demanded a share of kola nuts distributed after the official naming. For some time, Aunt Aissatou only referred to baby Aissa as Buubu Ñooge and performed the name in front of Rune, the baby's father, "mi andaa mo [Aissa] . . . miŋ ko Buubu Ñooge mi andi" (I don't know her, I only know Trash Owl). Such utterances were often accompanied by negative evaluations of the naming ceremony, during which Aissatou and some other women hadn't received their fair share. During this time, the teasing name provided a way for other women in the community to voice their dissatisfaction with their level of inclusion in the naming ritual. For these women, uttering "Buubu Ñooge" interdiscursively harkened back to Aissatou's original moment of dissent in getting passed over. Rather than overt challenges to their status within ritual hierarchies, these performative, teasing voices provided useful tools for mobile individuals to test the limits of participation and inclusion.

As the teasing name began to spread throughout the village in subsequent interactions, it soon became a rallying cry for other women who felt they too had been passed over during the naming ceremony. Articulating the dissatisfaction in such terms offered a political strategy that did not require any conspicuous organizing of women across the village. Aunt Aissatou's teasing reinterpretations were about claiming not only a greater share of kola but also a ratified role for herself in the naming ceremony of her namesake, baby Aissatou. Without gifts of kola to ratify their participation in the official naming event, Aissatou and other disenfranchised parties disseminated Buubu Ñooge in order to rectify their exclusion. Eventually, their linguistic extortion paid off. In the evening of the day after the naming ceremony, I asked the village chief about baby Aissa, and he told me that the name, Buubu Ñooge, had finally been removed: "They [Aissatou and the other women] were given kola; they were given corn, they were given rice, they were given soap. Now it's baby Aissa. Now they forgot the trash part. That was removed now, we got rid of that now." I visited Aunt Aissatou soon thereafter and found her content with the resolution. I never again heard the name Buubu Ñooge.

While this teasing reenactment and extortion demonstrated a virtuosic individual performance, they should be viewed as part of a broader repertoire of economic and social strategies employed by women in Senegal. Amid exchange relations in Dakar during which cloth became a primary object, for instance, "exchange was not about relations between things, but rather about construction relations between persons" (Buggenhagen 2012, 31). As with the cases described by Buggenhagen, cloth, like kola, was an important item exchanged by women across affinal lines in Taabe. However, the importance of these dealings lay not in the acquisition of objects, like cloth or kola, but in making visible the relationships they facilitated. Aissatou's teasing performance demonstrates a creative example of the ways in which individuals rendered themselves visible in contexts of increasing mobility. Although this episode offers only one example of a woman's creativity in expanding opportunities for herself in the context of mobility, there is a rich literature on how Senegalese women in transnational contexts have been building economic success by expanding and occupying new social niches (Buggenhagen 2012; E. E. Foley and Drame 2013; Hannaford and Foley 2015; Hannaford 2017).

One's participation in a life cycle ritual was marked not merely through physical copresence but also through the giving and receiving of gifts such as kola. Distributed objects such as kola nuts thus held the potential to mediate inclusion in community events for mobile populations. Distributed to witnesses just after the naming of baby Aissa, gifts of kola thus mediated a person's ability to report on an event and to be a ratified authority on a naming ceremony. Rather than simply assuming bodily presence to be coterminous with participation, this encounter reminds us that participation is possible through chains of spoken witnessing and material objects like kola nuts. It is through such mediated connections that migrants could participate and maintain a presence in hometown activities. On a smaller stage, the chains of giving and knowing evidenced in this example demonstrate the social issues faced by many other African migrants living across Africa, Europe and North America who must continually negotiate their presence in faraway hometowns.

For a community spread out across Senegal, West Africa, and beyond, participating in important ceremonial encounters such as baby Aissatou's naming ceremony necessitated the maintenance of bonds constructed through gifts and efficacious language. Hosts like the village chief attempted to incorporate people into the village through the just distribution of gifts. Greetings, pledges, and other forms of "standing in" at a distance were integral to bringing a large range of people into the influence of the community. Those who, like Aissatou, had missed out on life cycle events could resort to creative use of relational routines to cement their place within a community. Participation was not merely a question of whether someone was there or not but an issue of how people mediated material, discursive connections through talk and exchange. Exchange enacted through the materialities of talk and gifts constituted social relations, thereby implicitly invoking the question of who counts and who might be forgotten. Mobility thus entails a verbal art of negotiating connections with a range of people who maintained various levels of contact and multimodal presence in each other's lives.

The example of baby Aissa's naming ceremony demonstrates the importance of hometowns as ritual anchors that mediated the inclusion of residents and migrants who only occasionally spent time in places like Taabe (Piot 1999; Kane 2011; Whitaker 2017; Whitehouse 2012). Dispersed communities of kin, colleagues, and neighbors across regional economic centers have increased the stakes of distribution in ritual ceremonies. Across Africa and much of the world, villages like Taabe have become points of origin for cyclical rural migrations in which many residents spend much of the year in regional economic centers. Such hometowns have increasingly become ritual and communal anchors for peripatetic residents who spent much of the year in more economically vibrant areas such as Kédougou City or the gold mining concessions.

For decades now, villagers in Taabe have perceived a collapse in the social life of the village, with fewer youths remaining amid the draw of work in Dakar, in gold mining areas, and in the Senegambian border area. While the naming ritual might appear to happen in a contained village, it provides an important site through which individuals measured, maintained, and built relationships with dispersed populations. Within this context, Aunt Aissatou balanced her involvement in agricultural trade with her participation in community rituals.

Aissa's teasing performance can therefore be seen as an articulation that actively shaped her place within the community, not mere linguistic representation. More broadly, teasing was thereby used to reveal social stakes and prompt others to insist on the value of social ties. Given the levels of in- and out-migration from rural zones across Africa, the perspective of teasing provides an unconventional perspective on how individuals prompt others to participate in natal communities. Deployed as a form of comic coercion, teasing can have far-reaching impacts across space. Baby Aissa's uncle (in Pular, older father) Mamadou—who left the village for long periods of time—was often teased about not being from the village, a charge he often had to counter with highly monitored repartees. Arriving in Taabe after a long period of absence, Mamadou often had to parry these tongue-in-cheek accusations of being a "stranger" who no longer had business in Taabe: "aŋ a jeyaaka ɗo" (you, you're not from here). These everyday forms of teasing formed a linguistic web of playful entrapment that was spun in casual exchanges by individuals coming in and out of Taabe. Such manipulative talk about people's whereabouts demonstrates the subtle ways in which language as infrastructure mediated connections to places and shows how acts of mobility emerge through the performance of verbal art.

Mobile traders frequently leveraged ritually sustained connections between people to facilitate connections and privileges in different places. As demonstrated by the naming ceremony, tracing name-based connections with others was consequential social work in West Africa. Although never automatic, sharing a name with someone could provide the grounds of a privileged relationship with them. In many cases, it carried along shared qualities across generations. One of Taabe's most prolific fonio traders, Neene Bouba, had used these linguistic affordances to build a social network with key entrepreneurs in Kédougou City. Drawing on the power of sharing names, she had named her eldest daughter after the female leader of a powerful women's group in Kédougou who coordinated interregional trade in fonio. As a tokora of this powerful women, Neene Bouba thereby benefited from connections between her family and this economic and social network. Through this onomastic affordance, the powerful groupement leader from Kédougou had been socially pressured to travel with gifts and companions to Taabe for the occasion of her namesake's naming ceremony. This name-based connection fueled a reciprocal exchange of greetings, visitations, and goods. Thinking of this example alongside Aissatou's teasing demonstrates the capacity of language to mediate distance and open communicative channels between people. Viewed in this way, both Aissatou's performance and namesake connections show how language can be usefully viewed as a form of infrastructure. Linguistic practices opened up enduring pathways of talk, movement, and exchange that sustained connections between people separated by many kilometers.

Across Senegal and West Africa, it was common practice to offer return gifts (*neldaari*) to family and friends upon one's arrival back home. While often analyzed in terms of remittances from migrants abroad, these gifts were not merely a source of economic support or a way to build one's status. More fundamentally, they were a medium through which returning migrants could make distant places palpable to their kin at home. For instance, it was important that return gifts be from and carry connections to these distant places. Some migrants slyly flouted these expectations by buying expensive-looking, name-brand knockoffs at local markets immediately upon returning home. Just as to receive kola at a life event was to become ratified as a witness who could speak authoritatively of particular events, to receive gifts from travels was often to become linked with these places and thereby ratified to report on them. As one market seller once explained to me, if you don't bring something back from one's travels, it's like you were never there. Gift giving and the surrounding talk through which it was rendered meaningful were not just a question of redistribution in terms of resources or social status but also a spatial question of navigating one's place within a dispersed community.

A House Built of Blessings, Salt, and Stone

Like Aunt Aissatou and so many other mobile men and women who made their way to and from Taabe regularly, I was confronted with basic questions of how I would invest myself in time and space. With responsibilities to visit, greet, and reciprocate with families across Taabe, Dakar, and Kédougou City, how would I honor relationships of individuals who had opened their lives up to me? At times, my career as an anthropologist felt like a way to fulfill these obligations as much as an end in itself. The pressure to maintain phone calls, send notes, and share resources across these boundaries was immense. Mobility was partly a product of negotiated greetings, reciprocities, and admonishments from their kin to return and remain connected. Visitations happened along pathways built out of the exchange of gifts and greetings.

Not unlike those of Mamadou and Aunt Aissatou, my absence from Taabe also became an object of frequent evaluation and (largely good-natured) critiques. Would I not spend more time in Taabe? What was keeping me away? Why would I want to spend so much time in Kédougou City? Even when I could not physically be in all places at the same time, steady messages and small gifts were highly valued means of keeping up relations with people who had invested so much of their lives in me. As with the distribution of kola nuts at naming ceremonies, doling out small gifts and greetings helped cultivate a social network around me. Although some of my fellow Western visitors balked at these oftentimes monetary investments, they were the same strategies through which any mobile individuals maintained their distributed lives in a diasporic context.

I spent the majority of my first year of fieldwork in the village of Taabe, where I focused on in-depth fieldwork with a more limited number of individuals. This, I ventured, would give me a solid ethnographic foundation—a chance to polish my Pular language skills and cultivate a social network that I could build on in my second year. As ideologies of language, rural villages like Taabe were said to be places where so-called "deep" or "good" Pular was spoken, unlike the so-called "mixed" Pular spoken by urban residents.[3] I spent one year doing linguistic ethnography in these rural borderlands, with only occasional trips back to Kédougou City to recharge batteries, restock supplies, and eat more varied food. And as had Aunt Aissatou, I did my best to avoid missing major life cycle events and to maintain my "presence" in disparate communities even while I was absent.

After one year, I expanded my research out from Taabe, exploring the regional capital of Kédougou City, the trading cities farther along the Gambia River, and the mining areas that attracted the hopeful from across the region. Using the city of Kédougou as a base in this second year, I rented a large hut that was part of a family compound of a Bassari family I had known for some time. In this area, Bassari were understood to be the autochthonous residents of Kédougou who had lived here before the later arrival of Fulɓe and Maninké. Whenever possible, Bassari built most of their dwellings out of the ferrous volcanic rocks that littered the landscape. Skilled Bassari stonemasons expertly fit these rocks together like giant three-dimensional jigsaw puzzles. The masters of this building method thus required very little mortar to build the walls.

This upscale hut that I lived in was in fact owned by a Canadian couple who had grown up in Kédougou in their youth as the children of missionaries. The broader compound that they shared with others was inhabited by an eclectic cast of characters. One was another Canadian child of missionaries who had been initiated as a Bassari member and now worked as a mechanic between Canada and Kédougou. He spoke Oniyan (the language spoken by Bassari) fluently and appeared to be more at home here in southeastern Senegal than in Canada, the land of his parents. The first time I met him, he told me of days roaming the forests with other Bassari children. One day something emerged suddenly and bit him in the leg. Having just sustained the bite of a venomous viper, he lost consciousness, only to awake later in a hut: his leg had ballooned in size; he was bleeding out of his eyes, ears, and mouth; and he was being force-fed salt water. Somehow, he survived, but thereafter, he felt illnesses more acutely. His protégé was a charmingly grumpy mechanic who spent a large portion of his time shouting up at the undercarriage of well-loved Mitsubishi Pajeros.

This Bassari family provided a welcoming and supportive place to trace the mobilities and linguistic practices in the broader region. I found it a comfortable refuge, partly because I considered it a place where I was not first and foremost an anthropologist. During the time I spent here, I took no field notes. I didn't feel self-conscious about whether I was "getting it"— whether I was understanding the layers of interaction or engaging in thick description worthy of anthropological investigation (Geertz 1973). Instead, I felt more comfortable letting myself sit and be. This experience taught me that it is important to operate at several levels of attunement rather than always attempting to furiously record everything. Sometimes it is more important to merely be present. At any rate, this mental rest was necessary. Only in the months and years after fieldwork did I realize how exhausting it can be, especially when you are in a linguistic and social context so different from your own.

Rather than speaking Pular, we spoke French together. After years of studying French, I had developed a best approximation of a continental French accent honed in dedication after many trips to France and college-level classes. After spending years in West Africa, however, I had, through no conscious effort, acquired more and more staccato rhythms and trilled *r*s that followed Senegalese French sound patterns.[4] I enjoyed learning bits and pieces of Oniyan but put no pressure on myself to learn it as a linguistic anthropologist. I developed close friendships with several young men in the family: we thatched rooves together, drank tea in the afternoons, and skimmed Frisbees across the rocky ground. Although most residents in Taabe and Kédougou City knew me by my adopted Senegalese name, Souleymane, here I was called "Niko," a shortening of Nicolas, which was not an uncommon name for Bassari men.[5] Every so often, we'd slaughter a pig, buy a case of beer or find some good palm wine, and invite others from all over the neighborhood for a party. As I did yoga in the courtyard of my room, the young Bassari children did their best to imitate my strange poses.

In my second year, however, I came upon an opportunity to acquire a bit of land not far from this Bassari family. Mamadou and I soon began to think about building a small compound that I could use as a field station. He planned on using it as guest lodging when he welcomed tourists from abroad. My aspiration was to build a small research station that I and other colleagues might use to continue to invest ourselves in this part of the world. Although our initial plans were modest, I expanded the huts somewhat after a colleague's archaeological field school needed a more reliable research space. Mamadou, who also worked as a tourist guide, would be able to co-own and manage this complex and uses it to house welcome Spanish tourists.

The land we had acquired sat a bit on the outskirts of town and was dotted with the ferrous, volcanic rocks that the earliest residents had first used to build their homes. It is these rocks that we used to build the main huts, a project that was led by a local Pular mason, Salam (Bassari masons would often critique his work). One day, as I dropped by to check on the work, I found him in a state of tense uneasiness. I was surprised to see Salam, who usually maintained a droll disposition, so concerned. While the entire outer wall and the first hut had gone up seamlessly, the construction of the second hut revealed a bad omen. Three times, Salam said, he had attempted to place a stone, and three times, this stone had fallen all the same. Although he talked about it obliquely, Salam took this to be a sign that there was an uneasy relationship with the spirits that dwell in this area. He immediately suggested that we perform a *sadaka*, a gift or sacrifice (of livestock) to put us on firm footing in this land.

As part of the rapidly expanding neighborhoods surrounding the older city, the land we were building on was recently claimed from the quail hunters who used it in recent memory. As newcomers in an emerging neighborhood, we turned our attention to those around us who had already developed relationships with the people and land we were settling in. We needed guides to help us mediate this uneasy relationship with the land. The closest occupied area to us was the village of Hodo, an older settlement that was originally founded as a leper colony on the outskirts of town. Half a century ago, residents had been looking for a place for people with leprosy to live away from other populations, and this village, a few kilometers from downtown Kédougou, became their final home. As the elders tell it, early residents defended themselves against hyenas in the wild bush. But this once distant outpost was becoming integrated as a neighborhood of the expanding city of Kédougou.

As with mobility, the work of establishing oneself in a community is a relational one. Rather than introducing oneself independently, in Senegal it is generally best to become acquainted with others through an intermediary. Just as mobility is a relational practice mediated through language, most Senegalese feel more comfortable expanding social ties along existing networks. It is for this reason that building ties with others is also implicitly a spatial exercise of mobility. In our case, old man Jango, who lived down the road from us, acted as the representative from our nascent neighborhood. He led us to the house of Hodo's imam, who would know how to make peace with the restless spirits underneath our dwelling. As instructed, we brought kola nuts, a large bag of salt, and a metaphorical "belt" (*boggol*) of cash money to bind all of these gifts together.

After a short introduction to the imam, we explained our problems with the new construction. I did not relay these concerns to him directly, but they were passed on to him through a chain of discourse. The imam listened to our concerns and welcomed us to the neighborhood. He reiterated that a sadaka, a sacrifice or gift offering, would help remediate our relationship with this bit of land. Sitting quietly on the floor of the imam's large compound surrounded by many neighbors and kin, we allowed the recited blessings from the Koran to soak into our bodies and the offerings we had bought.

As with those in the baby Aissa's naming ritual, these blessings were not merely a proposition to be interpreted symbolically. Instead, they forged a physical connection with the people who already dwelled here and, by extension, to the places we would inhabit. Such Koranic blessings are best understood as *inherently* beneficial rather than as symbolic words that have positive meanings. Work by Rudolph Ware (2014) on the deep history of Islam in West Africa shows that these kinds of recitations from the Koran are not merely to be interpreted for their meaning; they are the essence of goodness *in and of themselves*. A Muslim scholar who could recite the Koran from memory is known as a hafiz and can be understood as an embodiment of these qualities or, as Ware describes it, a walking Koran. For many in Kédougou, the act of uttering these positive blessings from the Koran was fundamentally impossible to those who were not themselves good Muslims: "Nafiq waawataa hunjaade" (Someone who is evil cannot recite [them]). It is for these reasons that ink water washed away from Koranic tablets was ingested as a direct instantiation of these blessings. Across Kédougou, practitioners frequently talked of the direct ability of Arabic blessings to affect others. The recitation of blessings could help control or calm the body. They could also bring children to sleep through their inherent qualities. It is also in this way that Islamic scholars, often called *serignes*, were able to facilitate migration. The Mouride brotherhood, for instance, has played a significant role in Senegalese diasporas around the world and has leveraged the religious community to build a significant transnational economic base (O'Brien 1971; Diouf and Rendall 2000; Riccio 2004). However, Muslim scholars and leaders enabled migration through more than brokering their followers' financing, international travel, and employment prospects; their blessings enabled mobility through the direct power of the words (Tall 2002; Gemmeke 2013; Kleist and Thorsen 2017). Viewing physical objects and language as material infrastructure in the same frame helps explicate these dimensions of mobility.

As with the baby Aissa's ritual naming ceremony, kola nuts were distributed to those present for the Hodo imam's benediction. In addition, the large bag of salt we had brought was divided into smaller bags that were passed out to those present. The imam's wives were then tasked with distributing out small bags of this salt to everyone in the neighborhood after our departure. In the days that followed, bits of this blessed salt infused the soups and stews of our fellow neighborhood residents. Like the kola nuts distributed during baby Aissa's naming ceremony, these objects expanded the number of people who were connected to this powerful ritual moment. As neighbors received and ingested this salt, they became invested in our concerns and aware of us as ratified newcomers to their neighborhood. This offering can also be thought of as a gift of sorts to the spirits that occupied this land before us. A powerful tool used across much of West Africa, these kinds of sadaka could be used to attempt to bring into the realm of human action those things that we otherwise might not appear able to control.

Not merely metaphorical, the linguistic performance of these blessings could be understood as a material mortar that held together the walls of this hut. The efficacy of the blessing-infused salt lies in the inherent qualities of these Koranic sayings. In other cases, blessings from the Koran could be contained in amulets (*gris-gris* in French or *talkuru* in Pular) to grant specific physical or interpersonal qualities to the wearer. As I mentioned previously, consuming slate water becomes a useful way to embody qualities, given the real and physical properties of the written word in this Islamic tradition. The distribution of salt provided a material channel in which engagement with these blessings was spread across the neighborhood and, through this, a relationship with spirits that mediated our belonging on this piece of land. In a related context, Sabina Perrino (2002, 250) has shown that saliva, used in encounters between patient and healer, "serves as a carrier or vessel in which the phonated Qur'anic verses can be placed, verses that can then bring the patient into communicative contact with the transcendent power of Allah."

These blessings from the Koran and the assemblage of offerings can thus be seen as one instantiation of the verbal art of mobility. At key moments like the baptism of a newborn or the founding of a compound, migrants exchanged gifts and words strategically to account for nonpresent others and to weave themselves into the lives of others. These migrants and travelers resorted to linguistic exchanges to help negotiate relationships not only with human neighbors, but also those autochthonous spirits that originally inhabited the land. It is through such negotiated relationships of reciprocity, built on sadaka, that individuals across West Africa were able to spread out and build their homes in area that were previously occupied by spirits rather than humans. The house that Salam built—one that would become my field station—was formed not only from stone and mortar but also through the collective concern of my neighbors as articulated through linguistic blessings.[6]

In this section, I have shown that the infrastructures of houses were built on a foundation of linguistic exchange. Although the previous example concerns a compound I built with my friend Mamadou and his community, other migrants regularly encountered these same issues as they etched their lives into new places. Even the materiality of the houses built by migrants was an important factor in their mobility. For instance, in the case of the village of Taabe and most other dwellings in the region, residents made ingenious use out of freely available resources. With clay, cattle dung, earth from termite mounds, and water made into a sticky syrup by the *lakka* plant, a sturdy hut could be built by a group of three or four in a matter of days. This meant that individuals could, with little financial investment, maintain flexible living arrangements in Taabe in addition to homes in more distant economic centers. While concrete-walled huts with tin rooves increasingly marked one's status, long-standing techniques using clay and dung maintained a far cooler indoor climate during the dry season heat. Although construction techniques may appear to be small details, considering the materiality of homes has strong implications for how anthropologists have come to understand kinship and relatedness. Whereas the study of kinship used to entail an almost mathematical calculation of kinship terms as an abstract system, anthropologists later realized that the materiality of homes was an important constitutive factor in how people conceive of and enable relations between one another (Morton 2007; Melly 2009; Leinaweaver 2009). Being able to move, subdivide, or otherwise rebuild houses was an important social resource among individuals who were continually negotiating relationships with mobile neighbors and kin. In this view, the strength of a home is less a function of its building materials and more a question of the social and linguistic labor through which individuals interweave it and themselves with the concerns of their consociates.

Not merely a physical substance, concrete bricks can be understood as the material condensation of migrant labor. As such, they constituted an important social strategy of savings. Funds remitted back to Senegal were frequently turned into such building materials. In many cases, individuals might only have the funds to buy cement for the construction of bricks that could be stacked up and left out for years before they were finally put to use. Locked away in concrete, these resources defied any individuals who might want to make demands on a migrant's funds. In urban areas like Kédougou, individuals regularly locked their savings into the walls of their dwellings. For many families, these excess funds are used to construct cement walls around one's home or rooms that are added on to a central structure one at a time. While ten years ago most of Kédougou's concrete buildings were to be found in the market, these days families with sufficient funds are increasingly building multi-story buildings with cement.[7]

Language—viewed as a material infrastructure—also has the capacity to bind people together across great distances. Both examples in this chapter have demonstrated how linguistic practice enables migrants to enmesh themselves into the lives of others. These processes happen through the exchange of objects and language, which should be understood in the same analytical frame. Special occasions, such as the naming ceremony or ritual founding of my field station, offer particularly powerful ritual centers through which such connections can be reified. Viewing language as a form of infrastructure helps us understand how blessings offered from one place might help others become a part of a growing neighborhood and helps track the pathways of teasing, greetings, and gift exchanges through which migrants maintain their presence in distributed communities across West Africa.

Notes

This chapter is derived, in part, from the article "Ritual Contingency: Teasing and the Politics of Participation," published in the *Journal of Linguistic Anthropology* on November 25, 2019.

1. Earlier in the day she had come by carrying a small calabash filled with an assortment of old junk: broken flip-flops, shattered pieces of an old radio, a dirty sock, and shards of hard plastics. These were offerings to satirize the gifts of rice, cloth, and oil that were brought in by Rune's many in-laws from surrounding villages, so her intentions were perhaps satirical from the beginning. Alongside the teasing nickname, these gifts can also be viewed as an act of protecting incipient social beings from evil eyes and jealous gazes.

2. Although Buubu Ñooge might appear to be a cute nickname, to many West Africans, for whom owls are very real and terrifying incarnations of witches, this was perhaps a shocking moniker. I once witnessed a frenzied call to arms after an owl flew into a domestic compound one evening. With a piercing shout, the man next to me began to look frantically for his slingshot and soon sent sharp stones whirring into the branches around the owl. Many believed owls' presence could foretell the death of a family member.

3. Locals often used such terms to distinguish Pular that included more French or French-derived words. In a linguistic sense, these more "mixed" urban varieties are not inferior to other forms of Pular, since loan words and borrowed constructions from other varieties is a normal part of how language works. All varieties of language are systematic and rule- based. However, speakers may have strong feelings about such issues, and many have historically tried to insulate their language from other varieties understood to be foreign.

4. By this time, I could often pass for a Senegalese speaker of French on the phone. Once I encountered a French reporter in Kédougou who, upon hearing me speak, laughed at my accent for a solid two minutes before she could bring herself to talk again. While this could be considered good-natured teasing, these attitudes also betray a broader linguistic racism based on implicit assumptions of what constitutes legitimate French. Standard language ideologies rooted in the colonial experience have long stigmatized speakers of French deemed to be "nonstandard" despite the fact that their varieties are just as systematic and rule-based as Parisian French. My experiences are nothing compared to generations of Caribbean, African, or southern langue d'oc French speakers, whose varieties are deemed deficient—an assessment that often provides the basis for discrimination and exclusion.

5. Niko sounded just a bit better than the nickname I was accustomed to, "Nik," which, in French, can sound like a slang term for "fuck" (e.g., the French hip-hop group Suprême NTM, derived from "nique ta mère" [fuck your mother]).

6. The role of language as a discursive infrastructure through which buildings and homes were founded can also be seen in Rudolf Gaudio's discussion of modernization campaigns that sought to demolished unauthorized housing in Abuja (Gaudio 2021). In this case, the fixity of a building was to be found not merely in its material foundation but also, more importantly, in the social relationships owners cultivated with project administrators as well as in the social categories of autochthony they could embody.

7. Constructing buildings too large for one's immediate family unit has certain advantages. For one, surplus rooms that are not immediately needed can be rented out to a larger market of migrant renters. Since access to land has become relatively scarce, it is no longer possible for most incomers to find land and use locally sourced materials to construct adequate lodging. With this wave of increasing migrant labor, many of Kédougou's teachers, administrators, gendarmes, police, traders, and porters, therefore, have had to rent rooms in Kédougou. As such, an important savings strategy has been to convert surpluses into forms that are resistant to fluidity, thereby withstanding any claims by associates or kin. These kinds of strategies were important for migrants who found it harder to amass resources the closer they were to their home communities and kin, where the pressures to redistribute money was greater.

5

CONSTITUTING A BORDER THROUGH
LINGUISTIC PRACTICE

NATIONAL BORDERS HAVE LONG SERVED AS LANDMARKS THROUGH which scholars have traced the contours of culture and the flows of migration (Schiller, Basch, and Blanc-Szanton 1992; Appadurai 1996). Borders offer one conceptual foundation of methodological nationalism, a perspective that uncritically poses social scientific research questions within the frame of the nation-state (Schiller, Basch, and Blanc-Szanton 1992). In this tradition, most conventional analyses of (national) borders and mobility have focused on the movement of bodies across space. Historians note that such borderlands feature ongoing projects of citizenship and belonging given the unfinished projects of colonial state formation (Glovsky 2019). Such scholarship has usefully "deterritorialized" the study of culture and looked to global circulations as well as barriers across which individuals in an interconnected world live (Appadurai 1996; Larkin 2013a). Rather than taking the state for granted, scholars have posed questions of power and exclusion in the borderlands that interrogate the "politics of location" (Carter 1997) and how space and territory are mediated by state actors. These processes examine questions of power central to the mobilities of migrants. Approaches that emphasize language are useful to untangling issues of territoriality because they provide tools for asking how everyday social actors bring different kinds of places into relation. Rather than a symbolic practice that happens on top of a politically and environmentally defined place, language as infrastructure helps conceptualize how linguistic practices materially impact the world we inhabit. Through scalar assumptions, distinctions, and material channels etched through linguistic practice, migrants partly constitute the places they inhabit.

By focusing on the Senegal-Guinea borderlands, this chapter explores the kinds of broader linguistic and material exchanges that bring a border into being. It draws attention to the everyday, local actors as well as wider-reaching processes and events, such as epidemics. Out of these frameworks, the border between Senegal and Guinea emerges as a zone of discernment whose boundaries are largely brought into being through linguistic practices and evaluations. Rather than imagining mobility as a movement across an already constituted space, this chapter pushes us to consider that the boundaries and places across which mobility happens are constituted through human interactions and acts of distinction. As such, the border between Senegal and Guinea became materially enacted through situated human discourse. In this way, the space across which mobility happens emerges through the material processes of language as infrastructure.

Although sight and geolocation are often assumed to define borders, this chapter suggests that they can also be brought into being by hearing and speech. Defined as much by aurality as visuality, the borderlands of Senegal and Guinea became a zone of discernment that shaped the kinds of signs people attuned to. Border police, residents, and travelers paid close attention to linguistic signs, which were implicitly linked to certain kinds of imagined figures. As others have shown, a sense of oneself or the kinds of figures of personhood that make sense in a site are themselves a product of movement across borders (Yeh 2018). In this sense, borderlands come into being as a reflexive field in which individuals come to assess and interpret one another. In the case of Kédougou, the Senegal-Guinea borderlands emerged through their spatial liminality as well as their unique epidemiological and political context. Focusing on the Ebola epidemic of 2014–16 shows how the space of the Senegal-Guinea border was a function of repeated interactional practices.

"Mi yahay jooni Senegal" (I'm going to Senegal soon), a mechanic's apprentice muttered outside a petrol station on the west side of Kédougou City. The mechanic's oil-soaked pants were a sign of these difficult histories of travel and indexed the gritty work of bringing dusty, timeworn engines back to life. Kédovins often talk about trips to Dakar or to coastal Senegal in this way. Until relatively recently, going to Dakar was in many ways like traveling to a faraway country that was not your own. However, the construction of the Dakar–Kédougou–Bamako highway and the mining boom had quickly brought a steady stream of buses and lorries through

Kédougou. Not two years since its repaving, this road was already eaten away by the heavy wheels of uneven economic growth.

The mechanic was about to embark on an overnight trip to Dakar on a retired French Renault bus, where his expertise would come in handy in the likely case of a breakdown. I wish he had been there on my first trip to Kédougou to begin field work in 2014 when our overland bus broke down and we were stranded overnight in an unsettled stretch of highway. Hours went by in nervous discussions with the driver about when a second bus might be by to pick us up. However, by midnight, most of us had resigned ourselves to shallow nests burrowed into the pebbly ditches on the side of the road. In a cheeky escape, the chauffeur and his apprentice stole away in the dead of night as the rest of us tried to find solace in conversation. Drifting between wakefulness and sleep, I listened to the lamentations of my fellow travelers, whose stories of hardship in traveling portrayed Kédougou as a taxing destination. These stories were not merely representing the voyage as it happened, but they shaped our experiences. It is partly through such stories that Kédougou became the place that it is, forged in difficulty through distinction and distance. At sunup, a woman appeared, as if she had suddenly sprung up out of the earth, and prepared a table from which she began to set up a breakfast stand. Scrapping together every bit of change we could, we were soon revived through the power of bean sandwiches and Nescafé.

Linguistic Assumptions through Spatiality

Rather than a static thing that is then represented by language, space comes into being through linguistic practices. Important scholarship within the past decades has reframed thinking of space as self-evident and objective to thinking of it as an emergent cultural product coconstituted by relations of power, gender, and class.[1] Doreen Massey (1994), for instance, has shown how places are constituted through gender, an ideological process in which local, domestic spaces are often gendered as female and public spaces as male. In work that emphasizes how we experience space beyond the level of awareness, anthropologists such as Ingold (2000) suggest that we think in terms of landscapes that emerge through lived, habitual human activities. To simplify complex and wide-ranging discussions, many of these approaches rely on distinctions between space on an objective, Cartesian plane that can be cut up through mathematical calculations and the spatiality that emerges through the lived space of habitual collective action and through implicit forms of (often language-based) spatial reckoning.

Scholars of language, culture, and society have explored the emergence of space and place within linguistic practice. For the Western Apache described by Keith Basso (1988), for instance, place names encapsulate moral stances and personas through the recitation of narratives. Place names are thus interwoven with broader values and worldviews such that different people can inhabit the same so-called places very differently. From a broader perspective, the way speakers conceptualize space is partly a function of their language's spatial frames of reference. Whereas many languages conceptualize everyday spatial relations in relative terms (e.g., left and right), some speakers think primarily or exclusively in terms of absolute frames of reference (e.g., N/S/E/W) (W. A. Foley 1997; Majid et al. 2004). Thinking in terms of narratively and experientially constituted space, the world we inhabit is not merely a product of its physical attributes, narrowly conceived, but also a function of how it is articulated through human systems of signification. This also means that space is not merely "represented" by language—that is, described as an object in terms of its qualities. It also emerges through habitual human practices. Viewed as such, space is the laminated product of its physical characteristics and social practice. Thinking in terms of language as infrastructure helps us capture these processes.

However, assumptions that position language as a form of representation rather than a material practice—as I argue throughout this book—are implicit in scholarship on space. For instance, Henri Lefebvre (1991), an important theoretical touchstone in approaches to space and urban studies, made distinctions between *representations of space*, the supposed objective, Cartesian view of urbanists and scientists, and *representational* spaces as "directly lived through its associated images and symbols, and hence the space of 'inhabitants' and 'users'" (38–39). Lefebvre views the former as a "system of verbal (and therefore intellectually worked out) signs" and the latter as a more phenomenological and lived space of "non-verbal symbols and signs" (38–39). This contrast contributes to a referentialist ideology foregrounding denotation that views language as primarily a question of naming things in the world. In this view, habitual, lived action is reserved as a realm of nonlinguistic phenomena. In contrast, I have characterized language as a habitual, lived resource for intersubjectively constituting a world with others, which includes the space across which we envision mobility to happen.

Within the lens of a borderland that came into being through a particular political and epidemiological context, this chapter and the book more broadly highlight the ways in which individuals constructed social space through practices of mobility—by articulating connections between places through linguistic practice. Examining language in the context of mobilities reveals it to be a kind of emergent infrastructure. Rather than merely a vessel for expressing propositions, it is a material force that facilitates connections or even enacts borders. It is through repeated linguistic practices that places came into being and that pathways for social relations are constructed. While someone could attempt to delineate the border between Senegal and Guinea on a map, in practice the meaning of these boundaries and their consequences for the residents of this area were negotiated through everyday interactions. Not merely a geopolitical boundary, the Senegal-Guinea borderlands around Taabe and Takkopelel came into being through repeated discourses about border-crossing, rights to resources, and national origins. In particular, I draw on the epidemiological context of Ebola to show how this border became a materialized social boundary. Understanding these forms of boundary drawing and spatial distinction making is essential to understanding how mobilities are conceptualized.

Constituting a Border through Surveillance and Scrutiny—The Case of Ebola

Leaving to do fieldwork in Kédougou during the fall of 2014 was difficult. I had just finished my last year of graduate coursework and preliminary exams at the University of Michigan and spent a restorative summer of family visits in Maine and Germany with my partner, a fellow anthropology graduate student. News of the spreading Ebola epidemic in Guinea, Sierra Leone, and Liberia had been filling my news feed, and I felt somewhat nervous about going to a region that formed its penumbra. Assessing the situation within a Western media sphere—where West Africa was the imagined epicenter of suffering and disease—was particularly challenging. In talking with my friends and relatives, distinctions between perceived and actual risk were ever on my tongue in the weeks before my departure. I arrived in Senegal in September 2014, almost the peak of the Ebola epidemic that had torn through communities in nearby Guinea, Sierra Leone, and Liberia. For the first two months I stayed in Dakar and Saint Louis, visiting migrant families from Kédougou who had made coastal Senegal their home and reconnecting with friends from my previous time in Senegal as a Peace Corps volunteer and experiential education instructor.

Thinking across perspectives from medical and linguistic anthropology allowed me to conceptualize how the Ebola epidemic helped constitute the borderland between Senegal and Guinea. When I arrived for this trip in 2014, although from an epidemiological perspective Ebola had not yet made it into Senegal, it had nevertheless become a social and material reality that impacted people's lives and mobilities. As critical medical anthropologists have argued from cross-cultural perspectives, diagnosed illnesses are not preexisting, innate phenomena that affect all human societies in the same way as neat bundles of natural features (Lock 1995; Mol 2002; Fullwiley 2010). Viewing them instead as instantiated through socialized understandings of bodies and practices of healing helps us notice their situated emergence in different cultural contexts. Annemarie Mol (2002), for instance, argues that diseases are enacted through medical examinations, technologies of presentation, and medical interventions. Practitioners of biomedicine have largely limited its consideration of disease to the somatic symptoms bounded by the human form: this is most simply seen in the kind of diagnosis manuals used in most medical practices today. Other anthropological approaches to illness have expanded the notion of disease, locating its emergence across sociotechnical practices that cut across what is commonly assumed to be a nature-culture divide (Roberts 2013; Stonington 2012). These include ways of counting and assessing bodies, social stigma and forms of self-identification after diagnosis, and other ways in which disease is rendered visible.

Applying these insights to our context, Ebola emerged not merely as a viral disease in a biomedical sense. Looking to language as a material practice helps us insert language into these changing forms of evaluation and interaction on the border. Oftentimes, scholars of language examine genre, intertextuality, and interactional regularities in ways that make them appear to be nonmaterial properties of a speech community. Yet Ebola has affected the pragmatics and reflexive awareness of linguistic encounters in a material way. Language should be seen as an embodied practice that can be analyzed alongside epidemiology, which—wrapped up in webs of human meaning—has lasting effects on dynamics of interaction. Relating these insights to spatiality in the borderlands, it might be tempting to think of a border as an extant boundary that has the capacity to stop the spread of a disease such as Ebola. However, it is partly through changing routines of interaction and evaluation impacted by Ebola that this border became articulated. As cultural beings, we are socialized into particular habits of discerning others that shift according to setting and ongoing attunements generated through discourse. We latch on to particular signs of difference—all the while overlooking others—and use these as the basis for typifying and engaging with others (Irvine and Gal 2019). Irvine and Gal describe these as axes of differentiation, through which individuals make socially salient distinctions in the world, often based on linguistic features. These ideological processes of drawing distinctions can change, and in the context of the borderlands, Guinean versus Senegalese as well as Ebola versus Ebola free became more important distinctions.[2]

Many of these processes below the level of consciousness, a phenomena that scholars such as Pierre Bourdieu (1977) have understood as *habitus*: ingrained, embodied predispositions for moving, reacting, and evaluating. However, these intuitive frameworks do not exist independently from the changing and more-than-human world in which we find ourselves. They are historical and shift amid changing contexts. As such, habitus offers ingrained and embodied principles for dealing with new contexts like Ebola. However, the Ebola epidemic also exposed disjunctures in interaction and social practices that individuals performed intuitively, such as the proxemics of how far to stand from one another during face-to-face interactions. In the context of this emergent border, Ebola as a sociobiological entity impacted the kinds of interactionally performed signs and discernments that came to matter. In the case of Kédougou, this often meant that signs of Guinean origin gleaned from the comportment, clothing, and greetings of borderland travelers were increasingly scrutinized. Bodily contact and greetings in many places became increasingly fraught. Many debated conventions for greeting—for instance, a mere hello rather than the common handshake—which otherwise was an unexamined, habitual act.

As such, Ebola often subtly changed the ways in which people construed a border and gave evidence of their knowledge of it. Because this border was closed in the wake of the Ebola epidemic, people's claims about going to and from Guinea increasingly became couched in euphemism and obfuscation. Although epistemics—the linguistic issue of how people indicate how they came to know things—is most frequently analyzed as a structural, grammatical issue, it is also a product of interactional, social, and even epidemiological dynamics. For instance, during the beginning of my research, before I had fully understood the stakes of cross-border mobility, I came upon a young man I had previously met on the outskirts of Taabe. Standing on a path that ultimately led to Guinea and beyond, I asked him if he had been to Laabi, the Guinean border town where the border post was located. As a routine of placing fellow travelers, people frequently asked for each other's provenance and destination. While he did not outright deny his trip there, he insisted that Laabi was not, in fact, part of Guinea. In the face of an outsider's questioning, he was cautious in betraying his trips to Guinea at a time when the borders were officially closed. It is less useful to consider his answer to my question in terms of lying or truth value and more helpful to approach it as a product of shifting narrative epistemics in the wake of the Ebola epidemic. Similar discourses of obfuscation characterized interactions between locals and the gendarmes from coastal Senegal who increasingly roamed the area in an attempt to enforce the border closure. These considerations show that linguistic norms and practices often emerge in relation to exigencies of the material world.

The sociolinguistic construction of the Senegal-Guinea borderland was unique partly because of the absence of visible, official markers, such as barriers or cairns. Separated by several kilometers, the Guinean and Senegalese border stations framed a wide band of indeterminate social space. In between these places were situated a number of villages—some ostensibly in Guinea and others seemingly in Senegal. Taabe itself sat between these border stations. Most border posts along this area were small, backroad shacks that were easy to miss. In many cases, they were a good distance from the presumptive "border," located at the outskirts of towns or the forks of roads. Instead, lived boundaries were formed out of the discourses of local residents and travelers whose shared and repeated acts of storytelling brought a border into being. Occasionally, travelers from Guinea to Kédougou made their way through Taabe asking for directions, even if this was not the most direct route for international travel. Given the indeterminacy, this meant that the border was constantly at risk of being negotiated by ongoing human interactions.

Discourses about where straw could be harvested, for instance, were a narrative routine that partly instantiated the border in the lives of border residents. Claims about the location of borders were often grounded in dramatic articulations or interactional tensions that came to serve as narrative cairns. Establishing the border was thus not only an issue of space and boundary drawing but also a question of interdiscursivity—tracking the connections between speech events and places of utterance. One dramatic encounter in which two young Taabe straw cutters were drawn into a violent encounter with Guinean youth was such an event through which the border was discursively constituted. Blows were exchanged, bikes were abandoned, and counterclaims spit at one another—this intense activity became a marker of the site where the border was purported to be. During these tellings and retellings, claims to resources and concomitantly the notion of a border were incrementally established.

Of Gendarmes and Weekly Markets

Paying attention to the social relationships and linguistic interactions on the Senegal-Guinea border helped me understand it as a place of increased scrutiny and evaluation that brought into view origins and mobilities. In these borderlands, this anxiety over mobility in the wake of the Ebola epidemic manifested itself in the weekly market (*luumo*) located in Takkopellel, just at the base of the Fouta Djallon mountains. The Takkopellel market brought in villagers from surrounding settlements across Senegal and Guinea as well as traders from Kédougou. At its peak, the weekly market was a busy meeting spot where villagers could buy meat by the pound, exchange information about commodity prices, or buy knives or other tools without having to go to Kédougou. On off-days, the site of the weekly market appeared as a skeleton of bamboo structures with little bits of colored plastic sheeting sticking out from underneath the straw. The changing interactions in this weekly market town demonstrate some of the ways in which language and space impacted one another.

Soon after the closure of the Senegal-Guinea border in the wake of the Ebola epidemic, the regional government also closed borderland markets like the one in Takkopellel. In the weeks after the closure of the weekly markets and of the Senegal-Guinea border, patrols of Wolof-speaking gendarmes from western Senegal appeared in Takkopellel. Residents nervously remarked on the increased reach of the state. Indeed, the police offers were a new presence in this rural area, which was used to adjudicating its own affairs without official state agents. Encountering gendarmes on patrol was new for residents who had only known police officers to be stationed at the border posts. Formerly, police presence had been limited to the border post down the road, where officers stayed put in a small post on the edge of the main artery. Even Kédougou City residents were coming to terms with an increased mobile police presence. Until recently, only a few border police were stationed at checkpoints in and out of town where intercity transportation voluntarily stopped for occasional ID and customs checks.

Mariama, a woman who sold home-cooked meals from a small eatery that her family managed, complained to me one day about this new gendarme presence. With them, there is no negotiation she said to me: "negotiation alaa." What bothered her most was that they were inaccessible and that any attempts at social negotiation were rebuffed. As such, gendarmes could resist simple yet significant exchanges of social information all the while opening up others to scrutiny. In explaining this, she insisted on the importance of simple practices of greeting and, in so doing, opening oneself up to another person. Greetings across West Africa tend to be not merely a simple phrase but an often lengthy exchange of information, social identity, and substances that can be better understood as access rituals—the act of making another person accessible to you (Ameka 2009). As the seller of delicious roadside snacks, Mariama exercised this as her stock-in-trade: the ability to cut through a crowd and identify with potential customers through a knowledge of their kin, in-laws, last name, or origins. She did this by greeting people by name and by finding different kinds of social idioms in common with them.

But to have someone who flatly refused these techniques of sociality was uncomfortable to her. With the gendarmes "there is no negotiation," Mariama lamented. She continued to reflect on her inability to engage with gendarmes as available others with whom she might chat or establish a relational hook. Her tirade was interspersed with calls of "teyyil!" (shut up!), which mimicked the foreign voice of a gendarme who shuts down any possibility for sustained interaction. This inaccessibility is potent, given the myriad ways in which West Africans have built on interactional channels to creatively negotiate relationships with one another—often in the idiom of ethnic or patronymic joking relationships, generational relationships, or alliances of affinity. In many respects, the gendarmes' social insulation parallels Duke's unwillingness in chapter 2 to offer his name as a sign that his interlocutors might use to place him within webs of sociality.

What particularly bothered Mariama about the gendarmes was their reticence to make concessions or to recognize the claims of Guinean and hoore fello residents who had been coming to the market for years—many of whom had kin on this side of the border. Stories spread of Guineans being caught on the footpaths down the mountain to the market. Guineans entrapped in this way were escorted to the border by gendarmes, and any goods they were carrying were confiscated. While questions such as "ko honto wonuɗaa yahde" (where are you headed) were commonly interwoven amid greetings between travelers meeting each other on the road, the stakes of such questions were elevated in the context of a newly policed border.

In conversations with border police stationed in Kédougou, I often heard them explicitly talk about this strategy of interactional isolation. A police officer from the distant town of Kaolack, whom I had occasion to talk to over the course of several weeks, reflected on this explicit tactic of interactional isolation at the organizational level. He warned me that if you let them, locals would try to find some kind of relationship with you. It is partly for these reasons that police were cycled in and out of posts across the country. In this way, police were thus administratively discouraged from developing long-lasting relationships with the locals in their posts. Their rotating appointments, often on a six-month basis, shielded officers from developing and investing in social relationships that might compromise their positions.

Such were the techniques of the state, in which its agents were frequently insulated from instantiating relationships with individuals through interactional as well as technological means. Simple objects like dark aviator sunglasses, office furniture, and uniforms functioned as social skins (Turner 2012) to insulate their wearers and thereby prevent individuals from giving too much of themselves in interaction. At issue was the capacity to extract information about others without running the risk of giving signs of oneself. As I argue in chapter 2, the bureaucratic methods of statecraft like ID cards were used not just as tools for control but also often as creative ones for individuals to gain access to different opportunities. In practice, what this meant was that IDs were seen less as cornerstones of one's personhood and citizenship and more as documents that could be shared, exchanged, and in some cases altered to present oneself in novel ways.

Alongside these interactional dynamics, there were also basic language issues at play. The inability of gendarmes to speak Pular at times also had the effect of insulating them from interaction. Few of the predominately Wolof-speaking gendarmes tasked with patrolling the Takkopellel area spoke Pular, the lingua franca of this area. Those posted to Takkopellel spent their time patrolling the town and its environs, often lingering at the crossroads at base of the roads leading down from the Guinea border. During this time, patrolling gendarmes traveled with a member of Takkopellel's volunteer security detail, who served as their translators and guides. These volunteer security officers were normally tasked with managing local disputes but were not officially part of the police force.

Once while coming down the mountain to the Takkopellel weekly market, a small group of Taabe residents and I encountered two gendarmes accompanied by a member of Takkopellel's volunteer security force. Any Guineans entering town would have had to pass along the same roads as we did, and those traveling alongside me were suspected of coming from Guinea. Arriving in front of the gendarmes, we overheard the police officers ask the security volunteer about our presence as we entered town. The translating security volunteer responded by placing us as residents of the town of Taabe, "ko ɓe Taabe ɓeŋ" (they are people from Taabe), suggesting to them that this village was in the territory of Senegal. The security volunteer confirmed to the gendarmes—who were particularly concerned about one of our companions—that we were from the village of Taabe. It was warm, but one of my companions, Rune, was wearing a jacket. At moments like these, the gendarmes, with the help of the security force, attempted to pick up on cues involving dress, baggage, and footwear that might betray one's provenance. Indeed, warm layers like the one Rune was wearing were often identified as signs of being from Guinea, where the higher altitudes of the Fouta Djallon mountains could bring in cool evening air.

Standing across the lane from a gendarme, I noticed that he spoke only with his local security counterpart. Although he and the volunteer stood close together, he spoke loudly as if he intended for us to overhear him. Even though those in our group spoke Wolof, the gendarme eschewed any direct engagement with us, talking *about* those around him rather than *to* them. This was partly possible because the gendarme spoke Wolof to the security volunteer, who became his linguistic mediator. While many of the locals did speak Wolof, the institutional assumption seemed to be that this was not the case. The local security officer thus translated and transmitted questions to us at the same time that his role closed down direct contact with the gendarme. In so doing, the local guide transmitted this voice of authority while insulating the police officer from potential exposure of his personhood during interactions. Here, any point of connection, shared name, joking relationship, or affiliation might be used as mitigating context. "Negotiation alaa," Mariama had said (there is no negotiation). Not merely a question of cairns and quadrants, the border was traced and made intelligible by linguistic exchanges that brought it into being.

I can imagine that my presence also impacted the gendarmes' assessment of our provenance. I wondered how much the security volunteers resisted this scrutiny of those who did not belong. While in some cases the gendarmes accepted their guides' assessments of whether people were Senegalese or not, the production of a Senegalese national ID could become the final arbiter of such investigations. In theory, a passport, national ID card, or visa might appear to provide the grounds on which individuals were granted passage across borderlands. In practice, however, the border offered a field of evaluation in which actors assessed one another based on outward linguistic and embodied signs. For those from Taabe crossing into Guinea at the border town of Laabi, for instance, sufficient performed knowledge of language and kin networks precluded them from having to show official IDs. Other scholars have written of similar phenomena elsewhere. For example, in the context of racialized language practices in Brazil, to be able to perform upper-class "standard" language enabled Brazilian youth to inhabit privileged spaces such as beachfront areas, which were otherwise rendered inaccessible to them without IDs (Roth-Gordon 2016). In a similar manner, the Guinea-Senegal border was woven through the warp and weft of ongoing linguistic evaluation and performance. Signs of one's provenance included one's clothing, possessions, and linguistic signs gleaned through even the shortest of greetings. Guinean chauffeurs and travelers—often descending from the more temperate climate of the Fouta Djallon mountains—could be recognized by thick coats, scarves, and gloves, accessories that often betrayed their provenance by the time that they arrived in the heat of Kédougou. At a moment of social change and an epidemic, this contentious border became the site of shifting principles of discernment that guided what people paid attention to. It emerged as a material site for hearing and not merely seeing others.

The Sociality of Border Crossing

As I have argued throughout this book, mobility can be usefully thought of as an act of social negotiation. As such, borderland residents like those from Taabe thought about border crossing not as a legal or security issue but as a social practice necessitating the proper performance of respect. Like other interactional contexts in which individuals must mutually navigate appropriate principles, border crossing was also evaluated as an interactional act that necessitated the performance of greetings and respect. Even during the height of the pandemic when the border was officially closed, stories of Guinean youth storming over the border on motorcycles were discussed in these terms.

Talk of one particularly egregious encounter lingered in the air for some time in which two young Guineans on motorcycles ostensibly declined to stop at the request of a Senegalese border official and blew through on their motorcycles. Without any immediate means of transportation, Guinean and Senegalese officials were often incapable of pursuit. What bothered my local interlocutors, however, was neither that these youths had contravened legal entry procedures nor that they had put others' lives at risk in a time of Ebola. What bothered them was that these youth had shown themselves to be *disrespectful* (alaa needi).[3] Less concerned by the potential for viral spread, residents lamented their inability to recognize the Senegalese border guards through the arts of greeting and social recognition. Border guards themselves were often the subject of similar discourses of respectfulness. Locals often remarked on the respectfulness of Senegalese guards in contrast to Guinean border guards, who were often portrayed as uneducated and unsophisticated. In this part of the world, in fact, there was a whole genre of jokes dedicated to Guinean border guards. While bribery and informal negotiations have historically been common among Guinean police in the context of political dysfunction, any resistance of Senegalese border officials to bribery has frequently been interpreted by traveling Guineans as a sign of a functioning Senegalese state (Fioratta 2020).

With the border being a zone of intense social discernment, acts of border crossing and routines of vehicular travel came to be interpreted through such discourses on respect. Travel by car or motorcycle was not merely a technical mode of transportation but also a mode of sociality that became a part of processes of *enregisterment*, a linguistic anthropological term that helps track how certain typified behaviors and ways of speaking became models for certain kinds of people (Agha 2007). Border residents frequently read respect into the forms of movement in and through the materiality of vehicles. Asif Agha (2007, 55), for instance, views enregisterment as a process in which "diverse behavioral signs (whether linguistic, non-linguistic, or both) are functionally reanalyzed as cultural models of action, as behaviors capable of indexing stereotypic characteristics of incumbents of particular interactional roles, and of relations among them." As Agha rightly points out, these diverse behavioral signs need not be narrowly conceived of as linguistic and may include comportment, gesture, or style more broadly.

Travel along the Senegal-Guinea border shows that such forms of enregisterment not only concerned social actors, narrowly speaking. The behaviors of car and driver as sociotechnical hybrids blur boundaries between human and machine such that Guinean driving was seen as disrespectful driving and interactional mode. Along the Dakar–Bamako highway, for instance, Malians were broadly associated with the heavy, new vehicles of long-distance freight. This was partly due to networks of relatively wealthy Malians who dominated the long-distance freight networks and the mercury markets (used for extracting gold from surrounding rocks), along the Dakar–Bamako highway through Kédougou. At times, the weight of their vehicles appeared to parallel the weightiness of their conduct in interactional contexts, in which significance of a person (such as that displayed to one's in-laws) was itself conceived of in these terms.

Particularly in the context of the Ebola epidemic, Guinean travel was intensely scrutinized on the roads between Guinea and Kédougou City. As I traveled with Mamadou to and from Taabe, he and other fellow travelers sketched out pragmatic models that typified people in terms of their movement and travel. Local Senegalese cars were often construed as slower moving and therefore more polite than the overladen, hurried, and "rude" Guinean vehicles. Respect in motion was thus shown by slower cars allowing faster cars to pass and, in response, by faster cars honking in thanks. This peripatetic theory of respect informed Mamadou's understanding of which cars were Guinean and which were Senegalese. "Guinéens alaa respect," I often heard (Guineans know no respect).[4] Looking broadly at linguistic anthropological work, interactional approaches are very good at accounting for linguistic practice in neat, stationary face-to-face encounters. However, such approaches have a harder time accounting for diverse modes of social interaction that happen in relation to the built environment and via these different modalities of movement. Thinking of linguistic practice in the context of mobility helps us notice these forms of social practice on the move.

In an area with highly unequal access to means of transportation, different modes of mobility furthermore afforded different levels of social exposure and risk. Owning a car, for instance, could provide a measure of protection against the pressures of attending to social relations. While visiting with colleagues in the more distant city of Tambacounda, I had occasion to meet the former head of Kédougou's gendarme brigade, who was a well-known and respected man. For an individual of such renown, traveling in a car became a way to avoid the time-consuming exchange of everyday greetings. By the end of his career, he could barely walk down the streets of Kédougou without being consumed by greetings and solicitation.

In a palpable way, this example demonstrates the role of language to constitute, not merely represent, mobility. Ultimately, this state of affairs was so disruptive to his daily life that the retired gendarme took a car wherever he went—even if it was a short distance away. Attending to his phone while being shielded from the outside allowed him to slip in and out of areas where he might otherwise be carried into drawn-out conversations. Being driven around by a chauffeur also helped excuse him from any responsibility to make the decision to make social stops on the way since he wasn't at the wheel. While having a car could be used to project a consequential and successful persona, at other times vehicular travel helped to insulate individuals from the responsibilities of managing face-to-face interactions with others.

In contrast, for my friend Mamadou who often drove his four-wheel-drive SUV from Kédougou to Takkopellel, having a vehicle often set him up for notoriety and increased scrutiny. The road from Kédougou to Takkopellel was a route that often saw little public transport, and foot passengers frequently solicited him for rides. Such encounters frequently impelled travelers to insist on a particular relationship with individuals who, like Mamadou, had wheels. It was uncanny how often Mamadou was claimed by many to be a long-lost kinsperson. I teased him that he was "kinshipping" on these trips, a joke resulting from sun weariness and extended time in the field that would only make sense to a few fellow anthropologists who had taken courses in the now almost abandoned field of kinship. In fact, it is often *through* such trips with Mamadou that I learned the genealogy of his family and how they were related with surrounding communities. While most might envision an anthropologist interviewing locals about their kinship relationships under a palaver tree, I found that these fraught mobile encounters offered opportunities for self-distancing through which individuals came to reflect upon their relations with others (Keane 2015). Genealogies and social relationships between people are not merely questions of static facts; they can be seen as links mobilized by people on the move as forms of social action.

As such, moving across the borderlands in different vehicles and modalities afforded situated engagements with others. Mired in never-ending bottlenecks in the back of a taxi, Catherine Melly (2017) described how the act of driving through Dakar's traffic jams offered travelers affordances for their self-narration that emerged in concert with their surroundings. Forms of narration and the things a person might attend to can thus be seen as a function of their mobilities. Other anthropologists have reflected on these forms of mobility as ethnographic methods. For instance, in his exploration of a provincial town in Mali, André Chappatte (2022) chose a bicycle to encounter the urban environment and its residents with greater intimacy. From a phenomenological perspective, different modes of mediated mobility afford different forms of ethnographic engagement. For my part, I have tried to engage ethnographically through a range of different forms of mobility as transport. Walking through Kédougou allowed me to witness greetings and a recognition of others in face-to-face interactions. Riding a bike in southeastern Senegal afforded a quicker form of mobility that was nonetheless frequently interrupted by calls to stop and say hello. This vehicular mobility was frequently associated with being a Peace Corps volunteer in Senegal and thus is accompanied by a form of social typification. Purchasing a motorcycle during my period of anthropological fieldwork allowed me to reach greater distances more quickly, but it also constrained the kinds of paths I could take and brought me into relationships of reciprocity with many who wanted to borrow it. Riding a motorcycle also brought me into contact with the gas station owners and, more importantly, repairmen, who became a significant site of ethnography later in my fieldwork. Beyond the negotiation of social encounters through vehicular technologies that mediated mobilities on this scale, I have endeavored to show how linguistic practices constitute mobility in a very real sense.

Mountain Path Sociality

Just as broader processes and events, such as the Ebola epidemic and the ways of talking that arose because of it, could instantiate a border, so can affordances of the "natural" environment also mediate how people use and evaluate language. As I moved through the landscape of southeastern Senegal, I began to notice that certain routes and places were marked through the routines of interaction that occurred there. The mountain paths between Senegal and Guinea were such a space. Traveling between Senegal and Guinea in the Fouta Djallon mountains happened at the boundaries of what people considered settlement and bush—a network of paths that led Robyn, Steve, and me astray on our fateful journey. From Takkopellel in the lowlands, you had to first climb a precipitous foot trail up a forested slope to reach Taabe and other villages on top of the first rise. This narrow mountain path formed a liminal space that offered a place of play and linguistic freedom for many. Taabe's schoolchildren made this trip down and back up the mountain every day to attend school. Mamadou would occasionally take tourists up here to his hometown of Taabe, where they would take souvenir photos of the sprawling African savanna below.

For children finding themselves momentarily between the home, school, and market, these mountain paths along the border of Senegal and Guinea were a place of wondrous imagination. Their dreams etched into rocks and their voices echoing through the trees, local children inhabited the personas of famous rappers or forest animals as they played in the liminal space between settlements. It is here that Nigerian stars such as Davido found themselves inscribed and at home in the trees. Along these in-between paths through the forest, children would tease travelers by impersonating chimpanzees from high points along the canyon rim so that their animal calls resounded widely. Chimpanzees as well as baboons also traveled through these areas, and travelers were keen to pick up on sounds of movement around them.

Mobility in this area manifested itself through interactions. Seemingly a place of isolation and silence, these pathways also became a place of overhearing and social evaluation. For those slowly trudging up or down the mountain, the path opened down on miles of surrounding savanna and offered excellent cell coverage. Since the Senegalese cell network all but disappeared once you reached the top of the plateau, the forested paths up the hoore fello plateau were ironically a place of intense sociality. Plateau residents from Guinea and Senegal headed to the weekly market made use of the phone network as long as they could, exchanging news with distant relatives as they ascended the steep mountain paths. Whereas I huffed and puffed my way up the mountain, my fellow travelers often climbed these steep paths while negotiating family dramas on their cell phones. Indeed, discussions along these paths between towns were where I witnessed some of the most sensitive conversations. Talk of marital problems and disagreements with siblings were often kept private until we reached the spaces of discretion among the trees and pebbly footpaths.

Locals from this area were quick to remark on their secretive nature. They were proud of their ability to dissemble their speech to urban Pular speakers by adopting a "deep" (*luugungal*) variety. These were accompanied by a slew of hand signals and secret signs to those in-the-know. A common move was the tactic of *gundagol*, the act of slipping away with a subset of

Figure 5.1. On top of the plateau.

fellow conspirators to engage in secretive talks of a delicate nature. Passing by and encountering other groups of travelers, however, one could not help but catch bits and pieces of their talk in these ostensibly "private" zones. Following behind individuals, or momentarily spending time with them at places of rest, travelers caught bits of discussions and usually put pieces together to guess at what might be going on.

One day, Mamadou and I were climbing behind a man in conversation with his brother on speakerphone. We began to overhear him counseling his older brother about how to deal with his apparently intractable wife. She had, it seems, burned money as an act of marital defiance, and the man and his interlocutor were discussing how to proceed. Mamadou and I both listened curiously to these troubles as we continued to follow him up the mountain. Since hoore fello residents often stashed their bikes at the top of the mountain and descended the rest of the way on foot, a three-kilometer up section provided a particularly productive space of compressed sociality. As many travelers reclaimed their bikes on the top, they then made quick progress to their final destinations, and the liminal space of eavesdropping was abruptly ended.

Site Making

On another trip up the mountain, Mamadou and I had just summited the first rise and entered the outskirts of Taabe. Crossing paths with another traveler, we were greeted by the admonishing voice of his kinswoman: "aŋ a jeyaaka ɗo" (you, you're not from here), she said to Mamadou. He offered some faltering excuses in a laugh-speak. In one sense, these teases can be understood as a strategy of baiting Mamadou to invest himself more in Taabe, which, in his responses to her, he promised to do. The spatial language used by this woman, however, should be thought of not as representing preexisting places but as an ongoing articulation of the relationship between places as socially constituted. For instance, by insisting on his absence *here* (ɗo) in the village, which sits in contrast to places such as Kédougou City (*there*, "toŋ") that have kept Mamadou away, the young woman establishes a spatial distinction between socially meaningful sites. As I mentioned, Mamadou often split his time between his home village of Taabe and the city of Kédougou, where he had a primary residence. Instead of seeing these as two distinct places that are evidence of Mamadou's absence, the young woman might have seen them as linked sites that composed one integrated social sphere (i.e., a Kédougou-Taabe zone that sits in contrast to coastal Senegal). In the case of a diasporic context, inhabiting the same community is not always a question of inhabiting the same space in a Cartesian sense of dots on a map but of inhabiting the same social sphere as constructed through memory, gift exchange, or discursive reciprocity. Such forms of community building through linguistic and cultural practice are thus not dependent on geographical coordinates. The question of being home (here) or abroad (away) is one that is not entirely solved by judging distances on a map.

This distinction between Taabe (home) and Kédougou (away) thus could be constituted differently for those who see Kédougou City and surrounding villages as a local zone of action that together lie in contrast to more distant economic centers. Indeed, many Kédovins regularly traveled in between rural hometowns and Kédougou, where they often clustered together in a particular neighborhood. In effect, this young woman was engaging in an act of social site differentiation that implicated particular scalar assumptions (Irvine and Gal 2019). Such distinctions between places as socially relevant should be seen as emergent forms of social evaluation rather than a priori differences. When Mamadou's kinswoman thus utters "ɗo" (here) on top of the plateau, she is establishing a meaningful distinction that marked these two spaces as sociologically distinct.

A short kilometer's walk down the mountain toward Takkopellel sat a crossroads that brought together a few paths up the mountain. For Mamadou and many of his friends, this was a site of important sociological differentiation. As I gathered, going up the mountain was to be evaluated based on specific *villageois* expectations for dress and comportment. Up there, Mamadou tended to wear more "traditional" clothing; he monitored his speech for respectful greetings and shied away from flaunting things of value. The larger village of Takkopellel, down from the Taabe plateau, however, was a place where Mamadou put the successes he gained from previous migrations on display. This was a place where one could wear one's best clothes and show off.

Coming down from hoore fello villages like Taabe, Mamadou and his friends would sneak into the bush at this crossroads at the base of the mountain and change into their latest fashionable outfits on their way to late-night soirees. Mamadou's crew, drenched in the sweat of the mountain trek, would take off their simple T-shirts and trousers just off the path, where they could be hidden among the foliage. Donning sporty prêt-à-porter clothes purchased during the weekly markets in Kédougou or Dakar, Mamadou and his friends would then spray themselves with cologne and display their finest baseball caps and sneaks. Their language often changed too. I noticed more French phrases, more English thrown in for effect, and more Spanish as evidence of their knowledge of a cosmopolitan world. Here, he was as likely to greet his peers in a "que tal" as he was in Pular. The use of Spanish was becoming increasingly common in an area where Spanish tourists visiting the nearby waterfall and Spanish primatology enthusiasts had become steady fixtures. By choosing between traditional *bou-bous* or the latest fashions unwrapped from plastic, Mamadou and his fellow people of the world were crafting different understandings of themselves for different audiences.

In so doing, Mamadou and his friends were monitoring their own bodies as vehicles for articulating connections with fashions, ideas, and objects from faraway places. While my previous discussion of articulating mobilities rests on the analysis of linguistic performances, this episode shows the symbolic dimensions of embodied practice. Beyond the spoken word, this embodied practice could speak volumes about one's mobility and connections with distant lands. Capturing these as embodied articulations means that people are looking at one another as models—not merely things said, but signs given off by embodied comportment. For Mamadou, to insist on his belonging to the village as well as to return more frequently were both acts that could articulate an ongoing, negotiated relationships with his home village.

Conclusion

For much of its history, the region of Kédougou offered a shatter zone, an area just out of the reach of state control in which individuals could retreat to their own affairs. Many of the surrounding communities were formed by those escaping taxation from the Guinean state. This trend toward regularization accompanied not only the presidency of Macky Sall but also the mayorship of Hadji Cissé, which I discuss at greater length in the next chapter. In practice this meant that borders between places appeared to be increasingly fixed on the maps of land management bureaus, municipalities, and NGO platforms. In this chapter, however, an attention to linguistic practices reveals a borderland that was etched not only though cairns and crossroads but also through linguistic routines and processes of social differentiation. Events like the Ebola epidemic and the attention of NGOs, police officers, and international actors turned the borderlands into a zone of discernment of hearing as well as sight. Through these processes, this area became targeted as a space whose natural environment, social interactions, and population movements were intimately connected to the well-being and livelihoods of individuals elsewhere.

I have suggested that we can learn about mobility in West Africa and elsewhere by examining it as a social process mediated in large part through language. The Senegal-Guinea borderlands came into being as an intertwined product of linguistic practices, broader epidemiological-political processes, and the affordances of its natural and built environment. Rather than studying bodies crossing a line, an increased focus on interaction, language, and processes of differentiation shows that many insights on mobility and borders emerge in the intersubjective spaces between people. Border crossing was not merely a question of crossing from one side to another but of mastering certain linguistic performances in a highly scrutinized field of social interpretation. In the case of gendarmes, this meant insulating themselves from risky social interaction with locals.

For local farmers, this entailed successful performances of belonging in a way that potentially minimized signs of being from Guinea. These sorts of evaluations happened not only at the level of embodied persons but also through the technologies of travel like cars and motorcycles. Talk on the border rarely happened in neat configurations of face-to-face encounters; it was more likely to occur on the backs of motorcycles or within tightly packed buses. These interactions not only reported on existing configurations between places but also constituted spatial relationships, a process I describe as site making. It is through routines of verbal art that language becomes infrastructure—a web of everyday exchanges, stories, and articulations of social action that, woven together, form a laminated borderland.

Notes

1. Scholars have furthermore insisted that space also implicates an understanding of time, such as so-called distant, exotic tribes of ethnographic study that were therefore also held to be from a previous, more ancient time (Fabian 1983). M. M. Bakhtin (1981), who inspired work in linguistic anthropology, showed how time and space traveled together in the form of a chronotope.

2. As with the Ebola epidemic, these borderlands also became a prism for interpreting relationships between people and the environment through the lens of ecological conservation. Beginning in my time as a Peace Corps volunteer from 2006 to 2009, Spanish primate conservationists began to come to Kédougou region to observe chimpanzees. This part of Senegal and Guinea offers the most northerly reaches of West African chimpanzees and for these reasons offers an interesting case study for those interested in habitat loss and environmental change. By my fieldwork in 2014, the center in Takkopellel had become incorporated as an environmental research station associated with the Jane Goodall Institute (JGI). By this time, the center was offering tours for visitors interested in the chance to observe chimpanzees in their habitat. As part of their larger project, JGI Spain had established much of this borderland region as a *réserve*: a specific status that intended to provide the community a framework for engaging in conservation, though largely without local buy-in. Through this, the JGI was concerned with redefining how locals were to interact with the land and through this, with the chimpanzee populations. There were frequent miscommunications between parties; locals were often confused by JGI's exhortations to limit their collection of wild fruits and to refrain from urinating on reserve land. The way in which the nonhuman primate residents of these borderlands were framed as an international conservation issue furthermore impacted how this border was experienced and monitored. Although frequently resisted by Taabe locals, this borderland area thus became a function of international discourses on conservation, thereby impacting the horizons of mobility.

3. *Needi* tended to be used in reference to children who were learning basic manners and social norms.

4. Here the speaker uses a loan word from French. The Pular word for respect, *teddungal*, tends to be used in contexts of hospitality and behavior norms toward others, such as guests, in-laws, or elders. Related terms include *teddudo* (n.), an honorable person, and *teddingol* (v.), to respect (someone). Here respect took on an embodied meaning and the root (*tedd-*) refers to the weightiness of a person who is to be respected or the gravity of the context (for an example, see the anecdote about the Malian trucks in this chapter).

6

KÉDOUGOU MARKET

A Place of Wares and Words

A Place of Wares and Words

In 2014, Hadji Cissé, a well-known businessman and reform candidate, had just won Kédougou's mayoral race. In a region whose gold mining boom presented both pitfalls and opportunities, Cissé had built a thriving business out of importing used construction equipment from Europe. Central to Cissé's platform was a pledge to "regularize" Kédougou's economy and politics. This was a blanket term for reducing corruption and bureaucratizing processes that had long run through "informal" social networks. For the so-called informal migrant traders who worked from the sidewalks and makeshift tables across the market across Kédougou market, however, this was a risky proposition. Even before Cissé's term, migrant traders existed in a liminal position. However, Cissé's pledges to clean up the market put many in an even more precarious position, particularly given tensions between certain store owners and informal sellers who could often sell at a reduced price.

Indeed, in the months after Cissé's election, these administrative initiatives dislodged migrant merchants from the places they had been trading for many months or even years. Suddenly, my lived market landscape was upended. I had a hard time finding migrant sellers who had previously served as communal cairns in their habitual trading spots. Only the kola nut sellers, traders of a prized ritual good that imbued them with clout, proved to be relatively unaffected by these upheavals. Despite this precarity, migrant traders continued to inhabit the market, leveraging this instability as best they could. This chapter tells the story of how migrant market sellers negotiated their uncertain position during a time of change. Examining the routines of creative linguistic interactions helps show how migrants maintained their place in a changing market. While migrants are often studied in light of their mobility, a key to their success in places like Kédougou market was the ability to strategically root themselves in place for a time. Particularly in a time of Ebola where Guinea was held to be a source of contagion, the movements of Guinean migrant merchants who dominated Kédougou's market were highly scrutinized. While "ethnic solidarities" has often been used to explain how migrants associate in such contexts, an interactional approach to migrant lives shows that ethnic commonality was only the tip of an iceberg. Idioms such as kinship or affinity, which are often assumed to be structural and inevitable, were often useful resources for productively mediating relationships with a range of others.

Migrant merchants who sold Chinese goods imported from Guinea used a range of linguistic and interactional tools to negotiate their emplacement in the market. The Guinean migrant traders of Kédougou are a part of larger migratory patterns of Guinean Fulɓe Fouta seeking economic opportunities across Senegal and the broader region (Fioratta 2020). I highlight the experiences of kola nut sellers, who prove themselves to be relatively resilient actors in this time of upheaval. We will also meet other migrants, such as an elderly porter, Djiby Diallo, who resorts to numerous performances of relationship building to cement a stable community around him. A strong factor in the success of migrant market sellers was the cultivation of relationships achieved through the exchange of wares and words. Given these redistributive networks, succeeding in the market entailed the ability to invest in social networks while safeguarding one's money and goods. These migrants practiced the verbal art of being mobile, an infrastructure that emerged through situated linguistic practice. Through the cultivation of in-law relations, joking cousin correspondences, and other relationships, traders shaped the market around them into a place where they belonged. This last chapter, therefore, offers a reinterpretation of a classic topic in migration and mobilities: the market. I draw on all of the concepts developed throughout this book—mobility as verbal art, language as infrastructure, and the articulations of everyday encounters—to show how migrants negotiate their precarious position in times of change.

When I first arrived in 2006, Kédougou was a sleepy border town that was home to only a handful of motorcycles. But by 2016, hundreds of Chinese-manufactured motorcycles roamed the streets of Kédougou, employing a throng of mechanics. Sitting in southeastern Senegal at the crossroads of Bamako and the trading cities of northern Guinea, Kédougou City as well as the broader region were in the midst of a protracted economic boom. Although Kédougou's populations had long seen migrant and settling populations from Mali and Guinea, large numbers of Guinean migrants now flocked to Kédougou. These day laborers, merchants, and transporters came to pursue the economic opportunities that a new Dakar–Kédougou–Bamako highway and the mining economy afforded. These migrants often came to places like Kédougou far away from their kinship networks so as to avoid the pressures of redistribution. Even in distant markets, however, migrants needed to develop keen interactional strategies to protect their wealth while at the same time cultivating social networks.

While Kédougou was only loosely connected to the rest of Senegal by unreliable laterite roads until the 1970s, the Dakar–Bamako road that now routed through downtown Kédougou in 2009 further invigorated the downtown market area. This roadside market had become a trading and traveling nexus, offering economic opportunities for migrants who worked as porters, traveling merchants, and middlemen in what was a thriving regional trade. In recent years, it had increasingly served as a transport hub for the gold mining concessions and offered an important stop for those merchants and miners in transit. This new highway, the gold rush, and an increased connection with western Senegal all offered unprecedented challenges and opportunities for market goers and sellers. Not dissimilar from Julie Kleinman's (2014, 288) study of West Africans in Paris's La Gare du Nord as "a coming together of various trajectories from various places," Kédougou's downtown market was situated as a nexus for many forms of social and economic self-realization. While the traces of Kédougou's social and economic change were sometimes slow to detect in its more distant neighborhoods, the town's rapidly increasing connections with regional and international networks was most visible in this bustling district.

The market was one of the first places where artisanal miners and villagers from surrounding areas would stop on their way into town. The newly paved road ran alongside the border of Kédougou's labyrinthian inner market, composed of small alleys, makeshift tables, and corner stores. While a skeleton of permanent structures was hidden at the market's center, migrant merchants and peripatetic workers were its lifeblood: an infrastructure of people built through sociality and exchange. The alleys that crisscrossed its main streets were lined with sellers who had built their improvised displays into the sides of roads and buildings. Some sellers paraded

Figure 6.1. Kédougou market.

their wares around in their arms or pushed custom-built carts that allowed them to travel across the markets and neighborhoods in search of clients. Other sellers anchored themselves to pedestrian zones and built relationships with neighboring shops and sellers to stake their claims. As such, the effective range of migrant sellers was often underwritten by social connections negotiated with the shop owners, whose stake in permanent structures could grant access and shared space to others. Friendships cultivated among wholesale and small-scale merchants has helped solidify a trust that was paramount to sustaining successful economic activities (Warms 2014). This was a market built of wares and words.

Viewing the linguistic exchanges and social relations featured in this chapter as material channels of infrastructure resonates with ways in which economic anthropologists have examined exchange more expansively. Julia Elyachar (2010), for instance, describes the kinds of social relationships of women in Cairo as "phatic labor," which produces channels along which semiotic and economic value can flow. Not only can these processes be understood in a symbolic sense, but they can also, for Elyachar, be equated to material infrastructures: "In Cairo, 'phatic labor' creates a social infrastructure of communicative channels that are as essential to economy as roads, bridges, or telephone lines" (452). Linguistic interaction and exchange, in this sense, constitutes forms of infrastructure that enable the circulation of other material and symbolic forms. What many have described as "informal economies" can be understood as epiphenomena of these broader forms of phatic labor cultivated by women and migrants in places like Cairo and Kédougou.

A Linguistically Constructed Environment

Existing scholarship on African markets has shown them to be complex systems that are organized through patterns and relationships at different levels—spatial patterns made by the habitual movements of ambulatory sellers; broader (inter)national policies and economics; and interpersonal dynamics negotiated in interaction. Gracia Clark (1995, 3), for instance, describes Ghanaian markets as composed of processes that "create contradictory interests and pressures inside the marketplace . . . it is these very contradictions that constantly renew and transform the full range of trading relations, including their constraints." The linguistic practices I describe in this chapter present one complex patterning through which the market can be understood—both for analysts and for market goers. In what follows, I describe how linguistic practices as infrastructure were central to tracing the built infrastructure and spatiality of the market. For new incoming migrants who had yet to understand some of these broader relations, establishing themselves within this complex nexus required an effective use of linguistic and social capital. In this chapter, I describe how the interactional practices constitute a significant means through which individuals established themselves in the market and, in so doing, contributed to the spatiality of the market through their practices.

Rather than merely floating above the market as detached communication, language helped constitute the market in a material sense. As such, language can be thought of not only as a means to convey valuable information or even to build relationships but also as a force for shaping the place around them. As infrastructure built through linguistic exchanges, the downtown market emerged through the exchange of talk, food, and situated interactions. By likening people to infrastructure, Abdou Maliq Simone (2004) has argued against the design logic of architectural infrastructures and instead orients our attention to how people make use of and refashion aspects of their lived environment. People as infrastructure, is particularly apt in describing Kédougou's downtown spaces, and it demonstrates how humans creatively shape urban spaces, flexibly transmuting the built environment to suit their needs. Infrastructure can thus be thought of not only as walls, lines, and cement but also as the situated actions of people who break up and reshape any supposed teleologies of public space and urban planning. For instance, after a renovation of the market that coincided with the paving of the Kédougou–Bamako road, migrants repurposed a paved parking structure area at the entrance of Kédougou's downtown market. Sellers and porters had turned this area into a bustling business area that was the place to go if you wanted to purchase affordable goods like caps, radios, or flashlights of Chinese manufacture.

Market people creatively repurposed the environment around them to suit their needs. Much of this happened through not only individual action but also the intersubjective and shared practices of language use. Migrant sellers frequently shifted participant frameworks by assembling makeshift furniture in various formations or altering centers of social gravity through the sharing of tea. *Participant framework* here is a term that helps explore how interlocutors manage roles and responsibilities of interaction in space. Not merely a place of buildings, stalls, and carts, this market was also constituted through migrant interactions. Visiting at different times, I noticed how individuals slowly shaped the frameworks for interaction, creating circular spots that seemed to invite intense discussion on some days through the arrangement of chairs and selling carts. Other times, I would return to find these small oases of intense social interaction evaporated. These spots shifted between more closely managed conversations to relatively open configurations where tea or greetings might attract a new client. Market sellers often arranged themselves such that walking up to brick-and-mortar stores first entailed navigating the human pathways of mobile sellers who attempted to draw customers into interaction. Occasionally, this symbiosis between brick-and-mortar stores and mobile sellers was brought into question, with the former occasionally resenting the latter's ability to siphon off customers with lower prices and conversational finesse.

The participant frameworks of Kédougou's downtown market were contingent achievements, composed of shifting arrangements between small stools, umbrellas, and the temporary stages created by the bodily alignments of idle workers. Lurking on the edges, overhearers could pick up words here and there, thereby jumping in and out of modes of (over)hearing and participation (Goffman 1981a). Individuals might maintain conversations while seated at great distances from each other; at other times, they might yell greetings to passersby while they were simultaneously engaged in intimate conversation in close quarters. When regulars approached their usual spots, they were often greeted by their jammoore nicknames called out at a distance: mundane mysteries such as "France" or "millet man." These nicknames often made no sense to strangers, but they frequently harkened to migratory misadventures. Broadcast over the market, these secret nicknames were often addressed to a friend-in-the-know and sifted out those who had no knowledge of these secret stories and monikers.

The exchange of these names and gifts incited further exchange and movement. Once placed on a bed of charcoal embers, a pot of tea became a redistributive affordance for those who could create or draw on existing connections with the tea patron. Who was to count as deserving of tea in an environment where individuals were continually on their way in and out was often a recurring background negotiation in market interactions. Refreshments, snacks, or prayers that were publicly displayed similarly drew in people around them. While the exchange of greetings was often required payment to admit others into interaction, rights to sit and participate were generally monitored by implicit hierarchies among migrants, at the top of which sat kola nut sellers.

Greetings, nicknames, and the built infrastructure of the market thus all provided linked ways of managing access to resources and information. For market sellers, the display and management of their wares was a communicative art form that invited clients. Every morning, merchants displayed reams of flashlights, clothes, and other accessories and each evening, they carefully folded this merchandise away into compact blocks. Using rope or rubber straps cut from recycled bicycle tires, they tied plastic sheets and rice sacks around their stalls into tight bundles that kept their wares secure overnight. In the event of a rainstorm, merchants performed a more hurried improvisation of their habitual technique and quickly dashed off under the nearest roofed structure. Early in the wet season, rains were first announced by swirling dust storms. With an intuitive sense of the weather, traders responded more to the changes in barometric pressure and temperature than to the sky, which was often obscured by the cluttered market. These early season storms appeared first as a flurry of scurrying humans and livestock seeking shelter, who were soon set upon by plumes of dust and the stout first rains. Those unable to make it back home were swept up into corner shops, covered patios and private compounds. Laborers, shopkeepers, and shoppers suddenly found themselves thrust in atop one another. United against the dust, they were often brought into these improvised moments of greeting and commiseration—a sudden social effervescence witnessed through the loud din of staccato conversation bouncing off the cement walls.

Cultivating a Domestic Space through In-Law Talk

African markets have often been described as chaotic (Ferguson 1999). While such a description might betray an outsider's perspective, migrants also frequently spoke of markets as precarious places where you could get lost (in Pular, for instance, *majjegol*). Newcomers often navigated these places through the cultivation of social relations and everyday connections with others. Although much of these connections were assumed to happen along ethnic and kinship lines, my experiences indicated that the connections migrants mobilized were much more diverse and manifold. Much of this labor was performed through the exchange of goods, greetings, and entangling oneself in the fates of one's consociates. For instance, as I discussed in chapter 3, many migrants formed inchoate communities through the exchange of teasing nicknames related to migratory misadventures that bound them together through a shared precarity (Sweet 2021b). Success as a migrant thus rested in large part on the verbal art of building relationships. Linguistic routines drawing on social idioms such as kinship, affinity, and joking relationships (*cousinage* in French, or *sanakuyaagal* in Pular) were key to the cultivation of these relationships. Sellers thus succeeded in staying put by using greetings, reciprocal talk, and the exchange of social idioms to cement themselves into the social landscape.

Connections through affinity (i.e., in-laws, *esiraaɓe* in Pular), for example, offered many migrant sellers an opportunity to build a domestic space from the surrounding alleys and crates of Kédougou's downtown market. As such, repeatedly exchanging in-law talk with others in the market was not only relationship or identity work in a conceptual sense; it could also change the kind of place that migrants found themselves in. Inhabiting a domestic space rather than a foreign market these sellers could dispense hospitality and speak from the position of host, a powerful role across West African societies. Being someone who could offer food, give out blessings, and speak to the others as a host was one important strategy that helped market sellers cement their position.

Djiby Diallo, a middle-aged porter from a faraway village whom I came to spend time with, frequently employed the idioms of joking relationships and affinity to connect with others in a busy market. Djiby owned a wheelbarrow, which he made use of to unload goods from the lorries that brought supplies from coastal Senegal. In addition to being a tool for his livelihood, however, Djiby's wheelbarrow became a site through which he shaped the spaces and possibilities for interaction. From this site, he enacted displays of hospitality and generosity by using language of the domestic sphere and likening his wheelbarrow to his home. "Mi eggi taho, Souleymane" (I've moved, Souleymane), he told me one day as I came upon him slumped in his wheelbarrow deep in the interior of the Kédougou downtown market.

One day as I was passing time with Djiby between work shifts, an elderly man ambled across our view. Djiby leapt up and began to arrange the flattened cardboard lining the bottom of his wheelbarrow as if he was making a bed. Putting on the final touches with meticulous attention, Djiby addressed the man effusively, exclaiming, "He, ko esiraaɓe aŋ!" (Hey, it's my senior in-law!). Djiby continued, "Esiraaɓe bismillah moŋ esiraaɓe joodˇee, joodˇee esiraaɓe godˇdˇo wernay esiraaɓe muudˇuŋ" ("In-law, welcome to you, in-law sit down, sit down in-law. A person should offer hospitality to their in-laws"). Along with his embodiment of deference and the placement of his respected in-law in a place of honor (the wheelbarrow), Djiby employed honorifics such as *joodˇee* (*-ee*, plural/honorific) instead of the familiar form, *joodˇo* (*-o*, singular). After Djiby urged his "esiraaɓe" to sit in the wheelbarrow seat of honor, the other man reluctantly obliged. "Wona fii joodˇagol mi ari" ("I didn't come here to sit down"), his guest hesitantly countered, alluding to business with another man at the market. Djiby's deployment of affinity in this context not only articulates the relationship between himself and his ostensible in-law but also reshapes the kind of space they find themselves in.

Sitting not only entraps a person in a particular place, but it moreover demonstrates a bodily technique of honoring one's in-laws and visitors, individuals who are often beckoned to sit down upon their arrival in a compound or family house. Djiby's verbal honorifics combined with a deferential comportment contributed to a domestic chronotope (space-time setting) from which guests could be welcomed, seated, and even fed. Djiby's use of esiraaɓe here draws on a relational idiom that brings others into interaction in a busy market. His esiraaɓe's compulsion to sit down and spend time with Djiby, despite the former's unwillingness, attests to the compulsion of affinity in performance.

Kola Nut Sellers

While porters like Djiby resorted to broad strategies to situate themselves at the heart of the action, Guinean migrant kola nut sellers leveraged their important ritual wares to succeed in the market setting. They occupied nodal figures in Kédougou's linguistic economy. Kola nut sellers not only managed overland truck shipments, but they also loaned money, exchanged currencies, and traded in other big-ticket items such as motorcycles. Selling kola nuts was possibly one of the most difficult networks to get into, and its sale was very profitable with respect to other forms of commerce in the market scene. Many of the same kola nut sellers that I had known at the Kédougou market in my time during the Peace Corps from 2006 to 2009 were still present in 2014–17 when I conducted ethnographic fieldwork. The same could not be said for their peers: porters and small-scale sellers of other products. While some kola nut sellers had left for Congo or Angola, their spots were only to be replaced with another kin member or friend. Places like Congo and Angola represent important nodes in intra-African trade networks and had significant migrant communities (Whitehouse 2012; Gaibazzi 2018). While much literature on migration in Africa has emphasized international migration, intra-African migration to places like Angola, Congo, or Kédougou is frequently overlooked and constitutes the vast majority of migrations (Schapendonk 2013). Consequently, this book recognizes that the scales and distinctions across migration is held to happen can be partly studied through interaction.

As key nodes in the front market complex, kola nut sellers were rooted in their habitual spots from sunup to sundown, returning home only for evening rest. Most kola nut sellers rented small rooms in neighborhoods close to the market, where they often shared lives together. Many had wives and children back in Guinea, to whom they sent monthly remittances, though not all Guinean migrants were so successful (Fioratta 2015). Often working together as a unit, kola nut sellers organized regular transports of kola nuts and other merchandise. They frequently used these trips as opportunities to spend time with their families in Guinea, although many of these circular patterns of trade and reciprocity were disrupted during the time of Ebola.

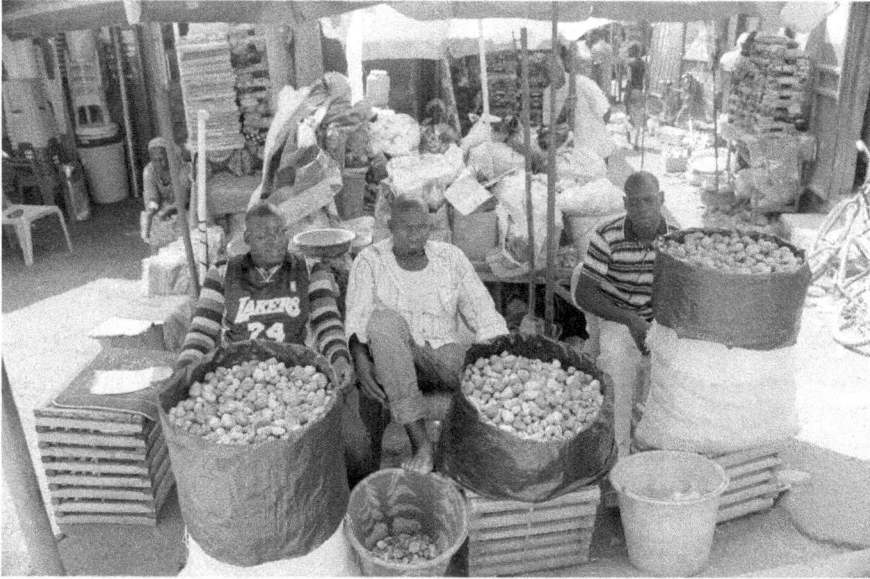

Figure 6.2. Kola nut sellers.

Kola nut sellers exemplify the social strategies of migrants across Africa in which distance from kin networks is used as a strategy of wealth accumulation (Jonsson 2012; Whitehouse 2013). While the pressure to share with kin can be very great close to an individual's local networks, economic activity abroad can make it easier to amass and hold on to wealth. This physical distance from one's homeland also made available a broader range of social and interactional strategies. Bruce Whitehouse (2013), for instance, describes how migrants who find themselves far from home are often able to engage in otherwise "demeaning" activities such as small-scale trade, which are understood to be below their social station. Free from more rigid social expectations, physical distance often enables migrants to articulate themselves in new and more flexible ways.

While some kola nut sellers sat clustered in groups of three or four, others claimed small alleyways in the market for themselves. Those who sat in larger groups could draw a larger crowd, but they also increasingly relied on their ability to create special relationships with *kiliyans* (clients) who might seek out specific kola nut sellers again and again. Kola nut sellers' spots could be minimalistic arrangements of a single sack, behind which they sat on simple stools with a moveable umbrella to protect against the sun.

Bringing in other chairs and clustering on small benches, kola nut sellers could quickly create a large space for others if need be. Market goers relied on verbal baiting and other strategies to sift through a diverse group of circulating individuals in the market. In order to stand out, market sellers created privileged relationships with market buyers, using a range of relational idioms to nurture kiliyan. A reciprocal term that sellers and buyers called each other, to be a kiliyan was to have a built a relationship with a seller to whom one might return over and over. In return, buyers could hope to get preferential prices or credit, drawing on established trust with sellers.

When providing long-term kiliyans with kola, for instance, Thierno, one of the most senior sellers in the front market, had a way of presenting the nuts in his open palm that made a demonstration of the choice merchandise he had selected for a particular kiliyan. He often began such an interaction by asking, "Ko kilo jelu faaleɗaa?" (How many kilos do you want?), even if the anticipated sale was often just a few kola nuts. With an initial assumption of a large order, buyers often had to construct palliatives that made excuses for smaller purchases. If Thierno noticed blemishes on a kola nut, he would remove it and search over the surface of his wares for a suitable alternative. Through a performance of meticulousness, he would often pause on three or four kola nuts before choosing a replacement. After being selected, kola nuts were then placed into clear plastic bags. Kiliyans were often given extra kola nuts in a separate bag. Since kola sellers could subtly reduce the quality of a kilogram of kola, long-term, friendly relations often won out over hard-nosed bargaining in buying kola nuts. As such, rather than bargaining over price, sellers would alter the quality and composition of kola to match the price as well as the relationship they had with their clients.

The migrant kola nut sellers proved to be the cornerstones of a living infrastructure that formed Kédougou's downtown market. During a time when a regularization campaign forced out and shuffled many other migrants, kola nut sellers managed to remain rooted. Achieving immobility in the market was a survival strategy for individuals who have otherwise been characterized by their mobility. Their success under these conditions could be found in a number of different factors. For instance, kola nut sellers frequently mobilized the ritual significance of their wares by leveraging gifts of kola and alongside them, blessings that materially ratified relationships with others. Repeated exchanges of wares and words could thus constitute a network of reciprocation that cemented their position in the landscape.

This was achieved by building client relationships with surrounding market goers, by spreading kola alongside Koranic blessings in order to increase good fortune, and by building a domestic sphere in this area through in-law talk and feasting.

Like Djiby, mentioned previously, kola nut sellers in part managed to bolster their presence in the market by cultivating a domestic sphere and by performing familial relations with others. Most kola sellers were from Guinea and rented rooms in the vicinity of the market, which most returned to only during sleeping hours. However, through the performance of in-law talk and hospitality, this market area itself often became a domestic home where they enjoyed considerable social gravity. For lunch, kola sellers would pool their money and have their female kin and friends cook for them. From their cooking spots deeper in the market, these women could carry half a dozen large, stacked bowls on their heads. All the while maintaining their center of gravity, they nudged their waists around the edges of protruding elbows, stools, and umbrellas. Soon small pods of kola nut sellers and their colleagues would form on the ground to eat, with most sitting in the style of Muhammad, who held one knee up and one folded beneath.

From this position, these migrants could share their meals and invite others in an idiom of hospitality. Having home-cooked meals brought over thus afforded kola nut sellers opportunities for performing a hospitality that was unavailable to those who snuck away to low-cost eateries tucked into corners of the market. As with other analyses of patron-client relationships, the giving of food, particularly as a form of household hospitality, has been a powerful force for ordering social relations in West Africa. The importance of these kinds of family meals is not to be understated. While in other parts of West Africa, restaurants and street food may be more common, most I met in this part of West Africa overwhelmingly preferred eating at home.

Inhabiting a flexible spot built up with shade umbrellas and small seats, kola nut sellers were able to outlast regularization campaigns partly by building places of social gravity where people came together. In the front market, kola nut sellers like Ibrahima, Thierno, and others I had known for a decade had managed to establish themselves as central market players. During the market regularization campaigns that saw most other small-scale traders removed from their tables and stands, only the kola nut sellers managed to initially retain their spots throughout the market. This flexible mobility, along with their trade in a ritually important item,[1] were likely factors that contributed to their not being removed in the waves of regularization campaigns in which other "informal" merchants were successively withdrawn by the municipal government.

The Verbal Art of Baiting and Protecting Wealth

For migrants who often traveled far away from their hometowns to accumulate wealth, building relationships and reciprocity with others while also safeguarding one's resources was a fine balance. Offering hospitality through food, blessings, and kola was a double-edged sword that entailed potential risks as well as benefits. While extending one's influence through the exchange of names, greetings, and blessings and gifts was at the heart of their success, these same strategies of patronage and reciprocity could render one's own wealth vulnerable. The art of carefully protecting one's resources while at the same time building relationships with others required a great deal of interactional shrewdness. For migrants, safeguarding one's wares and money all while remaining open to opportunity and collaboration was a key to succeeding as a migrant.[2] This occurred not only through the building of relationships such as kiliyan, as previously mentioned, but also through a manipulation of the space through linguistic practice—the art of language as infrastructure.

In the market, a kola nut seller's wares were particularly susceptible to claims. Sellers each sold from their own bag of kola nuts, wrapped in the large leaves of the kola tree. During small outings to take care of other business, other friends or sellers replaced them and took momentary charge of their goods. Sellers generally cut or folded down the giant sack as they sold down their wares. After opening a new bag, sellers spent the first several days peering from behind its towering form. As their wares diminished, their presence slowly came to overshadow the diminishing bag in front of them. Care was taken to ensure that kola nuts always lay flush, spilling over the top level of the bag. However, the largest and choicest kola nuts were displayed prominently on the top surface. With such desirable wares sitting out so openly, kola nuts were often the target of friends on the lookout for a freebie or those seeking alms.

With strong ritual importance, kola nuts were a particularly vulnerable target of alms and charity. Offered to market officials and clients, kola alongside Koranic blessings could provide pathways for cementing a seller's position in the market. It is in this way that many casual selling spots became destinations that people would be drawn to. Nevertheless, the management of kola required a subtle balance of dispensing and protecting these ritually significant goods. Those seeking alms often announced themselves by repeated calls on their daily trips to the downtown market: "sadaka ngiiri Allah" (alms for the sake of Allah). Like other market customers, alms seekers often headed toward their kola seller kiliyans, but they relied on the exchange of prayers rather than cash. When they received goods like kola, sugar, or coins, alms seekers would say a prayer for their benefactors. On a Friday morning as a kola nut seller and I sat under the shade of his umbrella, an elder strolled by the stand. "A yakay?" asked Thierno (You chew?). The elder held out his hand and, as he was walking away, responded, "Mi yahay ka julirde ɗoo, si a yi'ii laŋ a anday" ("I'm headed over here to the mosque, and if you see me you'll know"), hinting at the prayers that would be coming Thierno's way.

Sitting in positions of potential vulnerability, kola nut sellers nonetheless benefited from the prayers they received in return for their valuable wares. These forms of linguistic-material exchange not only demonstrate the materiality of language in a palpable way but also exemplify long-standing strategies through which West Africans accumulated wealth by investing in social relations (Berry 1989; Guyer 1995). These examples are understood as the kinds of multifaceted economic practices of Atlantic Africa that Jane Guyer (2004) describes as marginal gains—ways in which individuals translated value across different regimes to create wealth. Drawing on the example of a transport hub in Abidjan, Simone (2004, 410) similarly describes how "regularities thus ensue from a process of incessant convertibility—turning commodities, found objects, resources, and bodies into uses previously unimaginable or constrained." Not merely different kinds of material and monetary wealth, the market practices I describe show how wealth in the form of people, relationships, blessings, goods, and money were all exchanged and rendered equivalent in trading markets such as Kédougou.

In Senegal and more broadly across West Africa, Islamic prayers provide a liquid form of exchange that could be offered in the immediacy of a quick conversation. Prayers as material word were often given in exchange for good deeds, presents, or support. As such, they provided fluid currency that could be used as part of exchanges in everyday negotiations. Contributions of alms to wandering talibé, who recite the Koran in exchange for coins or food, is another important example (Ware 2014). Considered as a prayer economy, many scholars of West African Islam have explored the role material gifts play in the devotion of members of West African brother-hoods toward their leaders (Soares 2005). Even as kola nut sellers benefited in the clout of prayers offered by well-wishers, I also heard Koranic blessings pass from kola nut sellers to tax collectors in everyday interactions. These exchanges were also significant for kola nut sellers from northern Guinea, speakers of Pular, who had a deep history of Islamic scholarship and piety.

At a broader level, the exchange of wares and cash were potential targets for redirection as they passed from hand to hand. In this market of crisscrossing exchanges, migrants attempted to accumulate and maintain wealth—if even in small increments—while limiting its access to others. These practices provide one aspect of conflicting strategies of what has been called sharing and hoarding, which constitute the precarious nature of managing one's wealth in West Africa (Shipton 1989). A central aspect of these strategies is described by Parker Shipton (1989, 257) in his work on Gambian saving: "saving strategies are mainly concerned with removing wealth from the form of readily accessible cash, without appearing anti-social." The market thus provided a setting for elaborated forms of verbal and physical play in which migrants attempted to unearth or divulge each other's resources. As a verbal strategy, market goers attempted to render their wealth inaccessible through the monitoring and parrying of prying language.

Over the longer term, making wealth inaccessible entailed material transformations, for instance from cash into cement (see chapter 5). In the everyday, this entailed the monitoring and management of one's speech over the course of conversational routines in which one might be tricked or baited into indexing one's holdings. Market goers not only protected wealth through measured speech but also baited each other to divulge resources through conversational play. Even money exposed to public trajectories over the course of errands and exchanges was frequently subject to playful but probing attempts at redirection. For instance, upon spying a bit of loose change in the corner of a kola nut sellers' bamboo chair, a porter nearby announced to others present, "Dee ɗoo ko miŋ jeey?" (This here, is this mine?), in a subtle bid to protect the unclaimed coins.

In Kédougou's market, it was therefore necessary not only to watch one's kola and pockets but likewise to monitor one's speech. In Erving Goffman's (1967) analysis of face, engaging in communicative interaction entails risk. For the purposes of this context, risk entails the divulging of one's possessions or positionalities, which might be exploited by one's interlocutors. In a first instance, the habit of downplaying one's achievements during casual conversation fits this pattern. Migrants frequently were drawn in conversational routines that endeavored to bait interlocutors to reveal or defend material possessions. Those who knew taboo jammoore nicknames (see chapter 3) would often playfully bait unratified individuals to speak them and then extort money from their victims. Through such routines, interlocutors prompted and parried attempts to reveal the material standing of others, whose success could garner small gifts, tokens, or concessions.

In the context of the Kédougou market, viewing language as infrastructure helps us understand how market traders were able to successfully navigate a shifting market. The encounters from this chapter show language to be not merely a symbolic medium through which information is exchanged at a virtual or ideational level. Instead, linguistic practice brought people into physical contact, providing an interactional resource for influencing space and the trajectories of objects. This spatial and material role of language should be seen as a form of infrastructure that shapes the possibilities of contact and interaction. In this vibrant market, objects were intensely contested in linguistic practice through the conversational tactics of protection and solicitation. For many market goers, the strategic performance of social idioms offered a way to make connections with others in a jumble of action. Words here can be viewed as akin to the walls, doors, and physical structures that mediate the capacity of people to interact with one another.

Phatic Connections through Language

A common strategy of connectivity in the Kédougou market is something that can usefully be called *phatic baiting*: the act of relying on relational idioms, unavoidable questions, or other hooks to draw others into interaction. *Phaticity* is a term frequently used in linguistic anthropology to conceptualize the way in which language is used to establish contact between people or channels of communication.[3] Many greetings, for instance, aren't best understood as the exchange of information necessarily but as a way to draw attention to the presence of another.[4] Analyses of language have tended to focus on its ability to refer to things—a referentialist language ideology—at the expense of how linguistic practice mediates space and copresence. For instance, literature on joking relationships has attempted to characterize its primary functions as a mediator of positive social relations or, alternatively, as interethnic tension (Canut 2006). However, routines like the joking relationships I examine in chapter 2 were so powerful precisely because they could effectively capture the attention of others and lure them into interaction. More broadly, phatic language in the market setting shows how people draw on linguistic routines to manipulate space and impact the mobilities of others.

Djiby the porter's attempts to draw the attention of those he positioned as his in-law offer a good example of this kind of tactic. He also commonly drew on joking relationships to bait passersby into his orbit. Lying down in a wheelbarrow between jobs, he would often call out the name of his joking partners to an open market, hoping to bait someone into uptake: "Hee, aŋ ko Ba?" (Hey, are you a Ba?). By calling out this common last name into the crowded market, Djiby was often successful in baiting Bas into a joking relationship based on the correspondence Diallo-Ba. After this initial connection was achieved, it was difficult for those individuals to ignore him.

Not only enabled through language narrowly conceived, Djiby also set up his wheelbarrow between rows of kola nut sellers at the entrance to the front Kédougou market. Those wanting to pass into the depths of the market needed to pass by him on their way through. As such, Djiby's verbal performances combined with his bodily alignment positioned him to be able to capture social relations in the market. For instance, one morning as Djiby sat at the narrow entrance to an alley, he managed to waylay a young man who was squeezing his way through. Djiby quickly grasped his hand, asking him about his last name: "Ko Diallo kaa?" (It's Diallo, right?). "Ba," said the young man softly. Diallo and Ba formed one of the most common joking relationship correspondences that pitted these two against each other.

As the young man awkwardly attempted to distance himself, Djiby continued to play on bodily exchange between joking partners seen to be a source of pollution, exclaiming, "He faut mi sooɗo" (I need to wash my hands now). After these and similar exchanges, Djiby would often ask those he met for a small contribution, "Addii goɗɗuŋ" (Give me something). Djiby's use of first pair part questions which beg a response (such as questions, demands, or even claims of joking correspondences) demonstrates an extreme strategy of mobilizing responses from a chaotic market. The placement of his body along the axes of foot traffic to and from boutique shops furthermore demonstrates a future-oriented strategy of eliciting response and participation.

"This Guy Went to Dubai"

Given these tactics of capturing attention and wealth, monitoring others' impressions of your personal wealth was imperative among West African migrants, particularly those who had made it to places like Europe, North America, and the Middle East. As I discuss in chapter 3, coming back to natal villages or Kédougou often entailed an evaluation of how successful itinerant migrants had been. Theirs was a fine balancing act between performing success while at the same time not giving evidence of deep pockets that could readily purchase gifts for family and friends back home. In the exchange in table 6.1, for instance, a man comes up toward a cluster of porters and kola nut sellers who sit between the road and a bulk goods shop. As a well-dressed man greets the group, a voice soon calls out from the crowd, "This guy went to Dubai!" By invoking this place associated with lucrative commercial opportunities, the shouter marks the well-dressed man as a potential patron. In the transcript on line 6, Djiby the porter bluntly asks the man if he brought back any money. Beginning to respond, "I did," the man slowly gets sucked into revealing signs of potential wealth and resources. Right after line 8, he remains silent and leaves, no longer able to maintain the conversation without divulging his assets to Djiby's insistent prodding. Silence and departure offer the man a last-ditch strategy to insulate himself from compromising interactions. Though potentially effective in the moment, this kind of abrupt leave taking also carries the risk of disrespecting others, thereby leading to future interpersonal costs.

Other baiting techniques could be as blunt as "Ko honɗuŋ adorɗaa laŋ?" (What did you bring me?). This question alludes to neldaari, host gifts that were expected after migrants and travelers returned home. Responses could be disarmingly blunt in return. When a boy once asked an adult friend of mine, "Ko honɗuŋ adorɗaa laŋ" after returning from a trip to Spain, the latter responded with a stock insult: "bottere maa" (your balls). A common insult between young boys, such a response as strong rejection could be successful only across great distances in age or familiar relationships. Another possible response was silence or unintelligible speech. "Diallo, ko honɗuŋ maruɗaa laŋ, ko eŋ ñaatigi" (Diallo, what did you save for me, we are friends) elicited only a mumbling, unintelligible response. Not responding or tactfully avoiding such a direct question were two strategies for eschewing direct engagement with these solicitations or to conceal having come back empty-handed. These kinds of baiting questions were often

Table 6.1. "This Guy Went to Dubai"

#	Speaker	Speech	Gloss
1	Traveler	oui salamalaykum	yes greetings
2	Djiby	malaykum salam	greetings
3	Bystander	o yahno Dubai	he has been to Dubai
4	Djiby	a yahno Dubai	you have been to Dubai? ((to traveler))
5	Traveler	eey	yes
6	Djiby	a addi kaalisiiji ɗiŋ	did you bring the money
7	Traveler	mi addii	I did
8	Djiby	jelu	how much?
9		((traveler leaves))	

posed to migrants returning from abroad. Mining areas, seen as a destinations where one could make money, were also a trigger for similar searching questions.

I was not immune to these kinds of probing solicitations since my appearance gave off obvious signs of connections with places of privilege. Having parked my new motorcycle in the market one afternoon, a market porter came up to me and, after greeting, casually asked for my motorcycle: "okkaŋ moto maa" (give me your motorcycle). Someone less versed in these conversational routines might have been offended by such a solicitation. However, this form of appeal is not reserved only for strangers from away. This ubiquitous practice offers an interactional test of how one's interlocutor would respond. One of the most effective ways to parry such a request was to name the desired object after the person who requested it in a fleeting naming ceremony. This response powerfully demonstrates the commensurability of things and language as material substance. Such a solution was nevertheless valuable to both parties, constituting a material and relational channel through language that could often lead to future exchanges and opportunities.

This chapter has explored the verbal art of migrants in Kédougou's downtown market, highlighting the linguistic practices that allowed them to cultivate connections with clients, build relationships with fellow migrants, and bring others into one's orbit. All of this occurred during a time of social change that was felt most intensely in places like the downtown market. Kola nut sellers proved themselves to be particularly resilient. Rooted in place like the kola trees themselves—which maintained relations with those who planted them regardless of landownership—the kola nut sellers of the Kédougou market defined the space around them through strategic language, blessings, and reciprocity. Performances of hospitality formed the part of broader strategies that allowed migrants to root themselves in the space around them in a time when such informal selling spots were vulnerable. Not merely relational work in an abstract sense, these linguistic practices enabled migrants to shape the very market around them.

Notes

1. Often offered as a gift to open up channels of communication with strangers, kola nuts exemplify the overlaps between physical presents and linguistic exchange. For instance, when I first traveled to Taabe to ask if I could study language practices, I opened with a gift of kola and a statement of my purpose that locals referred to as *hunagol laawol* (showing the way). As such, kola nuts can be seen as an interpersonal mediator of participation and ratification. Kola nuts are also used as advance wedding gifts to show that a party wishes to pursue serious negotiation and provide an icon of marriage through the two halves of the kola, which fit together seamlessly. Kola have been central to trade between Sahelian and forest parts of Africa for centuries and have thus spurred large-scale patterns of mobility (Curtin 1975; Brooks 1993; Dilley 2004; Gestrich et al. 2021).

2. Using more specific terminology, sociologist Erving Goffman examines how interlocutors must protect what he calls their "face," or public persona, and understands this to be a central aspect of face-to-face interactions (Goffman 1967).

3. Beyond language as mere reference, phaticity (as contact and channel) is an example of the many possible functions of language as outlined by Roman Jakobson (1960). Roman Jakobson and later Michael Silverstein (1976) were among the first to emphasize this dimension of language beyond mere symbolic reference, a key perspective that this book draws on.

4. Charles H. P. Zuckerman (2016) has pointed out that phaticity need not be only positive and often encompasses negative, or disruptive, qualities.

CONCLUSION
Power and Mobility

Exploration and Mobility

Arguments about mobility in this book carry broader implications about power and social encounters. Thinking of mobility as relational, material, and constituted through linguistic practices helps us gain perspective on relationships of power. Exploitative exercises of power have historically occurred when people have assumed that they could map the world and encounter places on their own terms, independently of others. At a broader level, the Anthropocene is partly a recognition of this fact—that few phenomena on our planet can be analyzed independently of human activity.

Indeed, the extent to which mobility is viewed as a technical act of movement is a good gauge of power relations and the related ideologies that often obscure these processes. In many cases, this is possible through particular social distance offered by power and privilege in which interconnections with others are obscured, most blatantly in the case of colonial settler societies on a so-called frontier. For instance, in broader work on settler-colonial mobilities, Georgine Clarsen (2015, 42) writes, "Settler societies were constituted in, and continue to be structured by, ongoing processes of material, social, and cultural transformation that are predicated on—expressed through and measured by—motility and mobility. Foundational to settler colonialism are both the potential and actual capacities of settlers to roam as autonomous sovereign subjects around the world and across the territories they claim as their own—and conversely to circumscribe and control the mobilities of Indigenous peoples, to immobilize the former sovereign owners of those territories." As one important origin for these projects, the enlightenment was partly a project about obtaining and cataloging scientific knowledge about the known world (Tricoire 2017). This unleashed waves of explorers and merchants who aimed to map out and understand the world. Yet the maps produced during these eras belied the existence of places that were to be not found but revealed in relation to the people who lived there. Even during this seemingly rationalized endeavor, mobility was facilitated through others. For instance, Tim Ingold (2011) draws a distinction between wayfinding, a lived engagement through spaces in contrast to transport, which obscures our broader engagement with lived places under the guise of objective travel between destinations.

However, the social and relational facilitation of mobility has often been obscured. In *The Paper Road*, anthropologist Eric Mueggler (2011) describes the botanical expeditions of George Forrest, whose life's work was to discover and collect samples of Himalayan plants. He worked through local assistants from Naxi communities, who facilitated his access to these remote regions. Throughout this time, Forrest was searching for the epicenter of the genus *Rhododendron*. It might have seemed—even to Forrest himself—that he made decisions about such plant collections based on rational factors on a map. However, the regions he scoured were made available to him through the kinship networks of his assistants, who had hospitality relations in particular valleys and not others. The end result was not merely a map of natural history, but an exercise in social mapping.

In many cases, the travels of early colonial missionaries and explorers also tended to view the world as empty places to discover. Discussing the work of Fabian and Nerlich, Jean and John Comaroff (1991, 98) discuss how "the qualities of the scientific 'spirit' were identified with the heroic 'spirit' of the adventurer: the natural scientist's penetration into hitherto unknown realms had become one with the advance into regions unknown. The newly charted surfaces of the African landscape were to have a direct connection with the universe opening up within the person." In another example, Mary Louise Pratt (1985) describes in detail the travels of John Borrow, whose travel writings of his time in South Africa are illuminating. Rather than seeing it as a landscape to discover through people, Barrow was cataloging a place that could be known independently of the people who lived there. In Pratt's words, "Though he was traveling as a colonial official, charged with mediating disputes between Boer colonists and indigenous peoples, and though he was traveling with a large party of Europeans, Boers, and Hottentots, human interaction plays little role in his narrative. Instead, page after page catalogs without a thrill what Barrow likes to call 'the face of the country'" (122).

Anthropological perspectives are useful here. Rather than a landscape as merely an objective reality that sits independent of the people who inhabit it, most anthropologists consider our world to be hybrid—a laminated product of both its physical, material character and its cultural representations. Mobility takes into account power relations by engaging with a world that is knowable through other people. Mobility and even places themselves are largely constituted through ongoing linguistic exchanges.

The Importance of Contact

Some of the material in this book may appear to be the stuff of anthropological investigations from years past: ethnography of village settings, face-to-face interactions, and the back and forth of joking cousins or in-laws. Indeed, many of the first anthropologists planted themselves in small villages, examining such practices that they considered to be representative of larger structures. However, the linguistic practices they may have found there were not features of bounded communities. Instead, these linguistic resources facilitated broader networks that allowed people to travel widely and negotiate relationships with a wide range of people. These practices not only tell the story of broader migrations and interactions but also enable these mobilities. And despite a significant lack of cell service and access to computer technologies, many of my interlocutors in Kédougou—and especially its youth—were avid consumers of cell and computer media. As I describe throughout this book, they used these media alongside other forms of verbal exchange to maintain contact across great distances. Face-to-face interactions and facilitated media such as cell phones, radio, and the internet all provided opportunities to connect with and move oneself to places beyond the here and now.

However, one of the most precious things to many of the people I met throughout West Africa was the value of spending time with people. Speaking the names of others, recognizing their presence, and connecting those you meet to webs of relations was a passionate concern. They did everything they could to bring people together. The theoretical approaches adopted in this book capture the spirit of their enduring efforts to mobilize copresence through creative interactional and linguistic means. And yet I also don't want to paint a romantic picture of harmonious communal relations. Living people in close quarters, especially in the context of a small rural community, is also fraught with conflict, resentment, and frustration. Having an abundance of time to spend with others sometimes reflects systematic unemployment and economic hardship (Ralph 2008). Yet despite all this, the importance of visitations, greeting others, and navigating face-to-face interactions cannot be overemphasized. These are the aspects of life that the people I met in West Africa deeply cared about.

When I explained my ethnographic research, most Kédovins immediately recognized the importance of what I was doing. Even something as simple as an everyday greeting carried a deep significance to people— particularly for migrants. To my interlocutors, my interest in language didn't seem like an obscure academic topic at all. West Africans not only practiced this verbal art but also reflected deeply about their relationships with others and the linguistic practices through which they were enabled. These were not merely codes of behavior but also a set of strategies that people used to adapt to different circumstances. They enabled people to be mobile and to encounter places through people.

It is the value of this sociality that led me to become an anthropologist of West Africa. After many years of working there, these repeated interactions and relationships with others formed a web of relationality that had drawn me in. I often took on jobs and opportunities to maintain relationships with people. At times, my job as an anthropologist seemed designed to fulfill these relationships as much as it was an end in and of itself. In this, I am lucky. My career enables me to spend time with generous people with very different life experiences and to share in the everyday brilliance of their verbal arts.

As I am finishing this book, we are emerging from what has been an earth-shattering encounter with the global COVID pandemic, even if its effects appeared more tempered in Senegal. As with the Ebola epidemic in chapter 5, disease is not merely a viral phenomenon but one that is constitutive of our interactional lives. If anything, viral transmission exemplifies the materiality of language and interaction. Contact with others has become fraught, and it has shrunken our capacities to be mobile. If anything, COVID has revealed some of the taken-for-granted dimensions of our interactional practices, such as the proxemics of conversation that may have been previously hidden. If there is any silver lining, it is a recognition that interacting with others is a precious thing. Clearly isolation, quarantine, and masking have been important strategies for dealing with the COVID and Ebola epidemics. In one corner of the world, however, this book shows how difficult it is to escape face-to-face entanglements with others. These interactions are part of broader relational infrastructures built over the long term. An attention to these practices also shows how hard it can be to extricate oneself from the affordances of engaging with others. We often frame interactional behavior in the context of a pandemic as a personal choice, but our capacities to insulate ourselves from others are circumscribed by social practices under the level of awareness that may also be patterned in terms of socioeconomic class, race, or other factors. Hopefully this book has shown how these everyday interactional routines enable mobility in a complex world. For my part, I have learned that saying hello to others has revealed to me some incredible places and that greeting people makes me feel fulfilled. My hope is to share the richness of this everyday verbal art with others.

REFERENCES

Adey, Peter. 2017. *Mobility.* Abingdon, UK: Routledge.

Agha, Asif. 2007. *Language and Social Relations.* Cambridge: Cambridge University Press.

Ameka, Felix K. 2009. "Access Rituals in West African Communities." In *Ritual Communication*, edited by Gunter Senft and Ellen B. Basso. London: Taylor & Francis Group.

Amselle, Jean-Loup and Elikia M'Bokolo. 1985. *Au Cœur de l'ethnie: Ethnies, tribalisme et état en Afrique.* Textes à l'appui. Paris: Éditions La Découverte.

———. 1990. *Logiques metisses: Anthropologie de l'identite en Afrique et ailleurs.* Paris: Payot.

Appadurai, Arjun. 1996. *Modernity at Large: Cultural Dimensions of Globalization.* Minneapolis: University of Minnesota Press.

Babou, Cheikh Anta. 2008. "Migration and Cultural Change: Money, 'Caste,' Gender, and Social Status among Senegalese Female Hair Braiders in the United States." *Africa Today* 55 (2): 2–22.

Bakhtin, M. M. 1981. *The Dialogic Imagination: Four Essays.* Translated by Michael Holquist. Austin: University of Texas Press.

Barry, Boubacar. 1998. *Senegambia and the Atlantic Slave Trade.* Cambridge: Cambridge University Press.

Barth, Fredrik. 1969. *Ethnic Groups and Boundaries: The Social Organization of Culture Difference.* Essays presented at a symposium held at Bergen, Norway, February 23–26, 1967. Boston: Little, Brown.

Basso, Keith H. 1988. "'Speaking with Names': Language and Landscape among the Western Apache." *Cultural Anthropology* 3 (2): 99–130.

Bateson, Gregory. 1972. *Steps to an Ecology of Mind: Collected Essays in Anthropology, Psychiatry, Evolution, and Epistemology.* San Francisco: Chandler.

Bauman, Richard. 1975. "Verbal Art as Performance." *American Anthropologist* 77 (2): 290–311.

Bauman, Richard, and Charles L. Briggs. 1990. "Poetics and Performance as Critical Perspectives on Language and Social Life." *Annual Review of Anthropology* 19 (1990): 59–88.

Berry, Sara. 1989. "Social Institutions, and Access to Resources." *Africa* 59 (January): 41–55.

Bird, Charles S. 1999. "The Production and Reproductin of Sunjata." In *In Search of Sunjata*, 275–96. Bloomington: Indiana University Press.

Blommaert, Jan. 2010. *The Sociolinguistics of Globalization.* Cambridge Approaches to Language Contact. Cambridge: Cambridge University Press.

Bonte, Pierre. 2002. "L'esclavage: Un problème contemporain?" *L'Homme*, no. 164: 135–44.

Bourdieu, Pierre. 1977. *Outline of a Theory of Practice.* Cambridge: Cambridge University Press.

———. 1991. *Language and Symbolic Power.* Cambridge: Polity.

Bradney, P. 1957. "The Joking Relationship in Industry." *Human Relations* 10 (2): 179–87. https://doi.org/10.1177/001872675701000207.

Brant, Charles S. 1948. "On Joking Relationships." *American Anthropologist* 50 (1): 160–62.

Bredeloup, Sylvie. 2008. "L'aventurier, une figure de la migration africaine." *Cahiers internationaux de sociologie* 125 (2): 281–306.

———. 2014. *Migrations d'aventures: Terrains Africains.* CTHS Géographie, no 11. Paris: CTHS.

Briggs, Charles L. 1986. *Learning How to Ask: A Sociolinguistic Appraisal of the Role of the Interview in Social Science Research.* Cambridge: Cambridge University Press.

Brooks, George. 1993. *Landlords and Strangers: Ecology, Society and Trade in Western Africa. 1000–1630.* Boulder, CO: Westview Press.

Bruijn, M. E. de, R. A. van Dijk, and D. W. J. Foeken. 2001. "Mobile Africa: an Introduction." In *Mobile Africa: Changing Patterns of Movement in Africa and Beyond*, 1–7. Brill. https://hdl.handle.net/1887/21983.

Bucholtz, Mary and Kira Hall. 2005. "Identity and Interaction: A Sociocultural Linguistic Approach." *Discourse Studies.* 7 (4–5): 585–614.

Buggenhagen, Beth. 2011. "Are Births Just 'Women's Business'? Gift Exchange, Value, and Global Volatility in Muslim Senegal." *American Ethnologist* 38 (4): 714–32. https://doi .org/10.1111/j.1548-1425.2011.01332.x.

———. 2012. *Muslim Families in Global Senegal: Money Takes Care of Shame.* Bloomington: Indiana University Press.

Caine, Allison. "Herding at the Edges: Climate Change and Animal Restlessness in the Peruvian Andes." *Ethnos*, November 6, 2022, 1–21. https://doi.org/10.1080/00141844 .2022.2142266.

Canut, Cécile. 2006. "Construction des discours identitaires au Mali." *Cahiers d'études Africaines* 184 (4): 967–86.

Carter, Donald Martin. 1997. *States of Grace: Senegalese in Italy and the New European Immigration.* Minneapolis: University of Minnesota Press.

Chappatte, André. 2022. *In Search of Tunga.* Ann Arbor: University of Michigan Press.

Clark, Gracia. 1995. *Onions Are My Husband: Survival and Accumulation by West African Market Women.* Chicago: University of Chicago Press. http://ebookcentral.proquest .com/lib/uwy/detail.action?docID=488096.

———. 2010. *African Market Women: Seven Life Stories from Ghana.* Bloomington: Indiana University Press.

Clarsen, Georgine. 2015. "Introduction: Special Section on Settler-Colonial Mobilities." *Transfers* 5 (3): 41–48. http://dx.doi.org.grinnell.idm.oclc.org/10.3167/TRANS.2015 .050304.

Comaroff, Jean. 1991. *Of Revelation and Revolution.* Vol. 1. Chicago: University of Chicago Press. Ebook, http://hdl.handle.net/2027/heb02574.0001.001.

Cox, Stan, and Paul Cox. 2016. *How the World Breaks: Life in Catastrophe's Path, from the Caribbean to Siberia.* New York: New Press.

Cresswell, Tim. 2006. *On the Move: Mobility in the Modern Western World.* London: Routledge.

Curtin, Philip D. 1975. *Economic Change in Precolonial Africa: Senegambia in the Era of the Slave Trade.* Madison: University of Wisconsin Press.

d'Avignon, Robyn. 2018. "Primitive Techniques: From 'Customary' to 'Artisanal' Mining in French West Africa." *Journal of African History* 59 (2): 179–97.

———. 2022. *A Ritual Geology.* Durham, NC: Duke University Press.

De León, Jason, and Michael Wells. 2015. *The Land of Open Graves: Living and Dying on the Migrant Trail*. Oakland: University of California Press.

Derman, William. 1969. "Fulbe, Serfs and Peasants: Dimensions of Change in the Fouta-Djallon (Guinea)." PhD diss., University of Michigan.

Descola, Philippe. 2013. *Beyond Nature and Culture*. Translated by Janet Lloyd. Chicago: University of Chicago Press.

de Vienne, Emmanuel. 2012. "'Make Yourself Uncomfortable': Joking Relationships as Predictable Uncertainty among the Trumai of Central Brazil." *HAU: Journal of Ethnographic Theory* 2 (2): 163–87.

Diggins, Jennifer. 2015. "Economic Runaways: Patronage, Poverty and the Pursuit of 'Freedom' on Sierra Leone's Maritime Frontier." *Africa: Journal of the International African Institute* 85 (2): 312–32.

Dilley, Roy. 2004. *Islamic and Caste Knowledge Practices among Haalpulaar'en in Senegal: Between Mosque and Termite Mound*. International African Library. Edinburgh: Edinburgh University Press for the International African Institute, London.

Diouf, Mamadou, and Steven Rendall. 2000. "The Senegalese Murid Trade Diaspora and the Making of a Vernacular Cosmopolitanism." *Public Culture* 12 (3): 679–702.

Dougnon, Isaie. 2013. "Migration as Coping with Risk and State Barriers: Malian Migrants' Conception of Being Far from Home." In *African Migrations: Patterns and Perspectives*, edited by Abdoulaye Kane and Todd H. Leedy, 35–58. Bloomington: Indiana University Press.

Elyachar, Julia. 2010. "Phatic Labor, Infrastructure, and the Question of Empowerment in Cairo." *American Ethnologist* 37 (3): 452–64.

Fabian, Johannes. 1983. *Time and the Other: How Anthropology Makes Its Object*. New York: Columbia University Press.

Fahy Bryceson, Deborah, Jesper Bosse Jønsson, and Mike Clarke Shand. 2020. "Mining Mobility and Settlement during an East African Gold Boom: Seeking Fortune and Accommodating Fate." *Mobilities* 15 (3): 446–63. https://doi.org/10.1080/17450101.2020.1723879.

Ferguson, James. 1999. *Expectations of Modernity: Myths and Meanings of Urban Life on the Zambian Copperbelt*. Berkeley: University of California Press.

Fioratta, Susanna. 2015. "Beyond Remittance: Evading Uselessness and Seeking Personhood in Fouta Djallon, Guinea." *American Ethnologist* 42 (2): 295–308. https://doi.org/10.1111/amet.12131.

———. 2020. *Global Nomads: An Ethnography of Migration, Islam, and Politics in West Africa*. New York: Oxford University Press.

Foley, Ellen E., and Fatou Maria Drame. 2013. "Mbaraan and the Shifting Political Economy of Sex in Urban Senegal." *Culture, Health & Sexuality* 15 (1/2): 121–34.

Foley, William A. 1997. "Space." In *Anthropological Linguistics: An Introduction*, 215–29. Malden: Blackwell Publishers.

Foucault, Michel. 1977. *Discipline and Punish: The Birth of the Prison*. New York: Pantheon Books.

———. 1988. *The History of Sexuality*. New York: Vintage Books.

Freedman, Jim. 1977. "Joking, Affinity and the Exchange of Ritual Services among the Kiga of Northern Rwanda: An Essay on Joking Relationship Theory." *Man* 12 (1): 154–65.

Fullwiley, Duana. 2010. "Revaluating Genetic Causation: Biology, Economy, and Kinship in Dakar, Senegal." *American Ethnologist* 37 (4): 638–61. https://doi.org/10.1111/j.1548 -1425.2010.01276.x.

Gaibazzi, Paolo. 2015. *Bush Bound: Young Men and Rural Permanence in Migrant West Africa*. New York: Berghahn Books.

———. 2018. "West African Strangers and the Politics of Inhumanity in Angola: The Politics of Inhumanity." *American Ethnologist* 45 (4): 470–81.

Gaudio, Rudolf P. 2021. "Discursive Infrastructures of African Modernity: Indigenous Real Estate in Nigeria's Planned Capital." *City & Society* 33 (2). https://doi.org/10.1111 /ciso.12325.

Geertz, Clifford. 1973. *The Interpretation of Cultures: Selected Essays*. New York: Basic Books.

Gemmeke, Amber. 2013. "Marabouts and Migrations: Senegalese between Dakar and Diaspora." In *Long Journeys. African Migrants on the Road*, edited by Alessandro Triulzi and Robert McKenzie, 113–34. Boston: Brill. Ebook, http://ebookcentral .proquest.com/lib/uwy/detail.action?docID=1214120.

Geschiere, Peter, and Josef Gugler. 1998. "Introduction: The Urban–Rural Connection: Changing Issues of Belonging and Identification." *Africa* 68 (3): 309–19.

Gestrich, Nikolas, Louis Champion, Daouda Keïta, Nafogo Coulibaly, and Dorian Q. Fuller. 2021. "Evidence of an Eleventh-Century AD Cola Nitida Trade into the Middle Niger Region." *African Archaeological Review* 38 (3): 403–18. https://doi.org/10.1007/s10437 -021-09445-7.

Glovsky, David Newman. "Cross-Border Lives and the Complications of Citizenship: Migration, Belonging, and Alternative Geographies in the Borderlands of Guinea-Bissau, Guinea, and Senegal, 1958–1980." *Journal of West African History* 9, no. 1 (2023): 57–83. https://doi.org/10.14321/jwestafrihist.9.1.0057.

Goffman, Erving. 1967. "On Face Work." In *Interaction Ritual: Essays on Face-to-Face Behavior*, 5–45. Garden City, NY: Anchor Books.

———. 1981a. "Footing." In *Forms of Talk*, 124–57. Philadelphia: University of Pennsylvania Press.

———. 1981b. *Forms of Talk*. Philadelphia: University of Pennsylvania Press.

———. 1990. *The Presentation of Self in Everyday Life*. New York: Anchor Books.

Gokee, Cameron D. 2011. "Practical Knowledge and Politics of Encounter along the Lower Falémé River, Senegambia (c. AD 1500–1925)." *Azania: Archaeological Research in Africa* 46 (3): 269–93. https://doi.org/10.1080/0067270X.2011.609336.

Gugler, Josef. 2002. "The Son of the Hawk Does Not Remain Abroad: The Urban-Rural Connection in Africa." *African Studies Review* 45 (1): 21–41. https://doi.org/10.2307 /1515006.

Guyer, Jane I. 1993. "Wealth in People and Self-Realization in Equatorial Africa." *Man* 28 (2): 243–65.

———. 1995. *Money Matters: Instability, Values, and Social Payments in the Modern History of West African Communities*. Portsmouth, NH: Heinemann.

———. 2004. *Marginal Gains: Monetary Transactions in Atlantic Africa*. Lewis Henry Morgan Lectures. Chicago: University of Chicago Press.

Hannaford, Dinah. 2017. *Marriage without Borders: Transnational Spouses in Neoliberal Senegal*. Philadelphia: University of Pennsylvania Press.

Hannaford, Dinah, and Ellen E. Foley. 2015. "Negotiating Love and Marriage in Contemporary Senegal: A Good Man Is Hard to Find." *African Studies Review* 58 (2): 205–25.

Ingold, Tim. 2000. *The Perception of the Environment Essays on Livelihood, Dwelling and Skill.* London: Routledge.

———. 2011. *Being Alive: Essays on Movement, Knowledge and Description.* London: Routledge.

Irvine, Judith. 1973. "Caste and Communication in a Wolof Village." PhD diss., University of Pennsylvania.

———. 1989. "When Talk Isn't Cheap: Language and Political Economy." *American Ethnologist* 16 (2): 248–67.

———. 2006. "Speech and Language Community." In *Encyclopedia of Language and Linguistics*, edited by Keith Brown, 689–98. Oxford: Elsevier.

Irvine, Judith, and Susan Gal. 2019. *Signs of Difference: Language and Ideology in Social Life.* Cambridge: Cambridge University Press.

Jacquemet, Marco. 2009. "Transcribing Refugees: The Entextualization of Asylum Seekers' Hearings in a Transidiomatic Environment." *Text & Talk* 29 (5): 525–46. https://doi.org/10.1515/TEXT.2009.028.

Jakobson, Roman. 1960. "Closing Statement: Linguistics and Poetics." In *Style in Language*, edited by Thomas A. Sebeok, 350–59. Cambridge, MA: MIT Press.

Jones, Rachel A. 2007. "'You Eat Beans!': Kin-Based Joking Relationships, Obligations, and Identity in Urban Mali." Anthropology Honors Projects, Macalester College.

Jonsson, Gunvor. 2012. "Migration, Identity and Immobility in a Malian Soninke Village." In *The Global Horizon: Expectations of Migration in Africa and the Middle East*, edited by Knut Graw and Joska Samuli Schielke, 105–120. Leuven, Belgium: Leuven University Press.

Kane, Ousmane. 2011. *The Homeland Is the Arena: Religion and Senegalese Immigrants in America.* New York; Oxford: Oxford University Press.

Keane, Webb. 1997. *Signs of Recognition: Powers and Hazards of Representation in an Indonesian Society.* Berkeley: University of California.

———. 2005. "Signs Are Not the Garb of Meaning: On the Social Analysis of Material Things." In *Materiality*, edited by Daniel Miller, 182–205. Durham: Duke University Press.

———. 2015. *Ethical Life: Its Natural and Social Histories.* Princeton, NJ: Princeton University Press.

Kleinman, Julie. 2014. "Adventures in Infrastructure: Making an African Hub in Paris." *City & Society* 26 (3): 286–307. https://doi.org/10.1111/ciso.12044.

———. 2019. *Adventure Capital: Migration and the Making of an African Hub in Paris.* Oakland: University of California Press.

Kleist, Nauja, and Dorte Thorsen, eds. 2017. *Hope and Uncertainty in Contemporary African Migration.* New York, NY: Routledge.

Kopytoff, Igor. 1987. *The African Frontier: The Reproduction of Traditional African Societies.* Bloomington: Indiana University Press.

Larkin, Brian. 2008. *Signal and Noise: Media, Infrastructure, and Urban Culture in Nigeria.* Durham: Duke University Press.

———. 2013a. "Making Equivalence Happen: Commensuration and the Architecture of Circulation." In *Images That Move*, edited by Patricia Spyer and Mary Margret Steedly, 237–56. Santa Fe: School for Advanced Research.

———. 2013b. "The Politics and Poetics of Infrastructure." *Annual Review of Anthropology* 42:327–43.

Latour, Bruno. 1993. *We Have Never Been Modern*. Cambridge, MA: Harvard University Press.

Lefebvre, Henri. 1991. *The Production of Space*. Oxford: Blackwell.

Leinaweaver, Jessica B. 2009. "Raising the Roof in the Transnational Andes: Building Houses, Forging Kinship." *Journal of the Royal Anthropological Institute* 15 (4): 777–96.

Levitt, Peggy, and Deepak Lamba-Nieves. 2011. "Social Remittances Revisited." *Journal of Ethnic and Migration Studies* 37 (1): 1–22. https://doi.org/10.1080/1369183X.2011.521361.

Lippi-Green, Rosina. 2011. *English with an Accent: Language, Ideology and Discrimination in the United States*. 2nd ed. London: Routledge.

LiPuma, Edward. 2000. *Encompassing Others: The Magic of Modernity in Melanesia*. Ann Arbor: University of Michigan Press.

Lock, Margaret M. 1995. *Encounters with Aging: Mythologies of Menopause in Japan and North America*. Berkeley: University of California Press.

Lowie, Robert Harry. 1912. *Social Life of the Crow Indians*. New York: Trustees.

MacGaffey, Janet, and Rémy Bazenguissa-Ganga. 2000. *Congo-Paris: Transnational Traders on the Margins of the Law*. London: International African Institute in association with James Currey, Oxford; Bloomington: Indiana University Press.

Majid, Asifa, Melissa Bowerman, Sotaro Kita, Daniel B.M. Haun, and Stephen C. Levinson. 2004. "Can Language Restructure Cognition? The Case for Space." *Trends in Cognitive Sciences* 8 (3): 108–14. https://doi.org/10.1016/j.tics.2004.01.003.

Malinowski, Bronislaw. 1984. *Argonauts of the Western Pacific: An Account of Native Enterprise and Adventure in the Archipelagoes of Melanesian New Guinea*. Prospect Heights, IL: Waveland Press.

Massey, Doreen. 1994. *Space, Place and Gender*. Cambridge: Polity.

Mauss, Marcel. 1925. *Essai Sur Le Don: Forme et Raison de l'échange Dans Les Sociétés Archaïques*. Paris: L'année sociologique.

———. 1935. "The Notion of Body Techniques." In *Sociology and Psychology: Essays*. London: Routledge and Kegan Paul.

McGovern, Mike. 2012. "Life during Wartime: Aspirational Kinship and the Management of Insecurity." *Journal of the Royal Anthropological Institute* 18 (4): 735–52.

———. 2013. *Unmasking the State: Making Guinea Modern*. Chicago: University of Chicago Press.

Melly, Caroline. 2009. "Inside-Out Houses: Urban Belonging and Imagined Futures in Dakar, Senegal." *Comparative Studies in Society and History* 52 (1): 37. https://doi.org/10.1017/S0010417509990326.

———. 2011. "Titanic Tales of Missing Men: Reconfigurations of National Identity and Gendered Presence in Dakar, Senegal." *American Ethnologist* 38 (2): 361–76.

———. 2017. *Bottleneck: Moving, Building, and Belonging in an African City*. Chicago: University of Chicago Press.

Miers, Suzanne, and Igor Kopytoff. 1977. *Slavery in Africa: Historical and Anthropological Perspectives*. Madison: University of Wisconsin Press.

Miller, Daniel, ed. 2005. *Materiality*. Durham: Duke University Press.

Mol, Annemarie. 2002. *The Body Multiple: Ontology in Medical Practice*. Durham: Duke University Press.

Morton, C. 2007. "Remembering the House: Memory and Materiality in Northern Botswana." *Journal of Material Culture* 12 (2): 157–79.

Mueggler, Erik. 2011. *The Paper Road: Archive and Experience in the Botanical Exploration of West China and Tibet*. Berkeley: University of California Press.

Ndiaye, Raphael. 1993. "Ethno-Patronymic Correspondences and Jocular Kinship:" *African Environment* 8 (3–4): 93–124.

Newell, Sasha. 2012. *The Modernity Bluff: Crime, Consumption, and Citizenship in Côte d'Ivoire*. Chicago: University of Chicago Press.

Newman, Andrew. 2021. "'The Afterlives of Infrastructure.'" *City & Society* 33 (2). https://doi.org/10.1111/ciso.12324.

Niane, Djibril Tamsir. 1965. *Sundiata: An Epic of Old Mali*. London: Longmans.

O'Brien, D. B. C. 1971. *The Mourides of Senegal: The Political and Economic Organization of an Islamic Brotherhood*. Oxford, UK: Clarendon Press.

Ong, Aihwa. 2007. "Neoliberalism as a Mobile Technology." *Transactions of the Institute of British Geographers* 32 (1): 3–8.

Perrino, Sabina. 2002. "Intimate Hierarchies and Qur'anic Saliva (Tefli): Textuality in a Senegalese Ethnomedical Encounter." *Journal of Linguistic Anthropology* 12 (2): 225–59.

———. 2020. *Narrating Migration: Intimacies of Exclusion in Northern Italy*. Routledge Studies in Linguistic Anthropology. New York: Routledge.

Piot, Charles. 1999. *Remotely Global: Village Modernity in West Africa*. Chicago: University of Chicago Press.

Pratt, Mary Louise. 1985. "Scratches on the Face of the Country; or, What Mr. Barrow Saw in the Land of the Bushmen." *Critical Inquiry* 12 (1): 119–43.

Radcliffe-Brown, A. R. 1940. "On Joking Relationships." *Africa: Journal of the International African Institute* 13 (3): 195–210.

———. 1973. "On Social Structure." In *High Points in Anthropology*, edited by Paul Bohannan and Mark Glazer, 304–16. New York: Alfred A. Knopf.

Radcliffe-Brown, A. R., and Cyril Daryll Forde. 1950. *African Systems of Kinship and Marriage*. London: Published for the International African Institute by Oxford University Press.

Ralph, Michael. 2008. "Killing Time." *Social Text* 26 (4): 1–29. https://doi.org/10.1215/01642472-2008-008.

Riccio, Bruno. 2004. "Transnational Mouridism and the Afro-Muslim Critique of Italy." *Journal of Ethnic and Migration Studies* 30 (5): 929–44.

Riley, Emily Jenan. 2019. "The Politics of Teranga: Gender, Hospitality, and Power in Senegal." *PoLAR: The Political and Legal Anthropology Review* 42 (1): 110–24.

Roberts, Elizabeth FS. 2013. "Assisted Existence: An Ethnography of Being in Ecuador." *Journal of the Royal Anthropological Institute* 19 (3): 562–80.

Roth-Gordon, Jennifer. 2016. "From Upstanding Citizen to North American Rapper and Back Again: The Racial Malleability of Poor Male Brazilian Youth." In *Raciolinguistics: How Language Shapes Our Ideas about Race*, 51–64. New York: Oxford University Press.

Salazar, Noel B. 2011. "The Power of Imagination in Transnational Mobilities." *Identities* 18 (6): 576–98. https://doi.org/10.1080/1070289X.2011.672859.

Schapendonk, Joris. 2013. "Sub-Saharan Migrants Heading North: A Mobility Perspective." In *Long Journeys. African Migrants on the Road*, edited by Alessandro Triulzi and Robert McKenzie, 9–23. Boston: Brill. Ebook, http://ebookcentral.proquest.com/lib /uwy/detail.action?docID=1214120.

Schapendonk, Joris, Matthieu Bolay, and Janine Dahinden. 2020. "The Conceptual Limits of the 'Migration Journey': De-Exceptionalising Mobility in the Context of West African Trajectories." *Journal of Ethnic and Migration Studies* 47 (14): 1–17. https://doi.org/10 .1080/1369183X.2020.1804191.

Schiller, Nina Glick, Linda Basch, and Cristina Blanc-Szanton. 1992. "Transnationalism: A New Analytic Framework for Understanding Migration." *Annals of the New York Academy of Sciences* 645 (1): 1–24. https://doi.org/10.1111/j.1749-6632.1992.tb33484.x.

Scott, James C., John Tehranian, and Jeremy Mathias. 2002. "The Production of Legal Identities Proper to States: The Case of the Permanent Family Surname." *Society for the Comparative Study of Society and History* 44 (1): 4–44.

Shipton, Parker MacDonald. 1989. *Bitter Money: Cultural Economy and Some African Meanings of Forbidden Commodities*. Washington, DC: American Anthropological Association.

Silverstein, Michael. 1976. "Shifters, Linguistic Categories, and Cultural Description." In *Meaning in Anthropology*, edited by Keith H. Basso and Henry A. Selby, 11–55. Albuquerque: University of New Mexico Press.

Simone, Abdou Maliqalim. 2004. "People as Infrastructure: Intersecting Fragments in Johannesburg." *Public Culture* 16 (3): 407–29.

Smith, Daniel Jordan. 2004. "Burials and Belonging in Nigeria: Rural-Urban Relations and Social Inequality in a Contemporary African Ritual." *American Anthropologist* 106 (3): 569–79.

Smith, Etienne. 2004. "Les cousinages de plaisanterie en Afrique de l'Ouest, entre particularismes et universalismes." *Raisons politiques* 13 (1): 157.

Soares, Benjamin F. 2005. *Islam and the Prayer Economy*. Ann Arbor: University of Michigan Press.

Spitulnik, Debra. 1996. "The Social Circulation of Media Discourse and the Mediation of Communities." *Journal of Linguistic Anthropology* 6 (2): 161–87.

Stivers, Tanya, and Jack Sidnell. 2005. "Introduction: Multimodal Interaction." *Semiotica*, no. 156: 1–20.

Stoller, Paul. 2013. "Strangers Are Like the Mist: Language in the Push and Pull of the African Diaspora." In *African Migrations: Patterns and Perspectives*, 158–172. Bloomington: Indiana University Press.

Stonington, Scott D. 2012. "On Ethical Locations: The Good Death in Thailand, Where Ethics Sit in Places." *Social Science & Medicine* 75 (5): 836–44.

Strathern, Marilyn. 1988. *The Gender of the Gift: Problems with Women and Problems with Society in Melanesia*. Berkeley: University of California Press.

Sweet, Nikolas. 2019. "The Poetics of Relationality: Mobility, Naming, and Sociability in Southeastern Senegal." PhD diss., University of Michigan. https://deepblue.lib.umich .edu/handle/2027.42/151392.

———. 2021a. "The Socio-Poetics of Sanakuyaagal Performing Joking Relationships in West Africa." In *African Performance Arts and Political Acts*, edited by Naomi Andre, Yolanda Covington-Ward, and Jendele Hungbo, 39–68. Ann Arbor: University of Michigan Press.

———. 2021b. "Talk on the Move: Articulating Mobility in West Africa." *Journal of Ethnic and Migration Studies* 49 (13): 1–18.

Tall, Serigne Mansour. 2002. "Mouride Migration and Financing." *Isim Newsletter* 9 (1): 36.

Tamari, Tal. 1991. "The Development of Caste Systems in West Africa." *Journal of African History* 32 (2): 221.

———. 1998. *Les castes de l'Afrique occidentale: Artisans et musiciens endogames*. Nanterre, France: Société d'ethnologie.

Tricoire, Damien, ed. 2017. *Enlightened Colonialism*. Cham, Switzerland: Springer International Publishing. https://doi.org/10.1007/978-3-319-54280-5.

Triulzi, Alessandro, and Robert McKenzie. 2013. *Long Journeys. African Migrants on the Road*. Boston: Brill. http://ebookcentral.proquest.com/lib/uwy/detail .action?docID=1214120.

Turner, Terence S. 2012. "The Social Skin." *HAU: Journal of Ethnographic Theory* 2 (2): 486–504. https://doi.org/10.14318/hau2.2.026.

Vom Bruck, Gabriele. 2006. "Names as Bodily Signs." In *The Anthropology of Names and Naming*, 225–50. Cambridge: Cambridge University Press.

Walsh, Andrew. 2003. "'Hot Money' and Daring Consumption in a Northern Malagasy Sapphire-Mining Town." *American Ethnologist* 30 (2): 290–305.

Ware, Rudolph. 2014. *The Walking Qur'an*. Chapel Hill: University of North Carolina Press.

Warms, Richard. 2014. "Friendship and Kinship among Merchants and Veterans in Mali." In *Friendship, Descent, and Alliance in Africa: Anthropological Perspectives*, 119–32. New York: Berghahn Books.

Warner, Michael. 2002. *Publics and Counterpublics*. New York: Zone Books. Distributed by MIT Press.

Whitaker, Beth Elise. 2017. "Migration within Africa and Beyond." *African Studies Review* 60 (2): 209–20.

Whitehouse, Bruce. 2012. *Migrants and Strangers in an African City: Exile, Dignity, Belonging*. Bloomington: Indiana University Press.

———. 2013. "Overcoming the Economistic Fallacy: Social Determinants of Voluntary Migration from the Sahel to the Congo Basin." In *African Migrations: Patterns and Perspectives*, edited by Abdoulaye Kane and Todd H. Leedy, 34–49. Bloomington: Indiana University Press.

Wittenberg, David. 2002. "Going Out in Public: Visibility and Anonymity in Michael Warner's 'Publics and Counterpublics.'" *Quarterly Journal of Speech* 88 (4): 426–33. https://doi.org/10.1080/00335630209384389.

Wolf-Meyer, Matthew J. 2020. "Facilitated Personhood." *Journal of the Royal Anthropological Institute* 26 (1): 167–86.

Wright, Donald R. 2010. *The World and a Very Small Place in Africa: A History of Globalization in Niumi, the Gambia*. Armonk, NY: Sharpe.

Yeh, Rihan. 2018. *Passing: Two Publics in a Mexican Border City*. Chicago: University of Chicago Press.

Yount-André, Chelsie. 2018. "Gifts, Trips and Facebook Families: Children and the Semiotics of Kinship in Transnational Senegal." *Africa* 88 (4): 683–701.

Zuckerman, Charles H. P. 2016. "Phatic Violence: Gambling and the Arts of Distraction in Laos." *Journal of Linguistic Anthropology* 26 (3): 294–314.

INDEX

NIKOLAS SWEET is Assistant Professor of Anthropology at the
University of Wyoming.

FOR INDIANA UNIVERSITY PRESS

Tony Brewer, *Artist and Book Designer*
Gary Dunham, *Acquisitions Editor and Director*
Anna Francis, *Assistant Acquisitions Editor*
Anna Garnai, *Production Coordinator*
Samantha Heffner, *Marketing and Publicity Manager*
Katie Huggins, *Production Manager*
Nancy Lightfoot, *Project Manager/Editor*
Bethany Mowry, *Acquisitions Editor*
Dan Pyle, *Online Publishing Manager*
Michael Regoli, *Director of Publishing Operations*
Jennifer Witzke, *Senior Artist and Book Designer*

www.ingramcontent.com/pod-product-compliance
Lightning Source LLC
Chambersburg PA
CBHW020353270326
41926CB00007B/409